Eudora Welty: Thirteen Essays

Eudora Welty

Thirteen Essays
Selected from
Eudora Welty: Critical Essays

Edited by
Peggy Whitman
Prenshaw

UNIVERSITY PRESS
OF MISSISSIPPI
Jackson

THIS BOOK HAS BEEN SPONSORED

BY THE UNIVERSITY OF SOUTHERN MISSISSIPPI

Grateful acknowledgment is made to the following:
Farrar, Straus and Giroux, Inc., for permission to quote
from Susan Sontag's *On Photography*, copyright 1977;
Harcourt Brace Jovanovich, Inc., for permission to quote
from Eudora Welty's *A Curtain of Green and Other Stories*,
The Robber Bridegroom, *The Wide Net and Other Stories*,
Delta Wedding, *The Golden Apples*, *The Ponder Heart*, and
The Bride of the Innisfallen, copyright 1943, 1946, 1947,
1948, 1949, 1970, 1974, 1975, 1977 by Eudora Welty;
Random House, Inc., for permission to quote from the
following copyrighted works of Eudora Welty: *Losing Bat-
tles*, *The Optimist's Daughter*, *One Time, One Place: Mississippi in the Depression*, and *The Eye of the Story: Selected
Essays and Reviews*.

Library of Congress Cataloging in Publication Data
Main entry under title:
Eudora Welty, thirteen essays.
"Books by Eudora Welty": p.
Includes bibliographical references and index.
Contents: Traditionalism and modernism in Eudora
Welty / Chester E. Eisinger—The other way to live /
John Alexander Allen—The recovery of the confident
narrator / J.A.Bryant—[etc.]
   1. Welty, Eudora, 1909– —Criticism and interpre-
tation—Addresses, essays, lectures. I. Prenshaw,
Peggy Whitman. II. Title: Eudora Welty, critical
essays.
PS3545.E6Z674   1983   813'.52   83–6945
ISBN: 978-1-60473-396-9

Contents

Books by
Eudora Welty

A Curtain of Green. Garden City: Doubleday, Doran, 1941.

The Robber Bridegroom. Garden City: Doubleday, Doran, 1942.

The Wide Net and Other Stories. New York: Harcourt, Brace, 1943.

Delta Wedding. New York: Harcourt, Brace, 1946.

The Golden Apples. New York: Harcourt, Brace, 1949.

The Ponder Heart. New York: Harcourt, Brace, 1954.

The Bride of the Innisfallen and Other Stories. New York: Harcourt, Brace, 1955.

The Shoe Bird. New York: Harcourt, Brace and World, 1964. (Children's Book)

Losing Battles. New York: Random House, 1970.

One Time, One Place: Mississippi in the Depression: A Snapshot Album. New York: Random House, 1971.

The Optimist's Daughter. New York: Random House, 1972.

The Eye of the Story: Selected Essays and Reviews. New York: Random House, 1978.

The Collected Stories of Eudora Welty. New York: Harcourt Brace Jovanovich, 1980.

Preface

THIS COLLECTION COMPRISES thirteen of the twenty-seven essays published in 1979 in *Eudora Welty: Critical Essays*. Although it is good news that all copies of the earlier collection have been sold, I regret that the original hardcover edition is now out of print. Unfortunately, the high cost of production prevents a second printing. Nonetheless, I am pleased that the University Press of Mississippi has published this shortened, less expensive volume.

I have tried here to select essays that fairly represent the breadth of subject and approach that marked the earlier volume. Inevitably, many excellent essays are omitted; for these, I trust Welty scholars will have access through libraries to the 1979 collection.

The purpose of this collection of thirteen essays, like that of the earlier collection, is quite simply to increase the reader's enjoyment and understanding of Welty's fiction. Ultimately, the helpfulness of such literary criticism is measured by its influence in returning the reader to the stories with heightened insights and fresh appetites. I hope the essays here, through the variety of approaches they offer to a reading of Eudora Welty's work, will so serve the reader.

The range of these essays reflects that of the earlier volume and that of current Welty criticism. Themes, forms and stylistic features previously identified in Welty scholarship are given fresh treatment: the dualities of love and separateness as they operate in a family or community, the pervasive mysteries of the separate self, the functions of myth, the embodiments of a sense of history and of place in fiction. Other essays take up relatively unexplored areas of study: Welty's relation to twentieth century modernism, her achievement as a critic and literary theorist, her fiction's mirroring of time and myth through complex structural refractions, her intricate prose style in the longer works, particularly as revealed through a close stylistic analysis of *Losing Battles*.

In the opening essay, Chester E. Eisinger, who early wrote about Welty's fiction in his *Fiction in the Forties*, examines the modernist strain in Welty's technique—the emphasis on the rendering of detail, on the telling of the story—and shows how the impulse is linked to a steady traditionalist strain, which he locates in Welty's belief in certain codes of value and in the possibility of fiction's making thematic statements about them. The "uncommon combination . . . makes her, in the history of twentieth century American fiction, a transition figure, a writer who looks both backwards and forwards."

John A. Allen offers new perspectives on Welty's uses of myth, examining various thematic elements that recur throughout the fiction.

J.A. Bryant, Jr., author of the 1968 Minnesota pamphlet on Welty, explores some of the formal features that give unity and shape to the fiction. In fact, he shows that much of the successful blending of traditionalism and modernism discussed by Eisinger is accomplished through Welty's artful manipulation of the narrator.

John Edward Hardy discusses Welty's treatment of marriages and families, particularly the pattern of "marrying down," a theme reiterated in Welty's novels.

Albert J. Devlin looks beyond the "lyrical Welty," so often associated with *A Curtain of Green* and *The Robber Bridegroom*, to find in the works a "solid world, governed by time and causality and beset by social pressure." Devlin locates in the interrelation of the stories what he concludes is a "cohesive view of historical reality."

Drawing upon his wide experience as a scholar of American literature, Warren French places *The Robber Bridegroom* in the context of nineteenth and twentieth century American cultural history, finding that in the novel Welty employs fantasy, among other devices, to embody the country's experience of rapid transition from forest to marketplace and to suggest that the past, otherwise forgotten except in our stories, continues into the present.

Two essays on *The Golden Apples* chiefly concern the interplay of mythic elements that link the separate stories of the book. Julia Demmin and Daniel Curley discuss mythic parallels that shape one of the work's major themes—the competition between masculine powers and female mysteries—and that finally suggest a pattern for harmony and resolution.

In a detailed study of the book's structure, Daniele Pitavy-Souques shows how Welty's employment of mythic material, specifically the Perseus myth, results in a precise mirroring of theme: "the narratives that constitute *The Golden Apples* are dramatizations of the functioning of the myth of Perseus."

Robert B. Heilman applies his impressive literary sensibility to a study of the form and technique of *Losing Battles*. In a close stylistic analysis of this long and complex novel, Heilman explores the relation of the highly deliberate ordering of the novel to the view of life it expresses.

Seymour Gross, who has written earlier of Welty's place in the American comic tradition, discusses *Losing Battles* as the culmination of Welty's comic fiction.

Discussing Welty's early photographic career, represented in *One Time, One Place*, Barbara McKenzie examines the relation of the photography to the fiction.

Michael Kreyling, who has written a book-length study of Welty's fiction, discusses Welty's critical writings collected in *The Eye of the Story*. He looks closely at certain recurrent words in Welty's reviews and essays, finding that they not only indicate her views about literary art but provide a useful guide for reading her fiction.

Ruth Vande Kieft, author of the 1962 *Eudora Welty*, writes the concluding essay. Reading *The Eye of the Story* as a unified whole, she follows the special line of vision these essays offer for looking at Welty's views of life and art. For all the pleasure and wisdom one finds in reading the essays, however, Vande Kieft concludes that the fiction is ultimately more revealing of the aesthetic and moral patterns that define the Weltian vision. She ventures that "*The Optimist's Daughter* alone reveals more than the sum total of *The Eye of the Story*—both as criticism and as autobiography—about Eudora Welty's artistic vision of life and the patterns that have gone into its making."

In "Words into Fiction," Eudora Welty gives something of a warning about criticism, which "stands only to provide its solution, . . . a kind of translation into another language." A body of criticism has its time and place of application, she grants, but ultimately it is fiction that is "made to show forth human life" (*ES*, p. 137). In Ruth Vande Kieft's essay we find that criticism—Welty's own—performs the rightful function of all good criticism in returning the reader to the imaginative work of the artist. I hope the following essays will be similarly successful in exploring the world of Eudora Welty's fiction and returning readers to it, with all its radiant show of life.

Finally, in each case the quotations from Welty are from the first editions, which are listed under "Books by Eudora Welty." In general, abbreviated titles are used in the text.

Hattiesburg, Mississippi
March 1983

P.W.P.

Eudora Welty: Thirteen Essays

CHESTER E.   Traditionalism and Modernism
EISINGER   in Eudora Welty

WHEN T. S. ELIOT proposed his idea of the literary tradition in his famous essay, he did more than indicate a continuous line from the past; he indicated that every writer made a contribution which extended the line. He affirmed literary relationships. Different as he is, Harold Bloom is doing something of the same thing in our time. The assumption in his work on influence is that the poet, the writer, knows and is responsive to the work of the past; a continuity is affirmed in the effort of every poet to create, in his own distorted way, his predecessors. What both of these critics tell us, if indeed we have to be told, is that every writer has his place and takes his place in the great stream of literature.

What is true for other writers is no less true for Eudora Welty. A fine air of enviable independence and originality attaches to the view that Welty belongs to no school and is attached to no tradition, a view Vande Kieft expressed many years ago, but Welty herself knows better. She told Linda Kuehl that she feels close to Chekhov and that Virginia Woolf "opened the door" for her.[1] Those two writers begin to define the tradition to which Welty belongs, or, to put the matter more accurately, the traditions. Her work reflects the careful disorder of Chekhovian fiction and the accurate yet spontaneous rendering of detail that belonged to his slice of life technique. It reflects the modernism, in some of its facets at least, that characterized Woolf's fiction: the door she opened for Welty, she herself had passed through with Joyce, Kafka, Proust, Musil, and the other early twentieth century makers of experimental, avant-garde fiction. Welty is not a purely realistic writer; even Lukács knows that writers can rarely sustain pure realism in their fictions. She is obviously not purely an

[1] Linda Kuehl, "The Art of Fiction XLVII: Eudora Welty," *Paris Review*, No. 55 (Fall 1972), 75.

experimental modernist writer. But she is an uncommon combination of the two, and that makes her, in the history of twentieth century American fiction, a transition figure, a writer who looks both backwards and forwards. Her fiction reveals a tension arising from the mingling of traditional qualities that give it a teleological cast and of modernist qualities that elevate technique to a primary place and value the tour de force for its own self-contained sake.

The traditional novel, as I conceive it here, is the novel of Jane Austen or Balzac or Tolstoy. It is a realistic fiction that assumes an empirical epistemology and is dependent, therefore, upon the writer's grasp and perception of a sense-accessible world. It is a fiction resting upon mimesis in which the accurate or lifelike transcription of people acting in society is the sought-after goal. In this imitation of life, the writer seeks to bestow genuine identity upon his characters, and he assumes, therefore, the possibility of ontological integrity. He seeks to capture a culture's hum and buzz of implication, in Lionel Trilling's phrase, and to deal with the way in which manners, marriage, money, and morals work in the society of his fiction. The writer rests his fiction upon an idea of cosmic order in which time is linear, and the past is real and accessible; space is fixed, and the laws of cause and effect are operable. The traditional novel, as a final point in this synoptic description, is teleological: it has a goal, or a message, or a moral; or it even tries, in the view of some, to express a truth; or it is a form of knowledge.

The modernist novel emerges in part as a reaction against goal-oriented literature. Divorcing literature from those human concerns which center in meaning and idea, or, to use a shorthand term, in humanistic attitudes and activities, the modernist movement elevates aesthetics to a primary position and declares the autonomy of the literary work. It is not philosophy, sociology, economics, history, or anything of the sort, or dependent on any of these. It is literature and recognizable by virtue of its form, technique, language, the very process of writing itself. Ortega y Gasset's influential essay, "The Dehumanization of Art," is a model summary of such modernist tendencies. Preoccupation with the human content of literature, he says, is incompatible with aesthetic enjoyment. The object of art is artistic only insofar as it is not real. Aesthetic distance is necessary, since we can see a thing only when it ceases to form a living part of our being. Dehumanizing art creates distance between us and art. The road to art is the will to style; style involves dehumanization; to stylize is to deform reality.

Art has no serious purpose. It is just art. Here, Ortega concludes, is the source of irony and the reason why art, turning upon itself, laughs at itself. The modernist movement also begins to alter time and space concepts and to move in the direction of spatial form, as Joseph Frank pointed out in his well known essay; he demonstrated how modernist poetry began to abandon linearity and sequential thinking, thus making time epochs timeless and history ahistorical. When time and space can no longer be perceived in easy Newtonian terms, empiricism is rejected as a valid epistemology, and the idea of a fixed reality becomes an illusion. Each writer constructs his own reality. The disestablishment of certainties leads to an ontological crisis. In fiction, the result is to call into question the possibility of establishing identity and therefore of depicting individual characters.

This modernist movement, which owed a great deal to the poetry and critical ideas of Pound and Eliot, made no major impact upon American fiction in the first half of the twentieth century. One can find evidence of it in the work of Gertrude Stein and Djuna Barnes; parts of John Dos Passos's *U.S.A.* and of Faulkner's novels indicate the useful survival of this modernist mode in American fiction. But it is not until the post-World War II period, beginning with the work of John Hawkes and William Gaddis, that a modernist movement in fiction actually gets under way in this country. And then we get a wave of modernism with the fiction of Vladimir Nabokov, William Gass, Donald Barthelme, Stanley Elkin, John Barth, Thomas Pynchon, and William Burroughs, among others.

I should like to place Eudora Welty in the perspective of American fiction here outlined in order to describe her work and to discover if such placing will engender a useful reading of her fiction. My analysis, which will treat her work chronologically, is not intended to be exhaustive; it is instead designed to illustrate the two modes of fiction here distinguished as they appear in her books.

Let me begin by examining some of her own ideas about fiction. These are curiously mixed, but her eclecticism here is indicative of the richly varied texture of her novels and short stories. Some of her statements suggest that she is irrevocably committed to traditionalism in fiction. In "Some Notes on Time in Fiction," collected in *The Eye of the Story*, she writes: "Real life is not wished, it is lived; stories and novels, whose subject is human beings in relationship with experience to undergo, make their own difficult way, struggle toward their own resolutions. Instead of fairy immunity to change, there is the vulnerability of human imperfection caught up in human emotion, and so there is growth, there is crisis, there is fulfillment, there is decay. Life moves toward death. The novel's progress is one of causality, and with that comes suspense. Suspense is a necessity in a novel because it is a main condition of our existence. Suspense is known only to mortals, and its agent and messenger is time" (*ES*, pp. 164–65). The assumptions in this passage are that the writer is governed by real life and real people who have their being in real time and who change in accordance with recognizable and real laws of causality. No sense of either an epistemological or an ontological crisis disturbs Welty's faith that reality in all its dimensions is apprehensible. Fiction asks, she goes on to say, what a character can come to know of himself and others by working through a given situation. A plot is a device designed for the searching out of human truth. There *is*, then, a truth, and the novel is an illusion made by art in order to show "some human truth" (*ES*, p. 145). This illusion she speaks of is based on mimesis; the characters that writers portray must seem alive. Fiction must have passion and flame in its sympathy for the human condition. Every writer is committed to moral principles, she says, and these presumably define an attitude toward human experience. But of course the writer does not crusade or moralize. Place and the past also help to define a writer's attitudes; for Welty, place certifies the reality of the past, which of course means the reality of history. Her deep attachment to place and her firm sense of the past are among her most closely cherished mandarin pieties. They arise from her fierce defense of regional writing, which she expressed most sharply in a rebuke of Edmund Wilson, telling him that the independent imagination must be allowed to create in its own way in its own milieu. In all these ways, Welty appears a confirmed traditionalist.

The other strain in her comments on fiction is more difficult to trace because it frequently touches upon the ineffable. It seems present to her mind almost as a reaction against the certainties concerning knowledge, being, time and history, morality, and truth that we have just examined. For what really counts in the writing of fiction is the act of imagination; this is the medium in which stories are written, and this is what the reader must share with the writer. But what is it? Since she cannot convey the sense of the imagination in metaphysical terms as Coleridge does, she must rely, in her nonanalytical way, upon an explanation that is suggestive more than definitive. What is of interest in the writing process, she says, is "that subject, method, form, style, all wait upon—indeed hang upon—a sort of double thunderclap at the author's ears: the break of the living world upon what is already stirring inside the mind, and the answering impulse that in a moment of high consciousness fuses impact and image and fires them off together" (*ES*, pp. 114–15). Now of course writers of every kind, even Dreiser, are dependent upon the imagination; but it is those writers like the nineteenth century Romantics or Pound or Nabokov who in perceiving the world of imagination as an acceptable or preferred alternative form of reality clearly ally themselves with modernism. Nabokov says that memory and imagination release man from time and space and permit him to frame and embrace the image which is the instrument of his freedom, the freedom that art confers. And Pound in defining an image as that which presents an intellectual and emotional complex in an instant of time comes very close to seeing the work of the imagination in the same terms that Welty does when she speaks of fusing impact and image. Pound represents, of course, the first wave of modernism and Nabokov the second, and Welty stands between them and allied and at one with them in asserting the supremacy of the imagination.

She is in the same camp with them also with respect to style. "It's the form ... that gives a story something unique—its life" (*ES*, p. 109). The apotheosis of the writing process was, in the 1940s when Welty began to publish her books, a part of the movement we know as the New Criticism. John Crowe Ransom, whose book gave the movement its name, said that fiction will have style for its essential activity; what is memorable about fiction is its linguistic maneuvers.[2] Mark Schorer said that "when we speak of technique ... we speak of nearly everything."[3] This insistence on the importance of style was a way of distinguishing fiction as an art form and of asserting the autonomy of art as something independent and different from philosophy, politics, ethics, or whatnot. This doctrine of the autonomy of art based in good part on the centrality of writing as such—style or technique—brings together Welty, the New Critics, and the modernists. For a modernist like William Gass (who studied with Ransom, incidentally) language is all in all, and as with Nabokov and Barth, the play of language is an activity sufficient unto itself, the very process and substance of the novel. Welty's commitment to the oral tra-

[2] See John Crowe Ransom's essay, "The Understanding of Fiction," *Kenyon Review*, 12 (Spring 1950), especially 197–201.
[3] Mark Schorer, "Technique as Discovery," in *Forms of Modern Fiction*, ed. William Van O'Connor (Minneapolis: Univ. of Minnesota Press, 1948), p. 9.

dition of the South that, as the tale teller, she transfers into her fiction, attests to her effort to write "a pure talk story," the kind people would enjoy simply for the way in which it is told.[4] Southerners are talkers by nature, she says, and are used to an audience. These two factors influence narrative style.[5] They make for an affinity to the tale, and they elevate the *telling* of the story to a position of first importance. Technique becomes an end in itself.

Finally, against the certainties of realism and empiricism, Welty asserts the mystery of allurement, for mystery is a quality every good story has. Mystery obscures if it does not defy meaning, and when to this standard Welty adds reticence—the claim that the beauty of a story is often in what the author holds back—it is clear that she wishes to focus her attention more upon the text than upon anything that might lie beyond it (*ES*, pp. 88–89, 105). She has not gone as far as Susan Sontag, who opposes treating "the work of art as *a statement being made in the form of a work of art*,"[6] but she may share with Sontag the belief that in art we experience the form or style of knowing something rather than the knowledge of something. In these ways she at least approaches modernism if she does not indeed come fully into the modernist camp.

Welty's first volume of fiction fully reveals the workings of these two fictional impulses, some of the stories in *A Curtain of Green* seeming to yield most readily to a traditional reading and some to a modernist. "Lily Daw and the Three Ladies" is based upon a sense of community so strong in Welty that she scarcely seems to attend to community, even though its texture and its structure constitute the very essence or substance of the story. Without the particular idea of order represented by the ladies, who *are* the town, the possibility of deviation or abnormality, inherent in Lily, is inconceivable. The community provides a stewardship, and the ladies become the custodians of moral principles and norms of respectable behavior. It is this fully realized social fabric that provides the ground for the story as the ladies seek first to protect Lily from sexual exploitation and then to channel her anarchic but natural sexual drives into marriage. Although the ladies, almost a caricature of interfering respectability, may

---

[4] Charles T. Bunting, " 'The Interior World': An Interview with Eudora Welty," *Southern Review*, 8 (Autumn 1972), 717; see also Kuehl, p. 80.

[5] See William F. Buckley, Jr., "The Southern Imagination: An Interview with Eudora Welty and Walker Percy," *Mississippi Quarterly*, 26 (Fall 1973), 495.

[6] Susan Sontag, *Against Interpretation* (New York: Farrar, Straus and Giroux, 1966), p. 21.

be the objects of satire, they represent an idea of society, the community itself, which often achieves genuine reality in Welty's fiction and is more frequently displayed in honorific than pejorative terms.

If "Lily Daw" subtly reveals the social dimensions of Welty's teleological fiction, "Keela, The Outcast Indian Maiden" reveals the moral dimension in an uncharacteristically direct way. True, the protest in the story is not explicit, but the guilt the young man feels at the exploitation of the Negro and the violation of his dignity, the nauseating dehumanization imposed upon the Negro—all this attests to Welty's vivid consciousness of the human potential for the monstrous: moral freakishness is worse than the bizarre action of those who eat live chickens. But of course Welty's moral vision is not confined to this dark perspective on man, as "A Worn Path" movingly shows. The endurance of old Phoenix, her self-sacrificial love and her unremitting dedication to her lifegiving mission constitute Welty's affirmation of man's, or woman's, humanity. The celebration of these qualities makes this a traditionalist's "human" story. A final example of Welty's moral imagination in this volume is "Petrified Man," which allows the characters to reveal and condemn themselves much in the way of Ring Lardner's "Haircut." Welty's beauty parlor, heavy with sexual tensions in ways that Lardner's barber shop does not display, is the locus for the same kind of moral insensitivity as the barber shop; justice and compassion are overwhelmed by a perverse absorption in the abnormal or freakish and by bitterness at a failure to claim undeserved rewards.

This story is also remarkable for its stylistic achievement: Welty captures with exquisite accuracy the speech rhythms and diction of the beautician Leota and her clients. Such linguistic accomplishment does not in itself make a story modernist, especially when its moral content, so clearly present even though so totally implicit, is the real point of the story. But in "Why I Live at the P.O." the style, or more precisely the sound of the narrative voice, may well be the essence of the story. What we pay attention to here is texture not text, or as Madame Girard puts it in James Purdy's *Malcolm*, texture is all, substance is nothing. The story then becomes a performance, a term Neil Isaacs used to describe some of Welty's fiction, and what is performed is a tour de force, an ingenious accomplishment which is just that and no more: an exercise in the use of that voice simply for the sake of the exercise. The voice in its modulations and tonalities and in its idiosyncratic energies, existing for itself and in itself, is an artistic triumph. Seen in this way, "Why I Live at the P.O." is a wholly modernist fiction in the same manner and spirit that the Jethro Furber sections of William Gass's *Omensetter's Luck* are modernist: they are both triumphs of the preoccupation with the manipulation of linguistic resources. But the voice that each writer has imagined and so lovingly and carefully reproduced for us does not after all exist entirely for itself. It has, if nothing else, psychological reverberations. Nevertheless, to understand this Welty story as a fiction absorbed with its own language is to obviate the kind of speculation which finds that the narrator is suffering from dementia praecox, as Katherine Anne Porter long ago suggested.

I shall deal with only two more stories in this volume, stories which are "about" aesthetics in such a way as to suggest their modernist character. "A Memory" may be regarded as an exercise in aesthetics in which Welty is engaged in nothing more or less than framing contrasting pictures, an appropriate activity, since the narrator is studying painting. One picture grows out of memory and the others out of present observation, and the juxtaposition or doubleness is itself an illustration of an aesthetic principle. The pictures of past and present exist side by side in the narrator's consciousness. In the one cherished from the past, she brushed the boy's wrist, evoking a moment of unformed and unfulfilled passion. In the present, she deliberately frames one that is virtually pastoral, showing lake and pavillion and populated by statuelike persons. These pictures are the work of art, which is a compound of memory, imagination, and deliberately limited (or artificial) perception, qualities necessary to art. The second picture in the present is unframed; it comes into being with the entry upon the scene of the unruly and unlovely family that represents reality in all its crudity and resists with all its rough vigor the ordering impulses of art. This family represents the challenge to art posed by "reality," that sphere of experience which has not been brought under control. All three pictures constitute problems in aesthetics, which are the substance of this story.

"Powerhouse" is another story that can be read as an aesthetic statement and, in the light of Welty's critical ideas as they have been outlined earlier, even as a fictionalized statement of her own aesthetic. Music is of course the most ineffable of the arts, and Welty, dealing with this black musician and his group, makes it here suggest the ineffability, indirection, and obliqueness of all the arts, including the writing of fiction. Powerhouse shows that art proceeds by indirection, its plan or structure often interrupted by vagrant inspiration that produces elements which may or may not be worked into the whole: the free flow of the music is sometimes enough in itself. Unquestionably, the artist must command his medium—what Powerhouse has is power to master if not beat and overwhelm his piano—but he must not be a slave to his premeditated plan. He must know when to give way to the flow of his own improvisation. In this connection, Welty has spoken of her doubt that stories are composed "in any typical, predictable, systematically developing, or even chronological way. ... Each story ... thrives in the course of being written only as long as it seems to have a life of its own" (ES, pp. 107–108). Art is unpredictable, then, as the product of the imagination is likely to be, yet the group must make music as a group. The group moves between discipline and freedom, and Powerhouse moves with it, between power controlled and power liberated. All know the rules of the game, and the incomprehensible shouts and truncated statements as they play keep them together but then free them, especially Powerhouse, to soar off as his imagination impels him. Because art is imagination, as Powerhouse knows. The free-running imagination complements the improvised music: Powerhouse imagines the telegram, imagines Uranus Knockwood the sender of the telegram, imagines the death or perhaps the suicide of his wife. These imaginings are as much an art form as the music. They are the imagination at play—and play as art, just as in the music, where the imagination is powerful, rhythmical, affecting, and the artist both commands and bows to it. This is a story about art in which the processes of art become the story as Welty unfolds them in the writing. It is a masterful performance, much more effective than most modernist fictions of the post-war period, to which it can fairly be compared, that have as their self-reflexive subject the writer writing his story.

The Robber Bridegroom is, of course, a fairy tale, and as such it invites taxonomic speculation in the context of the present discussion. Insofar as it is a nonrealistic work of fantasy, it departs from the norms of the traditional novel and allies itself with that order of fiction which is more dependent upon the imagination than upon empirical observation. In its exaggerations of innocence and evil, with Clement and Salome, it willingly surrenders credibility of character. In its use of magic and miracle—the locket, the milk that won't spill, the talking head—it appeals to the suprarational more than to the reason. Insofar as it mythicizes history, with the Harpes and Mike Fink and even Jamie Lockhart, it deliberately distorts what passes for recorded fact. It thereby undermines the notion of a fixed reality, just as the use of disguise does, and in a more serious way, as the use of the theme of doubleness does. Clement tells us that all things are double, are divided in half, and in doing so, he casts doubt upon the certainty of any one thing. And finally the prose, appropriate to a fairy tale or a fable in its balladlike rhythms and its frequently sensuous images, is thoroughly artful in its contrived simplicity, the very antithesis of the even tone and orderly march of the sentences in, for example, the common-sensical Divine Jane: "New Orleans was the most marvelous city in the Spanish country or anywhere else on the river. Beauty and vice and every delight possible to the soul and body stood hospitably, and usually together, in every doorway and beneath every palmetto by day and lighted torch by night. A shutter opened, and a flower bloomed. The very atmosphere was nothing but aerial spice, the very walls were sugar cane, the very clouds hung as golden as bananas in the sky" (*RB*, p. 182).

But *The Robber Bridegroom* is a fairy tale, like others, with meaning, and not a purely autonomous prose work. Clement Musgrove is a comment, for example, on the cycle of history, seeing the historical process as part of the transitoriness of things and people and social structures. In the largest sense the book performs the task of many fairy tales by arousing fear and creating suspense, and then offering a catharsis by asserting the triumph of virtue and imposing an idea of order upon the total experience it relates. In the end, it is a fairy tale very different from those told by John Barth or Donald Barthelme. It does not turn the tale topsy turvy, as Barth wished to turn fiction on its head. It does not reduce the tale to meaningless shambles, as Barthelme does when he deals with Snow White and the Seven Dwarfs, which in his hands becomes a vehicle for the meaningless chaos he sees around him. Welty does not move this far toward modernism, but she moves far enough in this book to seek some of its freedoms from traditionally realistic prose.

The opening story in *The Wide Net*, "First Love," deals in good part with a question of communication much like the problem in such earlier stories as "The Key" and "A Piece of News." The characters in these stories have, for one reason or another, limited or impaired capacities for gaining knowledge. The stories are thus about problems in epistemology, or about how such characters come to know. All of them search for the sources of knowledge beyond the limits of empiricism. "First Love," which happened in extraordinary times and in a season of dreams, rests upon mystery—the mystery of consciousness and the mystery that lies in history. Joel Mayes, a deaf boy, comes to love a hero, Aaron Burr, simply through being in Burr's presence, although Burr of course never speaks to him. Joel had never before known love, and that is a species of knowledge that develops in his inner world or in his awakening consciousness; it is different from knowledge derived in an empirical and rational way. The boy's ways of knowing are clouded in dream and must arise from deeply embedded resources of memory and instinct. In the context of these same epistemological resources, the reader comes to a knowledge of Burr's plot and of his empire-building imagination. Welty deals with the past here not by invoking concrete historical detail but by trying to possess a mystical sense of how it was, by treating it, indeed, as a mystery. Thus the story cannot rest on demonstrable truth or the assumption of a fixed reality. Alfred Appel, Jr. pursues this relationship of dream to truth and reality in this and other stories in the volume, but he does not indicate how Welty is thereby linked to the modernists by virtue of shared epistemological assumptions.

"A Still Moment" is also an effort to repossess the past, but it is more mixed in its fictional modes than "First Love." It may be viewed as a fable that largely deserts realistic strategies, or as a fiction primarily dependent upon its manner of presentation: through the sheer force of style Welty creates the ambience for the story on the Natchez Trace which is as mythical as the Trace in *The Robber Bridegroom*, and she presents the symbolic abstractions who people the story instead of the rounded characters we have conventionally looked for in traditional fiction. When we have symbolic characters meeting in a symbolic wilderness, we inevitably think of Hawthorne, of "Young Goodman Brown," for example; and Hawthorne just as inevitably leads us to the tradition of the romance. The romance of mid-nineteenth century America was a legitimate offspring of European and English romanticism, and it sustained itself on dream (and sometimes nightmare) and mystery and lived in and investigated the underside of consciousness, in Richard Chase's much-quoted phrase. The romance as it comes to the twentieth century as the heritage from Poe and Hawthorne is thus an honored ancestor of modernism. Welty shows herself to be, in a story like "A Still Moment," an heir to this tradition and a recognizable descendant of Hawthorne.

But the romance is a two-edged instrument: it is teleological as well as nonrealistic; the symbols exist for themselves, but for more than themselves. The historical personages of Welty's story, shorn of their personalities, are all symbolic of monomaniacal, overarching, and unattainable ambition: Lorenzo Dow, God-intoxicated, who would convert all to his way; James Murrell, a paradigm for Evil, who would assert the sovereignty of the Devil over all; and Audubon, a paradigm for Science, who would assert man's sovereignty over Nature. These three men want, as Welty says, simply *all*. But the heron appears to them, holds them in transport at its beauty and mystery, and lifts the burden of ambition from them, dissolving their monomaniacal passions. They and we are made to see the limitations in each mode of perception and the folly of each kind of ambition represented among them. These thematic conclusions, the hallmark of traditional fiction, are more firmly presented than even Hawthorne might have done, since his were usually freighted with ambiguities.

In "The Wide Net," while William Wallace Jamieson and his friends are dragging the river for his wife's body, they see a train far below them that looks like a little festival procession. This apparently irrelevant detail is a key to the story, the whole of which may be seen as a rural festival which takes the form of an idyll on the river. The essence of this story is in the happy play of these characters as they experience the wonder and rich variety of nature. The essence of the characters is in their being and not in their meaning, to adapt Archibald MacLeish's notion. The story is a tour de force, insofar as it gives us these folk characters at play, at ease with themselves and existing for themselves. The dragging of the river is a happy, communal ritual which has virtually nothing to do with recovering the body. It seems to be a ritual that has lost its goal and its meaning, one devoted purely to self-pleasure. Yet one cannot ignore the passage in the story in which William Wallace, a kind of river god, dives into the deepest place in Pearl River and comes to some dim, unarticulated knowledge that his wife's trouble, her secret, was an elation coming of hope and change that she, no more than he, could articulate. The equivocal meaning of this passage is to hint at a meaning for the story as a whole, but to shroud it in mystery, as Welty so frequently believes in doing and does. That hint of meaning dilutes the reading of the story as pure play, and it suggests Welty's romantic faith in the possibility of meaning in that which is unspoken or that which is without and beyond words. Some modernists, especially those like Barth, Pynchon, or Gass who have an affinity with Wittgenstein, and who believe that language is all we have and that "what we cannot talk about we must pass over in silence,"[7] reject that possibility. Its hinted presence makes this story something (but not much) more than "mere play."

"At the Landing" has another river god, Billy Floyd. Theme in this story is not marginal, however, but central: Floyd is a natural force, and men and women must bow to that force or be a part of it. Floyd is a man who takes freely what is free—a wild, primitive character who takes fish from the river and game from the forest and the girl Jenny. He takes all these things because they are there and he has use or need, but he makes no commitments. For him having sex is like having food; both are natural acts. Jenny, stifled in her grandfather's house, is liberated to passion by Floyd and comes to know through him the mystery of love. And so she comes to know the secrecy and terror of life: "She knew from him nevertheless that what people ate in the world was earth, river, wildness and litheness, fire and ashes. People took the fresh death and the hot fire into their mouths and got their own life" (*WN*, p. 201). A happier version of this same theme, the inevitable workings of natural forces, is at the heart of "Livvie." Here is a January and May marriage which dissolves naturally in the spring of the year, without the play of will or reason. The characters simply bow to the change of seasons or the passage of time, which is symbolized as the old husband, dying, hands his watch to Livvie. That same natural movement brings the beginning of a new relationship for Livvie, this one with a young man whose sexual potency is as bright as his Easter garments.

Delta Wedding is essentially a traditional novel written in a realistic mode. I wish to concentrate here on showing how Welty works with a literary strategy that assumes certain social structures and demands a particular kind of treatment. She has always known that both the world of experience and the world of appearance must be within reach and that things and places, to be made credible, must be named and identified, treated concretely and exactly.[8] Welty's' dedication to this kind of realism is readily apparent, to choose minor but nevertheless convincing examples, in her sharply observed listing of things in the Fairchild store in town and

---

[7] Ludwig Wittgenstein, *Tractatus Logico-Philosophicus*, trans. D. F. Pears and B. F. McGuinness (London: Routledge & Kegan Paul, 1961), p. 3.

[8] Eudora Welty quoted in Ruth M. Vande Kieft, *Eudora Welty* (New York: Twayne, 1962), pp. 51–52.

in the precise detail of her account of the dinner table at Shellmound. The latter instance is of particular interest because the Fairchilds, at her command, bathe Shellmound in memory and family myth. In making the point of view character so frequently an outsider, that is, someone merely married or related to a Fairchild as Robbie and Ellen and Laura are, Welty shrewdly finds a way both to offer the family myth and to penetrate to a reality behind the myth. Robbie, George's wife, yearns for veracity at one point, "as hard and immediate a veracity as the impact of George's body. It meant coming to touch the real, undeceiving world within the fairy Shellmound world to love George . . ." (*DW*, p. 149).

The Fairchilds are the subject of the novel, or more exactly their family life is, which gives the texture of life, in Hortense Calisher's phrase. It is a life warm, various, confusing, and vital that Welty endows them with, and it recalls Chekhov, an acknowledged Welty model, and suggests also Tolstoy, who begins *Anna Karenina* by speaking of happy and unhappy families. The allusion to the Russians is useful, I trust, because Welty shares with both of them a technical problem. It is to imitate the confusion of family life through the necessarily formal and orderly processes of art: the artist imposes her will upon the confusion without destroying the rich sense and impact of that confusion. She shares with them further, especially with Tolstoy, the *idea* of the family. She makes all the outsiders conscious of the family's presence, but the child Laura dramatizes it most effectively. Her consciousness, her emotional life, and her choices are all dictated by the idea of family. That same idea is of course at play in the marriage of Dabney Fairchild to Troy the overseer. Dabney threatens the myth of the Fairchilds, their insularity, their unspoiled perfection as embodied in the virginal aunts, by seeking the realities of womanhood in love, sex, and marriage; all this is symbolized by her breaking the night light given her by the aunts as she runs up the steps of her house toward Troy. What Welty is pointing to in the wedding of Troy and Dabney is the way in which our social organization arises out of the elemental needs of our passional lives. In the contrast between Dabney and the aunts, Welty treats both society and sexual force realistically.

But Welty does not seem to be making a point. She seems instead simply to be writing about the troubles and tensions, the warmth and richness, the weakness, the property of the family. The social place of the Fairchilds is a given, although both Robbie and Troy are in the novel to make us aware that in a hierarchical society the Fairchilds occupy a comfortably high position. They are a well-to-do rural family of the Mississippi Delta in 1923, a year Welty carefully chose for its relative tranquillity and prosperity so that the socioeconomic base for the life of the Fairchilds would have total credibility. They are clearly the descendants of a plantation family, accepting as a matter of course and as their due a life revolving around big houses, Negro servants and field hands, an overseer, and cotton. Welty does not probe the question of class distinctions or racial justice or any other social problem that might arise in a novel dealing with a Southern family. All these matters having to do with property and money, marriage (beneath one's class or not), the relationship between the classes and the races, between Troy and the Fairchilds, between the Fairchilds and the Negroes, between Troy and the Negroes—all of this Welty gathers in without seeming to be aware that somehow she has projected out of her consciousness an entire social fabric, accurately and realistically woven. Standing in high relief on that fabric is the rich, nourishing life of the Fairchilds, a family as vital as the families in James Farrell or Eugene O'Neill, even if without their tragic pain, poverty, and degradation. The Fairchilds are satisfyingly believable even though their family myth escapes Southern decadence or the terrible guilt of Faulkner's families. Welty gives us cheerful realism.

In *The Golden Apples*, she reaches for and grasps a deeper strain, and she confronts the pain of loss, the powerful frustrations of unfulfilled quest, the high cost of isolation for the outsider, and the terror of life. The result is her masterpiece, as of this writing, a book that, by feeding on myth, takes on grandeur and size. If I treat it briefly here, examining two related aspects of the novel, I do not in any way wish to minimize its importance.

The first of these two is that it shares with *Delta Wedding* a solid, fully designed social fabric. Instead of the family as the central social structure, as in the earlier work, it is the community. Indeed, Morgana is so palpable a presence here that it clearly has the same weight as a major character. "Shower of Gold" may, with its title, take us immediately into the world of myth, but this first chapter is also grounded upon a network of mutually recognized responsibilities or exchanges of personal services, and that network establishes and validates the organic relationships which create the texture of the community. Katie Rainey cares for Miss Snowdie MacLain as, at the conclusion, Miss Snowdie will care for Katie. Katie protects Miss Snowdie against King and thus protects the integrity and order of the community against the anarchic forces of disorder introduced by the self-exiled outsider. Miss Snowdie lays out Katie's corpse in "The Wanderers," not only attending her in death but also thereby participating in the funeral, a communal rite by which Morgana comes to terms with death, as it imposes a preordained order upon the actions and emotions of the survivors. In "Shower of Gold," furthermore, Katie has no hesitation in commandeering the services of a Negro in protecting Miss Snowdie. He knows, without being told, what he must do: the black man tells his white lie in order to preserve the social fabric in which ironically he occupies an inferior position. Yet he has the security of having a place, as well as the knowledge of his function in that place.

So conscious is Welty of the society of Morgana that she lists its families at the beginning of the book. The MacLains are first, the Starks next, and so on down to the Raineys. Lumped together at the bottom, not given the dignity or importance of individual entries in the list, are Holifields and Bowleses; at the end of this group are two characters described as *colored*. I detect no irony in this list. It simply reflects, from top to bottom, the social order and range of Morgana, Mississippi, a hierarchical town society without a genuine aristocrat. But the MacLains are nevertheless the recognized leaders, even though the family has decayed: Ran MacLain, despite the marital trouble he gets into and despite the suicide he causes, is in the time span of the novel elected mayor of the town.

And it *is* a social order which imposes order when disorder threatens. It is out of assumptions about society that the principal tension of the novel arises. The major isolatos of the novel—King MacLain, at the top of the list of families; Virgie Rainey, at the bottom of the list but near the top in importance in the book; Miss Eckhart and Easter, who are not even on the list—dash themselves against the boundaries defined by the community, seeking a vision, a truth, a secret, a power beyond the community to give. In "June Recital" the ladies who parade to the rook game at the beginning and parade home again at the end provide the frame or order within which we see two related variants of disorder in action. Miss Eckhart, the outsider as foreigner and as artist, would yield to the order of art if she could, as her dedication to the metronome suggests: it represents art disciplined to the order of time. But she is made to feel terror and pain and is driven to madness, in good part because she cannot and does not know how to enter into the order of the community. Virgie, the outsider as the fey child full of airs of wildness, of abandon, is the unfulfilled natural genius whose frustration issues in teen-age sexual rebellion. At the end of this chapter, Cassie Morrison thinks about Miss Eckhart and Virgie meeting on the sidewalk, after they have emerged from the MacLain house, as if "they had been making a trip. . . . They were deliberately terrible." Then Cassie realizes that both "were human beings terribly at large, roaming on the face of the earth. And there were others of them—human beings, roaming, like lost beasts" (*GA*, pp. 84–85). In this story madness and rebellion are hemmed in by the ladies, and then, in an ironic counterpoint, by Bowles and Moody, representing the slapstick, lower class version of community order. The Virgie of "The Wanderers," however, knows that life is a prison that one must beat one's way out of, and she escapes Morgana by transcending it through the powers of endurance—knowing pain, loss, hate, and love—and imagination.

My second major point has, in essence, already been made. *The Golden Apples* is a teleological work of fiction. Of course Welty does not baldly state her aim, but she is making a statement about human experience. The benefits of the community in sustaining ritual and order, in giving continuity to life, in providing norms for personal relationships must be measured against the limitations of community. It bestows identity, but at the same time it can make for self-satisfied smugness. In "Moon Lake" Jinny Love Stark, whose position in the town is clearly defined, knows exactly who she is and does not, as a consequence, want to know any more; in other words, she foreshortens the horizons of her experience in contrast to Nina Carmichael, who yearns to identify with orphans, with others, who seeks an expanded consciousness which might take her beyond the limits defined by community and into the uncertain realm occupied by the orphan Easter. Or the community may be intrusive, as it is for Ran in "The Whole World Knows": "You can't get away in Morgana. Away from anything at all, you know that" (p. 144). These limitations suggest the price that must be paid for community and order. The price of separateness from the community is in part precisely that sense of loss and deprivation that results in being cut off from one's roots and from those sustaining relationships that flourish in the community—the family, or more particularly the father. Eugene feels this loss in San Francisco, in "Music from Spain." He and the Spaniard come together because they are alone and without love. The terrible roar the Spaniard lets out is a cry of undefined pain caused by a many-faceted isolation, the isolation of an artist cut off from his home and cut off from other men by language.

But the glory of separateness is in the quest and in freedom, is in transcending the order of Morgana and risking the dangers of liberation. Fulfillment cannot be an anticipated end when this choice is made. King is still a restless and unsatisfied man at the end of the book, although he has lived at least some of his life as a natural force (a sexual force, as in "Sir Rabbit"), as Floyd and William Wallace are natural forces in the short stories. But surely he was in quest of something more. Welty never defines it. The urgings of quest are enough in themselves. It is the same with Virgie. When she is finally liberated, in "The Wanderers," and will leave Morgana, she is able to hear "the magical percussion, the world beating in [her] ears" (p. 244). It is not the *meaning* of the running horse and bear, the dragon's slither, the trumpet of the swan that counts; rather, it is that once Virgie is made conscious of them, they are an irresistible lure that guarantees her a restless life spent in reaching beyond her grasp. In thus giving us the complexities of order and disorder, community and freedom or alienation, Welty gives us a vision of the polarized tensions in their many dimensions that govern human lives. That vision defines *The Golden Apples* as teleological fiction and beautifully makes of it a traditional novel of high artistry.

And artistry does not belong to the modernists alone, although it may be their sole possession. With them, the art of telling is an end in itself. *The Golden Apples* reveals, as I trust I have just shown, other ends. But *The Ponder Heart*, Welty's next book, is almost wholly dependent upon the art of telling, and it is a failure insofar as it seeks a farther reach. This novelette should exist simply for the sake of the narrative voice; if that were the case it would have escaped the sentimentality that arises from the vindication of lovable old Uncle Daniel. What is memorable here, as a virtuoso performance, is the voice of Edna Earle Ponder carrying on a monologue that testifies to the persistence of the oral tradition in the South and validates it with every turn of idiom and with the rhythm of every sentence. It is a more fully sustained performance than the one we get in "Why I Live at the P.O." But it is a modernist fiction manqué, indeed a fiction manqué, because Welty was not content with performance itself, with art alone; unfortunately all she had to add were warmth and whimsy.

In the title story of *The Bride of the Innisfallen* and in "Going to Naples" in that volume Welty seems to have more faith in the mode of telling alone and to rely less upon theme or moral. Both stories are Chekhovian in their meandering pace. The first seems without a center; it is made up of fragments that do not cohere. The characters seem to be assembled by chance, and their encounters are chanceful in ways that recall the Dos Passos of *Manhattan Transfer*. One notes an absence of orderly develop-ment. All this suggests a rejection of continuities and linear movement, and this same quality, this apparent randomness, marks the second story as well. These stories show a kinship with modernism, but not a total commitment to it. "Circe," on the other hand, is a conventional treatment of myth, even though Welty alters the *Odyssey* version by telling the story from Circe's point of view. When a modernist like Coover re-tells a myth, like the virgin birth, for example, his change of perspective—his point of view character is Joseph—makes such a radical change in the story that his version has the effect of demythologizing that event. Welty does not share this modernist skepticism, or cynicism, about the possibility of belief and values.

Losing Battles is further evidence of Welty's persistence in belief. It is an affirming novel drawing its strength from the strength of the people, the folk, whom it portrays. Its theme is the continuity of the family and the endurance of the people, who draw the strength to endure from their land and their place, their past, and their community, which is an entity larger than the family and the farm with which the family identifies. The novel is also about the resistance of the people to the efforts of the teacher, Miss Julia Mortimer, to educate them; they are intransigent in remaining what they are. Finally, it is the story of injustice worked by society upon an innocent and virtuous hero.

But thematic considerations in the course of this long novel frequently fade into the background, and the manner in which the story is told, or even the very nature of the story, assumes primary importance. What dis-tinguishes this novel is not those ordinary and obvious themes but the way in which Welty has mythologized her protagonist, making of him a hero in a series of tales. Jack Renfro is strong, audacious, selfless, and chivalric. He is impractical and unworldly. He does good for the sake of good. He is generous and forgiving, even with his enemies or those who have wronged him. He is a loving husband and father and a devoted son. He is a noble man, and Welty has cast him in the mold of a perfect Chris-tian knight of the Middle Ages or of a Renaissance courtier out of Casti-glione. The achievement of the book is largely in the effect of the incongruity between Jack's character and his social station; in other words, it is in the telling. She has also endowed him with supernatural powers.

He comes home, having escaped from prison, on the day of the family reunion celebrating Granny's ninetieth birthday, although he had no apparent way of knowing that the reunion was taking place on that day: he is privy to some mysteriously intangible source of knowledge. Jack's actual arrival at home from prison is magical. It occurs to a sound like a pistol shot in the yard and the frantic barking of dogs; a whirlwind of dust appears; there is a drumming and swaying of the house floor; a pan drops from a nail; and the new tin roof quivers. Later in the story he effects a miraculous return, rushing into the house in the nick of time to catch Granny as she appears to be toppling off the table. Thus the folk hero is a perfect knight who moves in mystery, magic, and miracle. This treatment, it need hardly be added, is antirealistic, as in *The Robber Bridegroom*.

Jack performs the exploits of the hero. They are in the epic spirit, but in scale they are appropriate to Jack as a hero of the folk. Jack is not mocked in the telling of these episodes; instead, he is honored. The first one is a tale, told by one of the family, and it is the first of many tales which occur in the novel. Talk is at the center of the story, and actions are frequently re-created in talk rather than acted out. The repeated use of the tale should be seen in the light of Welty's tribute to the master of the tale: "In our literature, what has traveled the longest way through time is the great affirmative soul of Chaucer" (*ES*, p. 152). Dependence on the tale reflects a love of story for the sake of story that is very like John Barth's attitude toward story and his practice in *The Sot-Weed Factor*, where the characters tell innumerable tales. The first tale in *Losing Battles*, to return to it, is told to the accompaniment of a chorus, made up of the listening relatives. Since virtually everyone in this audience knows the tale, its telling takes on the character of a rite. The story is that Curly Stovall, the villain, has taken a gold ring, a family heirloom that had belonged to one of Granny's daughters, from Jack's sister. Jack fights Curly, subduing him in order to reclaim the ring, which has talismanic qualities (like the garnet pin in *Delta Wedding*), and to avenge the injury done his sister. He stuffs Curly into his own coffin, tying him in. Then he carries the safe, in which he believes Curly has secreted the ring, from Curly's store to the family home. But the ring is not in the safe. Welty is at play with these various epic elements—the knight-errant fighting gallantly to avenge the injury done the damsel in distress by the villain, displaying courage and superhuman strength, and seeking or questing for the precious object of transcendent worth. The episode is full of vigor and fun. Jack is a comic character. But Welty is not writing mock-epic; Jack is not a mock-hero, but a genuine folk hero clothed in the habiliments of the knightly hero.

This adventure leads to Jack's conviction for theft and his prison term, harshly meted out by Judge Moody. Jack thus becomes a type of the folk hero unjustly treated by the law and forced outside the society: another medieval figure, a Robin Hood or the good man as outlaw. Welty's irony is that this figure becomes the benefactor of the man who did him injury. Judge Moody wrecks his car, which comes to precarious rest on the edge of a cliff. In a series of slapstick scenes, throbbing with the same wild disorder that informs Faulkner's spotted horses story, Jack undertakes to get the car safely down. Here Welty resorts to burlesque, as the country folk, led by Jack in their clumsy improvisations, barely avoiding disaster, stumblingly succeed in a thoroughly unorthodox way in rescuing the car. This tale of the Moodys' car, which is in two major parts, is propelled by comic energies which are their own excuse for being; joy is in the telling of the tale as an end in itself.

It is of this novel that Welty said, it is "just a pure talk story."[9] She wanted, she said, to translate "every thought and feeling into action and speech, speech being another form of action—to bring the whole life of it off through the completed gesture. . . ."[10] Talk and gesture—these are what the novel is about. Thus described, *Losing Battles*, despite its thematic content, comes close to being a modernist fiction which has as its subject the ways in which it is made. *The Optimist's Daughter*, however, the next and last of her fictions as of this writing, is a wholly traditional novel. It is a meditation upon death, as the last chapter of *The Golden Apples* is. Welty is here concerned with the difficulties and betrayals of dying. When Laurel, her protagonist, confronts these, she is overtaken by a flood of feeling, and she weeps "in grief for love and for the dead." She has won through to an earned catharsis of her emotions. Weeping for her recently dead father, she is able to confront and admit to her consciousness the earlier death of her husband. As a result, "the deepest spring in her heart had uncovered itself, and it began to flow again" (*OD*, p. 154). Facing his death for the first time, she is able to face all. She now recognizes that life is nothing but the continuity of its love. This recognition

---

[9] Bunting, p. 717.
[10] Kuehl, p. 77.

that love and death are tied together is one of the revelations of the novel. Another is that love and hate come together in the continuing of our lives. She frees herself to hate Fay, her father's disastrous second wife, who is one of those people upon whom almost everything is lost, one who is without "powers of passion or imagination in herself" (p. 178). Those powers, the sensitized consciousness, are qualities like those of an E. M. Forster heroine that make us human and make our lives worth living. Laurel considers them a part of her heritage from the past and from the ideals of order and community that ruled that past.

In the novel Fay represents the future, as she says at the end, and she is thus a threat to the past. She has married Judge McKelva, the optimist of the title, who lives in Mt. Salus, Mississippi. At the beginning of the novel, he is in New Orleans to see a doctor who is of a different generation from his but from the same place. Despite the difference in age, the judge trusts him and understands him because of that community bond. And for another reason: "I'm in good hands. . . . I know his whole family" (p. 11). But this faith is not enough. Enjoined to remain absolutely quiet in his hospital bed, he lies there near death. Fay seizes and shakes him. She was trying to scare him into living, she says much later, but Laurel sees the act as a murderous expression of petty deprivation and self-pity. It is, of course, an attack upon age and the past and all the pieties that support these by a person who does not know how to feel, a person of the present and future.

At Mt. Salus for the funeral, Laurel finds her own friends and the family friends, her father's crowd from the county bar, the Hunting and Fishing Club, and the church leadership. These constitute two distinct and orderly groups, a part of the community of support that Laurel may count upon, and they move in place like the "rim of a wheel that slowly turned itself around the hub of the coffin and would bring them around again" (p. 64). As in "June Recital," the people of the community bestow order upon the rites of the community. But Fay and her family disrupt the order with their improprieties. At Fay's insistence, the judge is buried in a new part of the cemetery and not beside his "old wife." The intrusion upon the expected order and ritual creates a tension between traditional modes of behavior and the impulsive, self-satisfying, accidental behavior of those without standards. Welty has created a clash between the traditional and the modern, the insider and the outsider. She does not find the former altogether blameless or the latter with nothing but shortcomings, but in contrast to *The Golden Apples*, where the outsider or isolato sought some transcendent goal, the insider here, Laurel, is the beneficiary of revelation and growth while the outsider is condemned as a desecrator and is vanquished. The handmade breadboard which Fay has ruined is a symbol of the spoliation and contempt she has visited upon the values of community, family, and home. Fay is a failure as a person. "Death in its reality passed her right over" (p. 131). In this clash, Laurel is Welty's victor, representing the victory of knowledge, sensitivity, character, a highly developed consciousness, all nurtured and shaped by the past and the community. No more fully traditional statement could be made in a novel. Clearly Welty is not moving toward modernism as time goes on. But there is reason to believe that she will have recourse to that mode again and that she will continue to draw upon both traditionalism and modernism.

JOHN
ALEXANDER
ALLEN

The Other Way to Live: Demigods in Eudora Welty's Fiction

THE READER OF Eudora Welty's fiction may be excused for sometimes feeling like Hazel Jamieson's cousin, Edna Earle, in "The Wide Net," who can spend a whole day wondering how the tail of the "C" got through the "L" in a Coca-Cola sign. Welty deals in all kinds and degrees of mystery and paradox. However prolonged and bemused one's pondering of them may be, one thing remains certain: they do not yield their secrets easily. Her work abounds in Delphic passages that, even when regarded with the care that love inspires, not only resist analysis but resolve themselves into further riddles without end, like the broom of the sorcerer's apprentice. Faced with such inscrutability, one can find a degree of comfort in the bafflement of certain of Welty's characters who are themselves engaged in threading labyrinths. We follow Eugene MacLain, in "Music from Spain," through a long, eventful day of seeking and share with him a striking vision, high on a cliff overlooking the Pacific. When he returns to his wife Emma in the evening, what has he learned, and what have we learned from him? The reader must proceed with caution. In "The Wanderers," the author remarks with uncharacteristic bluntness that poor Eugene, who at last went home to Morgana, Mississippi, to die, "had lived in another part of the world, learning while he was away that people don't have to be answered just because they want to know" (*GA*, p. 241). No doubt there is wisdom in the words of children. "You couldn't learn anything through the head" (p. 119), Nina Carmichael decides in "Moon Lake," banging her fist on the hot hair of know-it-all Jinny Love Stark.

Eudora Welty offers no rules for finding your way either in life or in her books. The map she supplies for *Losing Battles* is helpful up to a point, but we may need to supplement it with the one scrawled by Miss Julia Mortimer to guide Judge Moody to her house in Alliance; and that

/

map, as the judge remarks, is a maze, just a maze. He had not, as it happens, tried to go by it at all, but had become hopelessly lost on his own power. We may, like Dewey Coker in "Ladies in Spring," be familiar with every building on the main street of Royals where he lives, from the Baptist Church to the schoolhouse; but, on the day we spend with Dewey, he notices for the first time a Negro church, somewhere just beyond town, set back in a closet of trees. It has twin steeples and twin privies at the rear. Where has it been all of his life? At the end of the story, a little black dog sits on the top step of the church, looking as though he belongs to it. On the other hand, "there was no telling where he might have come from" (*BI*, p. 101).

A number of Welty's characters are as mysterious in origin as Dewey Coker's little black dog. Billy Floyd, in "At the Landing," is said to have the blood of a Natchez Indian, to be a descendant of the Natchez who escaped from Atlantis when that island sank under the sea. That helps to account for something very strange about *him*. Easter, in "Moon Lake," is an orphan; and, as though she were her own Adam, having no parent to give her a name, she has named herself. The little Morgana girls can scarcely credit such transcendent independence. Easter "remained not answerable to a soul on earth. Nobody cared! And so, in this beatific state, something came out of *her*" (*GA*, p. 112). Eugene MacLain's Spaniard, being a concert guitarist, is a traveling man, and, in the bargain, he does not know a word of English. And King MacLain, the scandalous manifestation of Zeus in *The Golden Apples*, may have roots in MacLain Courthouse, but that does not help his wife, Miss Snowdie, to keep track of his wanderings, even though she employs the Jupiter Detective Agency for the purpose.

We never enter the minds of any of these mysterious persons, nor of George Fairchild of *Delta Wedding*, or Miss Hattie Purcell or her niece, Opal, with whom Dewey Coker reckons in "Ladies in Spring." We must make what we can of them from what they do and from their effect on other characters, who find them as unsettling and provocative as the reader does. We share Nina Carmichael's fascination with Easter, Ellen Fairchild's with George. George adds reality to Ellen's world, leaving it, in all its imperfection, somehow pure, "fleeting and mysterious and hopelessly alluring to her" (*DW*, p. 80). Something similar might be said of any one of the characters mentioned above—or, for that matter, of Eudora Welty's work itself.

Jogged out of his watch repairman's rut by the unpremeditated act of slapping his wife, Eugene MacLain steps forth into the streets of San Francisco. A cat lies among the apples in a grocer's window, and its eyes inspire in him the thought that "he would know anything that happened, anything that threatened the moral way, or transformed it, even, in the city of San Francisco that day" (*GA*, p. 170). The thought is both frightening and inspiring to Eugene. In his sudden elation lies a clue to Welty's way with fiction and with us. As writer, she distrusts systems of every kind, together with preconceptions, pieties. The Spaniard, with his smouldering energies and passionate detachment, is everything that Eugene is not: one whom Eugene can imagine dancing with an alligator, floating like a bird up into airy distance, wearing horns on his head, shooting fire from his nostrils. He will, in fact, before the day is over spew out a torrent of confession in a bullish roar, while holding Eugene aloft, in an attitude of flight, over the abyss. It would be foolish to suppose Eugene could emulate the Spaniard. There is something intentionally comic about the very notion of such a transformation, and it is expressed in an explicitly comic way near the end of the story. The formidable waitress in the café where Eugene and the Spaniard stop for coffee announces, with reference to Eugene, her cure for misbehavior in her little husband. She simply picks him up and stands him on the mantelpiece. Not everyone is going to change just because he wants to; yet change is on its way for some and may occur exactly when they least expect it.

II

The Spaniard is one of a number of Welty's characters who possesses powers of a kind and degree that verge upon the godlike. Of the qualities they have in common, one is certainly passion, an intensity so great and overriding that it invites comparison with potent natural phenomena, like fire and flood. The Spaniard's outer calm, his aboslute control as artist, is like the quiet center of a cyclone. The same is true of George Fairchild, about whom Ellen asks herself with awe, "what on earth would ever be worth that intensity with which he held it, the hurting intensity that was reflected back on him, from all passing things?" (*DW*, p. 80). George's dramatic entrance at a critical point in her emotional life takes on for Ellen the effect of an apotheosis: "he stood with his shirt torn back and his shoulders as bare (she thought in a cliché of her childhood) as a Greek god's, his hair on his forehead as if he were intoxicated, unconscious of the leaf caught there, looking joyous" (p. 166). If one had to pick the Greek god that George resembles at this moment, it would surely be Dionysus. The association of that god with literal and emotional intoxication, with ecstatic states, combined with abundant kindness, fits George's character and role exactly. Like Dionysus, George is attuned to all realities, including death. Billy Floyd, on the other hand, the homeless boy in "At the Landing," clearly is associated with the god Poseidon, and the similarity of his name to "flood" is surely not an accident. He has a centaur-like rapport with horses and displays an animal's keenness of sense. His natural element is water, his habitat the river, and his emblem the enormous catfish that he carries. He has the primitive quality that belongs to Poseidon, as opposed to the almost feminine grace and gentleness that characterize Dionysus or George Fairchild in his propitious mood. King MacLain's exemplar in the pantheon explicitly is Zeus. He is the suave and dapper seducer of women, a guise that does not conceal but coexists with his square brown teeth and the pain of unappeased appetite that still afflicts him, modulated into hunger, even in old age.

Perhaps the most important attribute of the demigod in Welty's fiction is his intimacy with death. George Fairchild's brother, Denis (Dionysus), lost in the First World War, continues to be worshipped by the Fairchild family. As the living representative of the incomparable Denis, George is both the family hero and something like its sacrificial beast. No incident in *Delta Wedding* is more significant than the one in which George defiantly offers himself to death in the form of the Memphis-Yazoo City train that almost crushes him. Eugene MacLain's Spaniard, in his abstracted way, would actually have walked straight into the path of an automobile if Eugene had not caught hold of his coat and pulled him back to safety. Eugene himself later comes within a hairsbreadth of giving his enormous companion the little shove that would have sent him plummeting to his death from the high cliff over the Pacific shore. King MacLain's "dying," like so many aspects of his career as Welty presents them, is in the comic mode, but is no less essentially serious for that. After his assignation in Morgan's Woods with his wife Snowdie—the occasion on which the MacLain twins were begotten—Mr. King leaves his hat on the bank of the Big Black River to signify that he has drowned in it, though in truth, of course, he is more than ever wonderfully at large. As for Billy Floyd, he has an air of immortality, despite his perilous venturing forth on the flood waters of the Mississippi. He fears death no more than an animal does; and, like all men, but guiltless as an animal, he accepts the offerings of death. When the flood comes, it is a foregone conclusion that he will rescue Jenny, the reclusive girl who loves him. It is no less certain that he will violate her. In his boat he and Jenny pass over the graveyard where her mother and grandfather lie. He is a hunter, bringing meat and fish for her to eat, so that she learns from him how "people took the fresh death and the hot fire into their mouths and got their own life" (*WN*, p. 201).

Death is also associated with the girls who are the conquests of Billy Floyd and of King MacLain. After the flood, when Floyd has returned to the river, Jenny sets out in search of him. The fishermen who are encamped by the river do not object to her waiting there for Floyd. Near the end of the story, the men put Jenny inside a grounded houseboat; then, they go in to her, one by one, bringing with them the smell of the trees that have bled to the knives they throw at them. When Jenny, after a time, calls out, "A rude laugh covered her cry, and somehow both the harsh human sounds could easily have been heard as rejoicing, going out over the river in the dark night" (p. 214). The progressive, ritual-like assault upon Jenny is like the story of every woman's meeting with the beast in humankind. At the same time, Jenny is a celebrant of the life that had been denied her when she lived a prisoner with her grandfather in the house where her mother had remained mad and imprisoned until she died. Jenny's love for Billy Floyd is so great and multitudinous that it forms a night-long procession in her dreams. If she suffers a kind of death beside the river, it is of a different quality from that she had experienced in the house where she grew up. There, she had not dared to touch one of the innumerable prisms that hung in all the rooms, to sing out loud, or to visit her mother's grave without permission. Her grandfather had forbidden her even to speak to Billy Floyd.

Although Welty is staunchly sceptical of conventional moral attitudes, she deals in reality and therefore takes full account of evil. Most frequently, evil is associated in her work with imprisonment of one kind or another. When death takes that form, and only then, it is a true and unequivocal evil. One finds such death in the self-imprisonment of Octavia Farr and her mad kindred in "Clytie," and in the tyrannous rule of Miss Sabina in "Asphodel." The imperious will of Miss Sabina has made a prison of an entire town, for she supervises and controls every significant event that happens there and ministers, on her terms, to the needs of every resident. Long ago, wielding a horsewhip, she had driven her beast-like husband, Mr. Don McInnis, from her house. At last, she has died, and her maiden votaries wish only to conclude their mourning with a cozy picnic. Instead, they suffer a vision of the grand and naked Mr. Don, though he has long been dead and thought to have left the world a safe retreat for inoffensive ladies. Presently, he assumes the form of a band of horned, inquisitive little goats that devour all the delicacies that the ladies have put by from their little feast. Apparently it takes more than horsewhipping and the burning of his pillared mansion Asphodel to dispose of Mr. Don. Indeed, it takes more than death. "He ought not to be left at liberty," cries Miss Cora. "I have a good mind to report him to the law!" But, in the mind of Miss Phoebe, the disrupted picnic lives on "in a tender dream and an unconscious celebration. . . ." It remains, for her, "the enduring and intoxicating present, still the phenomenon, the golden day" (*WN*, pp. 112–13).

Eudora Welty often evinces something close to derision with regard to man-made law, as opposed to the law of nature or of the heart. King MacLain had once intended to become a lawyer, but he had never practiced law, preferring to travel in behalf of tea and spices. When Mr. King seduces Mattie Will Holifield in Morgan's Woods, the season is fall, but he looks, as always, like "the preternatural month of June." In theory, Mattie Will is protected on this occasion by her husband, Junior, a Negro boy named Blackstone, and a dog named Wilbur after Wilbur Morrison, publisher of the Morgana *Bugle*. In addition, Miss Lizzie Stark, who hates all men, has posted the family woods with signs reading, "No Pigs With or Without Rings. No hunting. This means You." But neither Miss Lizzie's defiance of the entire male sex, nor the bonds of matrimony, nor the legal code (a ghostly presence brought to mind by Blackstone), nor public opinion (duly voiced by Mr. Morrison in the *Bugle*), and least of all the fears of Mattie Will herself, can prevent her becoming one more instance of "Mr. MacLain's Doom, or Mr. MacLain's Weakness." King MacLain, whistling and smiling more sweetly than can be imagined, asks the girl politely to explain something to him, something mysterious; and Mattie Will can no more refuse him than stop breathing. The seduction itself, with its references to Yeats's "Leda and the Swan," figures forth the brute fact and the tragic and heroic consequences of mortal weakness overpowered by a god. The consequences of the rape of Mattie Will are not, of course, on the Homeric scale suggested in Yeats's sonnet. They are

properly accommodated to the town of Morgana, Mississippi. Nevertheless, both tragedy and ennoblement are let loose upon this little world by
the seed of King MacLain. As we discover in "The Wanderers," Mattie
Will in due course gave birth to a daughter (not a Holifield!), who, in
turn, brought forth Maideen Sumrall. It is the same Maideen, the unfortunate Kore of the Seed and Feed, who is ruined and driven to suicide by
Mr. King's son Randall. The story is completed when Randall is elected
mayor of Morgana not on merit in the usual sense, but "for his glamour
and his story, for being a MacLain and the bad twin, . . . for ruining a girl
and the thing she did. . . . They voted for the revelation; it made their
hearts faint . . ." (p. 210). The story is so carefully buried in *The Golden
Apples*, yet with such clear signs to call attention to a mystery, that a reader of that book, perhaps on his second or third go-through, feels, like the
voters of Morgana, he has experienced revelation, caught the hand of fate
in action, seen a mystery of life open before him.

III

The Kore figure so pathetically portrayed by Maideen Sumrall appears in
a strikingly different form in "Moon Lake" in the person of the orphan,
Easter. She emerges at once, among all the orphans and Morgana girls at
the camp beside the lake, as a magically dominant figure. With Easter in
her mind, Nina Carmichael lies awake one night in the tent she shares
with Miss Moody and other girls, including Easter. The others are asleep
when inspiration stirs in Nina and she puts her feeling into words: "The
orphan! she thought exultantly. The other way to live. There were secret
ways. . . . I've been only thinking like the others. It's only interesting, only
worthy, to try for the fiercest secrets. To slip into them all—to change. To
change for a moment into Gertrude, into Mrs. Gruenwald, into Twosie—
into a boy. To *have been* an orphan" (p. 123). Nina is no demigod. She is
something much more like a typical Morgana girl. In this story, however,
she serves as living proof that even the most ordinary person, circumscribed by well-defined customs, attitudes and habits of mind, can sometimes find her way to the crux of her experience and rise to it, imaginatively, in full. She will of course, in the grim phrase, revert to type. In "The
Wanderers," we see her for a moment as a married lady. She is Mrs. Junior
Nesbitt, and she is seated in the parlor of the Rainey house, "heavy with
child. . . , head fine and indifferent, one puffed white arm stretched along
the sewing machine." Her glimpse of the other way to live is buried far

in the past. Even at the time when it occurred, it was brief and unsustainable. Yet the brevity of her experience does nothing to invalidate it. It is only astonishing that such glimpses should occur at all. They are like little miracles, rare and precious, disproportionate in value to any external measure. As Ellen Fairchild concludes in *Delta Wedding*, "one moment told you the great things, one moment was enough for you to know the greatest thing" (p. 240).

At first glance, there seems nothing sufficiently remarkable about Easter to account for her profound effect upon Nina Carmichael. She might well be dismissed as only a stringy child who shares the institutional anonymity of the band of orphans to which she belongs. Her most immediately conspicuous physical distinction is a rising shock of hair which in contrast with the sun-bleached thatches of the other orphans is of a "withstanding" gold. But a closer look shows the quality of her eyes. Noticing them, Nina is reminded of her grandfather's collection of coins from Greece and Rome: "they had something of metal, flat ancient metal, so that you could not see into them. . . . Instead of round black holes in the center of her eyes, there might have been women's heads, ancient" (p. 106). The comment is not Nina's but the author's, yet Nina deeply feels the mystery of those remarkable eyes. She notices the way Easter drinks from the spring—flat as a boy, with her elbows cocked—and her reckless skill with her three-blade jack-knife. It is as though Easter bridges the gap between the sexes as well as that between the present and the distant past. Hard and boyish as she is, she has begun her breasts; and, when Mr. Nesbitt from the Bible Class takes her by the wrist and turns her around to stare at them, she promptly reveals the danger in her, to the other girls' delight, by biting his hand. Easter is self-contained and uncannily aloof, traits typified by her habit of rolling her eyes up into her head until only the whites are visible. On one occasion, when Jinny Love Stark suggests they pretend Easter is not with them, Nina finds herself saying, "But that's what *she* was pretending." Jinny Love is stunned by this observation. "But how could you ever know what Easter was pretending?" (p. 117). Perhaps for the first time in her life, Nina has gotten right outside herself and into the head of someone else.

Above all, Nina is struck by the intimacy between Easter and the grave figure of night itself when, as it appears to Nina, that dark giant brushes aside the flap and enters the campers' tent. To Easter, who lies asleep, he is "obedient and graceful." He knows all about her, loves her, even kneels down before her. This relationship is apparent to Nina's acute intuitive awareness from the gesture made by Easter's hand as it hangs down from her cot, palm outward. Like the sounds uttered by Easter in her sleep at nap time, it suggests "wholehearted and fateful concurrence with the thing dreamed." Although Nina lets her own hand hang down like Easter's, making a gesture identical with hers, night does not respond to her as to Easter; and when Nina finally falls asleep, she dreams that her helpless hand is being torn by the teeth of wild beasts.

Later in the story, when Easter has nearly drowned in Moon Lake, Nina with the others lives through the long minutes during which Loch Morrison, as Boy Scout life-saver, forces life back into Easter's body. Loch's necessarily brutal assault on Easter's inert form presents an exact analogy to rape, to violation. Yet Easter's stubborn passivity, her clinging, as it were, to death, makes her appear as brutal in withholding life as the Boy Scout does in ravishing it back from darkness. When the contestants, rescuer and rescued, seem to have reached a stalemate, Nina notices that Easter's hand has assumed exactly the same gesture that had seemed in the tent to ally her with night. The effect of this sign upon Nina is so powerfully emotional that she faints; but in the prior moment she has time to remember the things she loves at home. She has a fleeting vision of sweet-smelling grass falling in the wake of the lawn mower, the blazing four-o'clocks. When she is revived, she is visited by a moment from what seems the remote future: herself, as though released from time, picking up three little shells, while Easter lies beyond dying or being remembered. When Easter at last returns to consciousness, she falls from the table, but, in doing so, she kicks the Boy Scout. Nina's first reaction to Easter's resurrection, in her confusion of emotions, is a defiance of her own, to match Easter's. Then she is relieved, not so much that Easter is alive as that what had happened to her is out in the world.

Easter is by far the most memorable character in "Moon Lake," but the most important character is surely Nina Carmichael, who for a moment is transformed, liberated from her ordinary self, by the magic of Easter. Not even Welty, for all her art, can take us inside Easter's head. The other way to live *is* Easter's way, and it can be communicated only indirectly. It is, in its nature, wordless. In "At the Landing," Jenny finds an image that, for her, sums up the difference between her love for Billy Floyd and whatever it may be that he himself turns toward when he turns away from her: whatever it is that rules his life and leads him forward. Looking into the core of a lump of amber in a string of beads, she reflects that "nobody could ever know about the difference between the radiance that was the surface and the radiance that was inside. There were the two worlds. There was no way at all to put a finger on the center of light" (*WN*, p. 209). As Jenny is to Billy Floyd, so Nina is to Easter, Mattie Will to King MacLain, and Eugene MacLain to his Spanish musician. Likely enough, a parallel relationship exists between Welty's fiction and her inner vision, and between the reader and the core of radiance in her works.

IV

George Fairchild, the Dionysian figure in *Delta Wedding*, resembles King MacLain up to a point. Both have been trained as lawyers, but the law is not their destined calling. Both have magically winning ways, particularly with women. They share a knack for making the perfect gift. Both combine a self-contained tranquillity and sweetness of demeanor with inner passionate intensity. But George Fairchild differs from Mr. King in point of immanence. He has abounding love not only for every member of his family but for the whole world. Though he is capable of taking his pleasure with a runaway girl who chances to cross his path, he is no Zeus perpetually engaged in making conquests. He has chosen his love once and for all, begging her to return his love and marry him. He is dependent upon her for his very life, and the dream that comes to her when she has left him truly represents him as a desperate man with mouth agape as though in drunkenness or hunger. Whereas King MacLain's supposed drowning in the Big Black River serves conveniently to liberate Mr. King from domesticity, George is himself a liberator. Though he is himself at home in a domestic context, he inspires in women and girls an authentic Dionysian urge to cast off whatever bonds confine them.

The Fairchild family of *Delta Wedding* possess an abundance of all good things: beauty, talent, intelligence, inexhaustible energy. They seem, at first glance, to be free, and joyous in their freedom. They love one another fondly and, above all, know how to take full pleasure in the present moment. Happiness is so much their family legend that one realizes only gradually how circumscribed that happiness is, how quickly every Fairchild runs away from trouble or unpleasantness. Death is anathema to the Fairchilds. Old Aunt Shannon, who is eccentric if not downright mad, represents the family attitude more truly than they know when she converses with her husband Lucian Miles and other persons long since laid to rest.

Laura McRaven, a visiting cousin, has lost her mother during the preceding winter, and she is therefore "insistently a little messenger or reminder of death," but the family refer to Annie Laurie McRaven's death only as a kind of marker fixed in time, saying that such and such a thing occurred before or after Annie Laurie died. The loss of Denis Fairchild, in the war, is often called to mind, but his memory has been purged of every mortal taint—his drinking, reckless escapades, and disastrous marriage. He has in effect been sainted and established as the epitome, immune from change, of all the perfections that the Fairchilds of Shellmound Plantation worship in themselves.

A reminder that Denis was in fact very far from perfect is visible every day at Shellmound in the person of Maureen, aged nine. She is the only child of Denis and bears a superficial resemblance to all the other Fairchilds. However, she is "funny in her head" and regularly exhibits, between periods of docility, destructiveness like that of a young maenad on the rampage. She will capture a cricket and joyfully dismember it, stalk a bird with the same intent, or, crying "Choo choo," push a heavy pile of firewood onto her hiding cousin Laura. Yet the Fairchilds have grown used to looking through and around Maureen and the harm that lies inside her. They let her have her way in everything, outdo themselves in generosity toward her, and believe, as a point of faith, that "she bore no more breath of resemblance to [Denis] than she did to . . . the King of Siam" (p. 116).

It was in connection with Maureen that George Fairchild had dramatized, before a large family group, an attitude toward death that allies him in the reader's mind with both Maureen and Denis. Trying to free Maureen's foot from the railroad track in the middle of a trestle, George was nearly crushed by the Yellow Dog, the Yazoo-Delta train, before the action of *Delta Wedding* begins. The image of George nearly losing his life to the Yellow Dog while all the family and his wife Robbie plead with him to save himself, sticks like a portent in the minds of all the Fairchilds. But from the moment when the train stopped in the nick of time, the incident became officially a comic family anecdote, shorn of every trace of the tragic or heroic. Secretly, however—in the minds of Robbie, Ellen Fairchild, and Ellen's daughters Dabney and Shelley—the incident continues to represent a mystery that frightens, fascinates, and even inspires them.

The incident of the Yellow Dog is associated, more or less directly, with two events that followed it immediately: as though the heavens were responding to the event, there was a sudden threat of violent storm; and, while the dark clouds gathered overhead, Troy Flavin, the overseer of Shellmound Plantation, proposed marriage to Dabney Fairchild, and she accepted him. At the same time, Robbie had turned angrily on George, incensed because he had not jumped to safety when she begged him to. As she saw it, he had demonstrated that his love for any Fairchild, even Maureen, wrong in the head though she might be, exceeded his love for her. Soon after George and Robbie returned home to Memphis, Robbie's anger issued in defiance. First, she threw her pots and pans out of their apartment window, and then, in unconscious imitation of his own audacity, she ran out on George.

To Shelley Fairchild, aged eighteen, the incident of the Yellow Dog is unaccountably disturbing. She declines to tell the story publicly and has not even ventured to record it in her diary. Going over the event again and again, she recalls that George and Maureen, their faces fixed as the Yellow Dog approached, had struck her suddenly as looking alike. Then Maureen had pushed against George's chest. Falling backwards, he seized Maureen's hand, and "what he could not accomplish by loosening her foot or by pulling her up free, he accomplished by falling himself. Wrenched bodily, her heavy foot lifted and Maureen fell with him" (p. 87). Thus the incident gives rise to three related mysteries: that George and Maureen are, quite apart from ties of blood, closely related; that both unflinchingly "saw death on its way," even if the family did not; and that the meaning of their being saved is to be found not in the stopping of the train but in their mutual dependence and their common fall. Shelley remembers with shame that she had been afraid to walk on the trestle, and rebellion against her own timidity begins to stir in her. First, a sign occurs at the reception following Dabney's wedding. Like the others, Shelley has been dancing under the paper lanterns and the stars, drinking champagne provided in great quantity by George. She steps onto the screened porch to have a cool drink of water. Thinking of the world that Dabney has entered, she finds it unreal, a closed door to her, and she wonders in a visionary moment what lies behind it: "Shelley's desire fled, or danced seriously, to an open place—not from one room to another room with its door, but to an opening wood, with weather—with change, beauty . . ." (p. 220). Welty endows the animals in her work with an exact sense of timing. Hearing a sound at the door, Shelley opens it, and her cat Old

Beverley of Graustark comes in and deposits a mole at Shelley's feet. Not long afterward, Shelley dares the Yellow Dog herself, on a reckless impulse crossing its path in the car she is driving. With that act, she puts her childhood behind her and severs herself from the protectiveness of Shellmound, home of the fair children. Where death is concerned, Shelley is on her way to becoming no less "magnificently disrespectful" than her Uncle George.

The principal subject of *Delta Wedding* is the intrusion of the outside world upon the changeless demi-paradise of Shellmound. As the action unfolds, messengers from the world penetrate the Fairchild bastion, one by one. The reader first sees Shellmound and its occupants through the eyes of a friendly witness, Laura McRaven. Because the child is lonely after the death of her mother and associates with her the glamorous memories that stay in her mind from early visits, she is primed to see the Fairchilds at their most enchanting. Yet she is keenly intuitive and soon shows herself to be precociously discerning. She has been at Shellmound only long enough to bring it fully back to mind when she finds herself forming a mental picture of a cage of tropical birds she had seen once at the zoo. In that cage "the sparkle of motion was like a rainbow, while it was the very thing that broke your heart, for the birds that flew were caged all the time and could not fly out" (p. 15). In the end Laura will decline the offer that is made her to live permanently at Shellmound. Watching her Aunt Ellen and Uncle George attentively, she has identified in herself an emotion she had never dreamed of feeling—pity. They have too many secrets, too much pity for each other. It comes to Laura without words that the pulse of nature, storms to punctuate the seasons and clear the air, is scarcely felt at Shellmound, and she misses it. Going home to live with her father finally becomes, for her, a return to freedom.

While looking at Shellmound through Laura's eyes, the reader is also introduced to a second intruder, Troy Flavin. This time the point of view is that of the Fairchilds, who consider Troy an excellent choice as overseer but quite the opposite as Dabney's fiancé. He is not even a native of the Delta but has his roots in the poor hill country of Mississippi. He is twice Dabney's age of seventeen, a large, rough, red-haired man who terrifies the maiden aunts as hopelessly as though he really were half man, half horse. Fastidious Shelley finds Troy repugnant, calling him Hairy Ears, perhaps with Shakespeare's Bottom at the back of her mind. Fierce old Aunt Mac would throw Troy in the bayou and let "the minnows chew him up" (p. 67). Dabney's father Battle simply groans at the thought of losing Dabney to Troy. When Troy's mother in the hills sends her wedding gift of patchwork quilts straight from her beds, Troy suggests that Delectable Mountains is the one that he and Dabney will "sleep under most generally, warm *and* pretty" (p. 113). Aunt Tempe catches the eye of Ellen and holds it with a long, significant look, but nothing can be done about Troy Flavin. Dabney has chosen him, and if that choice is her rebellion, it was not premeditated but inspired. She associates Troy with a dark cloud and a blinding light, thunder and lightning. He is a river, rushing between its banks; and, even when she is lying in his arms, she feels like a drowned girl, timid of the element. Troy fascinates her because he is so obviously not a Fairchild, yet, in her thoughts, he is often linked with George, whom she adores. That is not altogether paradoxical because George is not what he seems, not altogether Fairchild, and Dabney has discovered this. George's sweetness, she reminds herself, "could be the visible surface of profound depths—the surface of all the darkness that might frighten her" (p. 37).

George Fairchild is the principal agent or catalyst in *Delta Wedding* of the other way to live. His influence works, in the most subversive fashion, from within. To begin with, he has married Robbie Reid, courting her "over the counter" where she worked at Fairchild's Store. To the Fairchilds, Robbie is as much beneath George as Troy Flavin is beneath Dabney. To make matters worse, George has displayed his enchantment with his wife without restraint. At one family picnic, for example, he and Robbie had "put on" what Battle somewhat acidly describes as "the Rape of the Sabines down at the Grove." He has compounded the family's discomfort by appearing for Dabney's wedding palpably in anguish because Robbie—as if *being* George's wife were not bad enough—has run off and left him.

A little past the midpoint of the novel, having skillfully seduced the reader with the Fairchild charm, Welty brings Robbie onto the scene, tired and angry and aggrieved, looking for George, who happens to be visiting at the Grove. As Robbie makes her way in blazing heat from Fairchild's Store, where she has taken refuge, through the fields that encircle Shellmound, the reader gains from her thoughts a new perspective on the Fairchilds. Her vision is as direct, unsparing and relentless as a battering-ram, and its effect is devastating. Robbie has no sooner breached the fortress of her adversaries than she is telling them, "You're all a spoiled, stuck-up family that thinks nobody else is really in the world! But they are!" And, a little later: "Once I tried to be like the Fairchilds. I thought I knew how. . . . But you all—you don't ever turn into anybody. . . . You're just loving yourselves in each other—yourselves over and over again!" (pp. 163, 165).

The entrance of Robbie at Shellmound coincides with a sign—the appearance of a chimney swift loose in the house—that sets the Fairchilds in a turmoil. "Bird in de house mean death," calls the housemaid, Roxie, from the kitchen (p. 159). They fly off, in their usual ecstatic response to crisis, making a game of tracking down the bird. Ellen Fairchild is left to bear the brunt of Robbie's anger. Ellen is a person gifted with tact. Her nature is both sensitive and thoughtful, and she deals with Robbie kindly. But she has been so long acclimated to Fairchild attitudes that Robbie's very truthfulness batters her sensibilities with "a quality of violation." The crisis comes when Aunt Mac remarks to Robbie, "Of course you only married George for his money." Robbie replies, "No, ma'am. I married him because he begged me!" (pp. 160–61). Fortunately, deaf Aunt Mac does not catch Robbie's response, for she has reached old age without once imagining that a Fairchild could be brought by any circumstance to beg for anything. Indeed, both Ellen and Robbie herself are "struck . . . humbly to earth" by Robbie's simple statement, "for it implied a magnitude, a bounty, that could leave people helpless." A moment later, George appears at the door, looking, as Ellen sees him, like a god, like Dionysus. The combination of this near-apotheosis with the bird fluttering about in the house, Robbie's grief and anger, and sudden awareness of the possible magnitude of love is more than Ellen can sustain. She gives George an imploring look, and, just before losing consciousness, "she seemed to commit herself even further to him and even more deeply by wishing worse predicaments, darker passion, upon all their lives . . ." (p. 166).

By the time of Dabney's wedding, George and Robbie, witnessed by the entire assembly at the wedding rehearsal, have made up. In one sense the wedding itself is an anticlimax, but its context clearly suggests that a more significant event is figured forth by it: the marriage of Shellmound with the larger and less manageable world outside its boundaries. The resemblance of Troy's role to that of Hades as the abductor of Kore in classical myth is suggested by repeated references to Troy's coming in out of the fields (that is, literally, entering by the side door) to carry Dabney off. On the surface of it, the wedding seems to be rather inanely decorative, what with the shepherd's crooks, the horsehair hats, and the brides-maids' gowns running from palest pink to American Beauty red. However, the costuming assumes a different aspect when one considers that Dabney has in fact unconsciously designed the ceremony to bring the pastoral out-of-doors into the house and thus provide an appropriate setting for her role as Kore. A hint of the significance of the pink to red color scheme is provided by Dabney herself when she awakens at dawn and looks into the morning light: "The sun, a red ball down East Field, sat on the hori-zon. Faint bands of mist, in the fading colors of the bridesmaids' dresses, rose to the dome of clear sky. And that's me, she had thought, pleased— that little white cloud" (p. 213). At the wedding, when Troy does enter from the fields, everyone realizes that an anomaly has unexpectedly sprung up to jar the pastoral harmony. Troy's American Beauty bouton-niere clashes violently with his flaming red hair. His surname, after all, is Flavin, meaning gold or reddish yellow. Bursting in on shadowy Shell-mound, Troy is, for the moment, like the sun, the other side of his role as the ravished maiden's gloomy Dis.

V

Ellen Fairchild is one of Welty's least domineering women, and as a result she is almost invisible in the Fairchild family. She has been well occupied during her twenty years of married life with ten pregnancies (including her present one), her eight children, none of whom resembles her in the least, and a large and socially hyper-active household. She has had little time for reflection, and this has meant a loss of self that she feels deeply. Her role in *Delta Wedding* gains dramatic force from her rediscovery of that self, the inner equivalent of Dabney, whom she is about to lose to Troy Flavin. One result of the magical presence of her brother-in-law George at this critical time in her life is her growing aware-ness of a depth of passion in herself, a passion that has nothing at all to do with her husband Battle or with sexual love for George. Her feeling for George is largely maternal; as such, it becomes a burden that she gladly casts off when she realizes that she cannot, and does not wish to, protect him from life—a surrender that equally applies to her letting go of Dabney.

Early in the novel, when George finds Ellen outdoors, waiting for Dab-ney, the first thing he does is untie and remove her emblematic white apron. Immediately, she knows that Venus, shining brightly overhead, is still her star. Freed to examine her feelings, she finds that "only George left the world she knew as pure—in spite of his fierce energies, even heresies—as he found it; still real, still bad, still fleeting and mysterious and hopelessly alluring to her" (p. 80). The revelation immediately follows George's matter of fact disclosure that he had met a runaway girl in the woods near Shellmound as he was riding in from Memphis on horseback, and that he had taken her over to the old Argyle gin and slept with her. Knowing that George has taken advantage of a stray girl in such a casual manner may give pause to the reader, who must reconcile this fact with George's kindness and acute sensibility. But if one is at first inclined to be censorious, the impulse is checked by Ellen's response. She is indeed shaken, but not by discovering something anomalous in George's character. As it happens, she herself had encountered the runaway girl, though at the time she did not know what had recently happened to her but only sensed that she had been either laughing or crying. To Ellen, the ravishing of the anonymous girl is part and parcel with the loss of her own daughter. In a curious way, she is "bitterly glad" that it was George who had caught the girl, for inevitably someone was going to do so, and at least it was over.

Ellen's own meeting with the girl is one of the most powerful passages in Welty's works. Its effect corresponds not to its literal but to its mythic significance. Ellen is cast in the role of the goddess Demeter, not in her angry and vengeful mood but in her mood of reconciliation, when she understands the loss of her daughter Kore, and Kore once again has been restored to her.

The herald of Ellen's experience is her dream of finding a lost garnet breastpin, with a setting like a rose, that had been a gift from Battle in the days of their courtship. She tells the dream to her youngest daughter, Bluet, to put her to sleep at nap time, so its context is initially protective motherhood. Ellen had dreamed that she put on her beautiful gown and went to the woods by James's Bayou, where, under a great cypress tree, the little breastpin was "shining in the leaves like fire." She "knelt down and took her pin back," pinned it to her breast, and wore it away. She adjusts the story to Bluet's understanding by leaving out the mysterious facts that the dream came in the form of a *warning* that she would find the pin and that the warning was rather pleasant than disturbing. The aspect of warning suggests that the finding of the pin is an event of magic significance. The hint of the forbidden relates the dream to the host of old tales in which the hero is told not to do a certain thing and takes particular pleasure in doing it all the same, precisely because it *had* been forbidden.

What Ellen finds in the woods under the old giant cypress is not the pin of her girlhood but girlhood itself in the form of the runaway girl. For Ellen, the girl has a beauty that is so great as to suggest the more than human, and Welty persuades the reader to accept this supernal beauty largely by drawing skillfully upon folk motifs that embody mysterious power. Going into the deep woods is of course a familiar event in old tales, and to do so is always to take the path of danger, discovery and change. Welty makes these woods seem very deep, with more trees than Ellen had remembered. The woods are very old and very still. The trunks of the huge cypresses stand open at the base like tents in biblical engravings. A connotation of death and loss enters through reference to the cinders on the bayou bank, "where the Indians burned their pottery, at the very last." Ellen is aware, even in her seclusion, of the hoofbeats of the horse Troy Flavin rides, "and once again, listening for them in spite of the quiet, she felt as if the cotton fields so solid to the sight had opened up and swallowed her daughter." In the intense quiet of the ancient woods, the runaway girl, like a hamadryad, steps out from behind the tree that had concealed her. "Stand still," Ellen tells the girl, as she habitually told one or another of her own daughters, "often on her knees with pins in her mouth." It is the right moment for Ellen to recall the feeling she sometimes has of being "a mother to the world." But, she thinks, as the girl in her torn dress does stand absolutely motionless before her, "she had never felt a mother to a child this lovely." Hers is a beauty that she had always hoped for when she told any one of her daughters to stand still. But this girl's beauty seems to go out from her, until Ellen believes she knows what poets mean by the phrase "to *shed* beauty." "A whole mystery of life [had] opened up" to her (pp. 70–71).

The climactic moment in the meeting occurs when Ellen tells the girl, "Look at me, I'm not stopping you," and the girl replies, "You couldn't stop me," speaking in the comfortable tone of a mother giving advice to her girls. It is then that a "half smile, sweet and incredibly maternal," passes over the girl's face. Then Ellen lets go of her hand. A muscadine falls "from a high place into the leaves under their feet," and their shared moment dissolves and is lost.

Before the girl goes off through the trees, Ellen admits to her that she had been frightened, as of a ghost, first by the girl's coming, then by the imminence of her going, so that her heart nearly failed her. As for the garnet pin, when Ellen explains what she had come there seeking, the girl of course denies any knowledge of it. "I wasn't speaking about any little possession to you," Ellen tells her. "I suppose I was speaking about good and bad, maybe. I was speaking about men—men, our lives." There is a delicate hint that the lost girl is what Ellen's dream had warned her she would find and that she *has* found, only to lose again. When later in the story the pin is actually found in an entirely different place by little Laura McRaven, she holds it in the pocket of her dress for only a few minutes. Then Roy Fairchild, aged eight, moved by an unaccountable impulse, throws Laura out of the rowboat where they are seated into the Yazoo River (the river of death); and Laura, who never tells her Aunt Ellen about finding the pin, imagines its progress down the Yazoo to the Mississippi and on to the sea.

The lost girl appears again, not in the flesh but like a ghost indeed. Aunt Tempe has permitted a newspaper photographer to come from Memphis to take a wedding picture. While Ellen stands waiting for him to snap the picture, the thought occurs to her that she and Battle are somewhat anomalous as married persons. He is regarded with amazement for having become "domesticated"; and she, a book-loving, town-loving girl from Mitchem Corners, Virginia, without much talent for domesticity, is still proving herself "a lady" by gamely submerging herself in every element of it. When the flash goes off, she is thinking of herself as a member of the little choral society of unmarried girls she had belonged to. As the photographer prepares to take another picture, he tells his captive audience that his satchel contains a picture of a girl run down by the Yellow Dog. Her torn body had been flung into the blackberry bushes beside the track. Thus between flashes, Ellen changes from being a virginal choral singer into a mother of eight who, although she looks at her daughter and her husband, sees "a vision of fate." In that moment the tragic is superimposed upon the festive, Ellen's middle age upon her youth, the brutal end of the lost girl upon the more than human beauty that Ellen had seen emanating from her when they met, deep in the woods.

The lost girl appears once more, obliquely, in the last pages of the novel. The Fairchilds, including Dabney and Troy back from their three-day honeymoon in New Orleans, are enjoying a picnic by the river. On the way there in the mule-drawn buggy, Ellen reflects upon "the repeating cycles of season and her own life." After all, she realizes, "there was something in the monotony itself that was beautiful, rewarding—perhaps to what was womanly within her" (p. 240). A little later, Laura McRaven and her cousin India are watching falling stars. "Stand still, India," Ellen says, wanting to look closely at her child for signs of coming beauty. It is a final sounding, like a musical theme, of the motif of the lost girl. "O beautiful!" says someone, of another falling star. Then, "bragging and in reassurance," Laura tells her Fairchild relatives that she had both seen the falling star and also where it fell.

VI

Compared to the mothers in Welty's fiction, fathers usually have a relatively minor role. King MacLain's function as the father of his twins does not extend beyond begetting them. When he appears at the MacLain house some years later, he is quite unaware that he is the father of two active boys, and the imps in Halloween masks who skate around him on the porch have soon convinced him that domesticity is less than ever to his taste. He promptly vanishes into Morgan's Woods again without even having said hello to the long-suffering Snowdie. The attitude of the adult Eugene toward his father approaches horror: "God forbid he'd find him! Old Papa King MacLain was an old goat, a black name *he* had" (*GA*, p. 178). Although Randall, at the time of his separation from his wife Jinny Love Stark, invokes his father's name often enough, wishing for guidance from him, his father's message has been written in his genes and will not be delivered orally.

Clement Musgrove, the innocent planter in *The Robber Bridegroom*, is typical of Welty's well-domesticated fathers, overmatched by sometimes darkly knowledgeable wives. Clement adores his daughter Rosamond, but is almost impenetrably blind to the wickedness of Rosamond's stepmother Salome, who will stop at nothing to be permanently rid of her. "I wonder," thinks Clement finally, reflecting on the contrast between his good wife, Amalie, and the witch-like creature who has succeeded her, "if even my own wife has not been the one person all the time, and I loved her beauty so well at the beginning that it is only now that the ugliness has struck through to beset me like a madness" (p. 126). If a similar revelation takes place in the mind of Judge McKelva in *The Optimist's Daughter*, while he lies dying, we do not know of it. It is, however, experienced for him by his daughter Laurel, who concludes that her father "died worn out with both wives—almost as if up to the last he had still had both of them" (p. 151). Clement Musgrove and Judge McKelva share the almost universal fate of husbands in folk tales who take second wives. The first is always good, the second, bad; and they can be taken as quite simply one and the same. The doubleness of woman's nature in Welty's fiction often recalls that of the Indian goddess Kali, one of whose hands is held in the gesture "Fear not," while the other displays a male head dripping blood. The same doubleness applies to male figures, but not in the domestic context. Jamie Lockhart in *The Robber Bridegroom* is both respectable merchant and Bandit of the Woods; the ambiguous personification of night in "Moon Lake" is balanced by Loch Morrison, in his equally paradoxical role as lifesaving rapist; and Troy Flavin is both a man of light and Zeus's dark brother, the abductor of young girls. No writer of our time has done more than Welty to keep myth vigorously alive, to give it new life. The power of her fiction derives in part from her compelling use of the essential truths and mysteries of myth in the service of unflinching realism. The result of this accord is that her work, though firmly rooted in both place and time, escapes all limitations of the local and particular.

In "The Wide Net" the father is presented as a purely mythic entity, a natural force not human in itself, yet known to every mortal creature as the power that manifests itself in all the acts and processes of procreation. We know nothing at all about either parent of William Wallace Jamieson, but we do know that he is soon to become a father himself and that his pregnant wife Hazel has grown so angry at his failure to assume that role that she has pretended to drown herself in the Pearl River, just to teach him a lesson. The dragging of the river by William Wallace and his helpers is educational for him in the broadest sense. First, he astonishes his friends by asking them the name of the river that he has fished in all his life. The familiar river has suddenly become a mystery to him, "as if it were some great far torrent of waves that dashed through the mountains somewhere, and almost as if it were a river in some dream . . ." (*WN*, p. 49). A second sign occurs when he dives beneath the surface of the river and stays submerged so long his friends begin to wonder if he will ever come up into the air again. In the depths, he begins to suspect that Hazel's real trouble was that "she had been filled to the brim with that elation that they all remembered, like their own secret, the elation that comes of great hopes and changes, sometimes simply of the harvest time ..." (p. 56).

The story never loses sight of death. Not only is Hazel supposedly drowned, but the group dragging the river includes Grady and Brucie Rippen, whose own father had drowned in the Pearl River. But the keynote is elation. After a huge mess of catfish has been harvested from the river by means of the net, all participants join in a gargantuan fish-fry on a sandbank in the river. Sated, William Wallace has a brief nap but soon awakens, inspired to act out his otherwise inexpressible joy by "doing a dance so crazy that he would die next," with a big catfish hooked into his belt and "tears of laughter streaming down his cheeks." Then all eyes turn from William Wallace to the river, where the King of the Snakes puts in his appearance, swimming majestically downstream. He looks William Wallace straight in the eye. Finally, the powers of the air put on a world-beating storm. Lightning bolts split two trees in half, one on each side of the river, and the wind blows so mightily that everyone is covered by leaves like scales and becomes a kind of fish. After witnessing this show of paternal might, the expedition marches into Dover to show off its astounding catch, and "the town looked somehow like new." Having experienced these revelations, William Wallace feels in his bones what fatherhood is, how he has been drawn into nature's most potent and ecstatic secret, and has become, without even knowing it, much more than just himself, or even himself plus Hazel. As he approaches his house, where Hazel is waiting to see how his education has proceeded, William Wallace gets one more sign, something he had never seen before in his life: although it has not rained at his house at all, a rainbow at night raises its arc in the moonlight over the roof. It looks gauzy, like a lady's summer dress, and he can see the stars shining through it.

VII

Losing Battles is perhaps Welty's most complex and inclusive dramatization of the other way to live. Despite the obvious difference between this exuberant extravaganza and *Delta Wedding*—for example, in tone, setting, and the social class of the principal characters—the two novels have much in common. They both deal with the incursion of a full life, a complete humanness, into the closed circle of a family that is in many ways admirable but has protected itself by shutting out the elements of life, those secrets, mysteries, strangers, who threaten its stability and self-esteem. This novel, like *Delta Wedding*, also has outsiders who penetrate the closed circle, though here the emphasis is on their reluctance to do so. As in *Delta Wedding*, the overall objective of the main characters, whether they know it or not, is to become a part of a grand human and natural alliance. This means the abandonment of parochial pride, fear and exclusiveness under the stimulus of a great individual, a demigod. In *Delta Wedding* that individual is George Fairchild, and in *Losing Battles* it is the teacher who for many years held Banner School, in Banner, Mississippi. But in *Losing Battles* the catalyst of change, Miss Julia Mortimer, has died on the morning when the action begins. The story presents one colossal lesson in humanity, conducted from beyond the grave. The book could be called The Death and Resurrection of Miss Julia Mortimer.

The pattern of *Losing Battles* differs from that of *Delta Wedding* in that, whereas the Fairchilds universally admire and idolize George Fairchild, though often for the wrong reasons, the great bulk of those who must reckon with the life and death of Miss Julia were her staunch opponents during her lifetime and continue, after learning of her death, to regard her as the bane of their existence. Even those who have been Miss Julia's protégés and admirers at some point during her life—Judge Oscar Moody, Miss Lexie Renfro, and Gloria Renfro—have, for one reason or another, come to resent her willful intrusion into their lives. They all turned their backs on her when she was most in need of friends, isolated and miserable after being "put out to pasture" at the end of her long and notable career. The reader of *Losing Battles* is therefore in the position of learning about the book's hero through the recollections of largely hostile witnesses. But if Miss Julia begins as a prophet not without honor save in her own country, she ends by achieving a kind of apotheosis, despite all resentment, all that can be said against her. Her spirit quite simply refuses to die, and *Losing Battles* could bear the epigraph, "O death, where is thy sting? O grave, where is thy victory?"

Like everything else in *Losing Battles*, the story of Miss Julia unfolds largely through the storytelling art of various participants in the ninetieth birthday celebration and Beecham family reunion, a hundred strong, at the farm of Granny Vaughn, five miles by winding clay road from the little town of Banner. The story comes out in four major phases: first, a mixed chorus of heartfelt distaste and reluctant praise from the six living Beecham men and their wives, all except one of whom (Cleo) have been students of Miss Julia's. This chorus is augmented by a number of lesser voices. Among these is the voice, both jocular and sinister, of Willy Trimble, who had learned his trade as carpenter and handyman from Miss Julia. Mr. Willy plays the role of gloating, insinuating death; and in that capacity he is cheated of his prey. The coffin he has made as a gift to Miss Julia is refused; he is denied admission to the wake at Miss Julia's house, across the Bywy River in Alliance; no one will ride with him in his wagon that carries the rejected coffin; and, although he broods like a thwarted vulture over Granny Vaughn's reunion, the old lady has the last word. She sends him on his way, telling him, with reference to his mule, to "take that jade of yours off somewhere and leave her. . . . She's been cropping my flowers" (p. 351).

The second phase of Miss Julia's story features the recollections of Gloria Renfro, bride of Granny's great-grandson Jack. Gloria has lived in Granny's house in determined isolation while Jack was serving a two-year sentence, with time off for good behavior, at Parchman Penitentiary. Gloria has mixed feelings about Miss Julia. She acknowledges a debt of gratitude, for Miss Julia had personally seen to it that the orphan girl received the training necessary for her to take over Miss Julia's place as teacher at Banner School. Her admiration of Miss Julia's generosity, unflagging energy, and iron determination emerges clearly in almost every word she speaks. From her, we learn that Miss Julia in off hours had used the mail to distribute fruit bushes, flower plants and vegetable seeds, "trying to give some of her abundance away" (p. 243). One year, she had "sent out more little peach trees than you can count, sent them free," with directions wrapped around each one of them. "She wanted," Gloria says, "to make everybody grow as satisfying an orchard as hers." While Gloria tells how she helped Miss Julia in this work—digging and dividing flowers, saving seed and measuring it in an old spotted spoon—an unexpected note appears in her voice. "You sound homesick," says Aunt Beck, astonished. In Gloria's account, Miss Julia thus appears as a devoted Lady of Plenty, a Demeter, or Athena as the patroness of agriculture. Like Athena, the great teacher among the Olympians, Miss Julia fostered both the handicrafts and the professions that sustain the civilized world. Although Rachel Sojourner could not do mental arithmetic, Miss Julia did succeed in teaching her to sew a straight seam. Willy Trimble, the carpenter, learned from Miss Julia to square off ends and to rabbet joints as well as she did, though she herself had a true eye and "was ever the least bit hard to please" (p. 232). Most of the professionals among Miss Julia's ex-students, contrary to her wish, had left Boone County and the state. But Judge Moody had remained, and so had the judge's doctor and Miss Julia's, Gerard Carruthers. Another alumnus is the Episcopal priest who astounds the mourners at Miss Julia's interment in Banner Cemetery by offering prayers in a language none of them can understand. "She's made her a Superior Court judge," says Judge Moody proudly, "the best eye, ear, nose, and throat specialist in Kansas City, and a history professor some-where . . ." (p. 305). What is more, the Ford coupe she drove when she left her home in Ludlow to give her life to Banner School was "a thank-you present from Senator Jarvis the year he went to Washington."

Although Gloria had failed Miss Julia when the time came for the torch to be passed to her, the cause had not been a deficiency of love for Miss Julia but an excess of it for her student, Jack; for, as she confesses, she loved him "worse than any boy I'd ever seen in my life, much less taught" (p. 320). When Gloria proudly told Miss Julia that she would give her teaching all to Jack, Miss Julia had laughed at her, something that was hard for Gloria to bear. Worse than that, Miss Julia, for whom mysteries existed only to be solved, had launched an inquiry into Gloria's parentage that threatened to make her Jack's cousin and thus under Mis-sissippi law render their marriage null and void. Welty does not deal in miracles of the more obvious sort. Gloria is not ready for a change of heart. She can spare Miss Julia no part of the love that belongs to Jack. But she does find the tears that she had refused to shed during Jack's long absence. She feels the awful pathos of Miss Julia's waiting, day by day, for Gloria to visit her, and being disappointed, day by day. Despite her anguished protests, Gloria is initiated by the Beecham women into the clan from which she had remained so proudly aloof. The secret of her parentage—of her mother's identity, at least—is revealed after all. If she is not Jack's cousin, she is still a good deal less exalted in her origin than she had wished to be. While Gloria is thus being welcomed, in spite of herself, into alliance with Jack's family, that alliance is assisted by the busy needle and scissors of Miss Lexie Renfro, who snips away at the voluminous folds of Gloria's resurrected wedding dress, with Gloria right inside it. At last the outline of the girl's figure is revealed for all to see. As Aunt Birdie tells her, "At least we know who it is, can see who you are now, Gloria" (p. 285).

The third phase of Miss Julia's story is supplied by the only unmarried

Beecham relative, Miss Lexie Renfro, even while she is bringing Gloria's figure into view. Before Gloria's arrival in Banner, Miss Lexie had for a time been Miss Julia's protégée and at that time had worshipped her; but a combination of Virgil, which she could not master, and bad nerves that were inadequate to the stringencies of Banner School had been too much for her. She had failed, earning the contempt of Miss Julia. Having no other means of livelihood, she had become a practical nurse. Ironically, it was she that the Presbyterian ladies chose to be Miss Julia's nurse in her decline. The battle of wills that ensued between the former allies, turned bitter enemies, is unflinchingly detailed by Miss Lexie, despite the protests of Miss Beulah Renfro, who dreads the intrusion of death and disgrace into Granny's celebration. Miss Beulah has good reason for her fear because the friendlessness, isolation and growing despair of the two ladies sequestered in Miss Julia's house of death in Alliance soon begin to arouse in Granny Vaughn the spectre of her own approaching death and to remind her of the absence from her own house of the large family of grandchildren whom she had raised after they were orphaned as small children. The hostility between Miss Lexie and Miss Julia soon becomes so intense as to preclude any semblance of humane feelings: Miss Julia becomes Miss Lexie's prisoner, and Miss Lexie, at her worst, the most cruel of jailors. Having persuaded Miss Julia that no one—no one at all—was going to come and visit her, Miss Lexie devotes her efforts to thwarting Miss Julia's attempts to communicate with the outside world. She has only one method left to her: writing letters and, at the cost of almost indescribably laborious pains, getting them off by mail. The nadir in the relationship comes when Miss Lexie at last succeeds in depriving Miss Julia altogether of the means for writing letters: "I hid her pencil, and she said, 'Now I want to die.' I said, 'Well, why don't you go ahead and die, then?' She'd made me say it!" (p. 284). But Miss Lexie, harsh and death-dealing as she is, is not incapable of shame. "Some things," she tells the reunion, "you don't let them make you say. . . . And I don't care who they are." Miss Lexie is lost almost beyond recall, yet her part of the story—her confession, really—is the very one that makes the deepest impression upon those in the reunion who are in the process of turning "the complete and utter mortification of life" in Miss Julia into the foundation of a new life for her and for themselves.

"It could make a stone cry," says Judge Moody of Miss Julia's final days on earth. His is the fourth voice to be heard in the recounting of her story;

and, like Gloria and Miss Lexie, he is both a former protégé and, more recently, a betrayer of Miss Julia. He is also one of her oldest friends. Judge Moody has reason to suspect that he has somehow been *maneuvered* to the reunion on the day of Miss Julia's death. He had received a letter from her while she was still of sound mind, a month or so before her death. She had summoned him to Alliance, but out of certain lingering resentments and a dread of finding out what had become of her, he had delayed complying with her summons. Unaware that she had died, he had traveled the twenty-one miles from Ludlow to the bridge between Banner and Alliance, only to suffer a failure of courage just at that bridge, where a rusty sign warned, "Cross At Own Risk." A few hours later, after sundry nudges from the hand of fate, he had left his wife's Buick balanced precariously on Banner Top and joined the reunion as a guest of the very boy, Jack Renfro, whom he had sentenced to imprisonment in the penitentiary. The role of Judge Moody at the reunion is deftly suggested by the fact that he sits throughout the long afternoon of storytelling in a school chair long ago carried up to Granny Vaughn's farm, as if for the purpose, by a cyclone that ripped the roof off Banner School. The judge, who has been obliged since fire destroyed the Ludlow courthouse to hold court in the Primary Division of the Ludlow Baptist Church, has started school again from the beginning. He is a principled and competent man of law, but he has suffered from an overdose of legalism and an attendant shrinkage in his store of human warmth and sympathy.

The judge's contribution to Miss Julia's story proves properly to be its cap and climax, because, in reading to the reunion the letter he had received from Miss Julia, he becomes the instrument through which she speaks from beyond the grave. What she has to say, in brief, is that she has spent her life, fueled by inspiration, in a battle against ignorance. In all but a handful of instances she has lost every campaign in that battle. Yet she knows, and in effect can prophesy, that those who go down battling with all their hearts in a good cause, as she has done, are the first to arrive at the truth. One might suppose that this truth for her was only a vision of pain, leading on to oblivion. But although she anticipates that vision, Miss Julia also foresees that her story does not end with it. Her victories lie before her, and we witness the first fruits of them. She writes, "When the battle's over, something may dawn there—with no help from the teacher, no help from the pupil, no help from the book" (p. 298). No help, that is, from the *living* teacher; and from the pupil—from Judge

Moody and the others—no help that they could ever have devised so well on purpose, or carried out, despite themselves, with such astonishing and radiant success.

The effect of Miss Julia's story on its auditors is perhaps best epitomized by two characters—Jack Renfro and Granny Vaughn—who have not been taught by Miss Julia and who contribute little to the telling of her story. Jack Renfro can respond fully to the Miss Julia that enters his mind and heart through the words of the others because he has already shared a part of her experience. He has suffered exile and imprisonment, been deprived of the presence of all whom he loves, and deprived them of his. He has also had to suffer, on his return, blow after blow to his pride, to lose battle after battle, simply in getting himself back home. With these credentials, added to a naturally warm and loving nature, Jack finds building in himself a strong and unequivocal love for the lady he has never known. Her losing battles are also his, and his are hers. In no less degree, he shares in her victory after death. When the smoke of the battle clears, he has emerged from defeat, heart-whole and as victorious as she.

The long process by which Jack Renfro gets back home reaches its successful climax when he has heard Miss Julia's story and is at last recognized by Granny Vaughn. Indeed, in her sometimes confused vision, he becomes not only himself, returned at last, but also the living embodiment of her favorite grandson, Sam Dale Beecham, who had gone off to war at Jack's age and died away from home. Throughout the day of her birthday celebration, Granny Vaughn has had Sam Dale on her mind. Sometimes she knows that he has long been dead; sometimes, confusing him with Jack, she thinks that he has been away and will return; and, at another moment, she believes that he is living and present at the reunion and will appear the next minute. To Granny, Sam Dale is the epitome of selfless goodness, loving kindness. In fact, Jack is as close in character as one could wish to Sam Dale in a second incarnation. One likes to think that the extension of Jack's loving sympathies to include Miss Julia helps Granny to recognize Sam Dale in him. Jack's return at last becomes, for Granny, the restoration of her dearest loss, the one birthday present that she had longed for above all and that had seemed, if not denied her altogether, at least almost intolerably delayed in its arrival.

As Granny struggles to retain her courage while she learns of the last days of Miss Julia, she tries to find Sam Dale in Jack. Her first attempt, which follows Miss Lexie's account, results in failure. Her hands reach for

Jack's face, and then "a faint cry came, and her face, right in his, broke all to pieces. 'But you're not Sam Dale!' " (p. 308). Later, when all the grandsons and their wives at last are telling her goodbye, she is almost overcome with grief and loneliness. " 'Thieves, murderers, come back,' she begged. 'Don't leave me!' " (p. 357). Finally, when all the men except Jack have gone, Granny wins her losing battle. Jack kneels at the foot of her rocker, looking up into her face. She sees that he is there and, for a little while, gazes at him silently. Then she says, "They told me . . . you'd gone a long time ago. Clean away. But I didn't believe their words. I sat here like you see me—I waited. A whole day is a long wait. You've found Granny just where you left her. You sneaked back when nobody's looking, forged your way around 'em. That's a good boy!" Granny tries to give Jack a present, a little silver snuffbox "that had been Granny's to keep for as long as anyone could remember." But as her hands approach him, they break apart, the gift rolls away, and she reaches for his face, traces all his features with her fingers, while Jack lets them wander; and Jack "still had not blinked once when her fingers seemed to forget the round boundaries belonging to flesh and stretched over empty air" (p. 357).

Later, in the front yard of Granny Vaughn's house, the old iron Wayfarer's Bell that had stood on its post for a hundred years or more is visible against the stars, "gathered into itself." In the old days, it had sounded every hour to guide travelers along a barely discernible trail through the forest. Its voice is the only one that has not been heard among the many that have spoken during the long day. But Granny Vaughn had told the reunion that she rang it "a little before sunup" that morning, and she adds, "Brought you running, didn't it?" If the great bell had rung in the old lady's mind, who is to say that it had not also rung in the mind of Jack Renfro, who was coming home, and of Judge Moody, who had lost his way and hung, like Mrs. Moody's Buick, poised over nothingness and destruction? The pages of Welty's work are full of ringing bells that are audible only to those who are intended to hear them. Mattie Will Holifield, when she crouches before the sleeping King MacLain, thinks that his snores are like all the frogs of summer, "Or to him little balls, little bells for the light air, that rose up and sank between his two hands, never to be let fall" (p. 97). To Ellen Fairchild, at a critical moment in *Delta Wedding*, the throbbing wings of the chimney swift that is loose in the house blend with her memory of a time when the gin caught fire and she lost the baby she was carrying. The "flutter of wings . . . softly insinuated in a strange yet familiar manner the sound of plantation bells being struck and the school bell and the Methodist Church bell ringing, and cries from the scene of the fire they all ran to, cries somehow more joyous than commiserating, though it threatened their ruin" (*DW*, p. 163). Miss Julia Mortimer, dying of neglect and frustration in her house at Alliance, demands to be given back her bell, the heavy brass one that she had so often swung with her strong right arm. Then she quotes Ariel's song from *The Tempest*: "Ding dong! Ding dong bell!" Surely Miss Julia's bell had also sounded again in the minds of those for whom sea change had power to transmute dead bones into something rich and strange. At the end of Granny Vaughn's reunion, as at the end of *The Tempest*, "no one was lost any more"; but, so long as human beings are at large on earth, there will be need for ringing bells. For this reason, among many others, the fiction of Eudora Welty will remain for all who know it "a heart's treasure." In the pages of her work, "there could be no bell that does not say 'I will ring again'" (*LB*, p. 365).

J. A.   The Recovery
BRYANT, JR.   of the Confident Narrator:
A Curtain of Green
to *Losing Battles*

THE TOTAL OF twenty-five stories in Eudora
Welty's first two collections, *A Curtain of
Green* (1941) and *The Wide Net* (1943), represented not so much the
artistic declaration of a new young writer with a distinctive style and point
of view as a performance by a mature artist prepared at the outset to make
fiction both her subject and her instrument and to demonstrate a confident
virtuosity in a wide variety of registers, styles, and methods of attack. "A
Piece of News," for example, was a specimen of perfection in its kind, but
it did not quite prepare the reader for the kind of perfection that was coming in "Why I Live at the P.O."; and nothing in either of these two stories
—nothing, that is, that the casual reader was likely to pick up—made him
entirely ready for "A Memory" or "Powerhouse" or "The Wide Net." Indeed, it would be hard to find a generalization to characterize the stylistic
diversity of Welty's early achievement, but one could make do with the
words of Katherine Ann Porter's Introduction to *A Curtain of Green*:
"She has simply an eye and an ear sharp, shrewd, and true as a tuning fork.
. . . There is in none of these stories any trace of autobiography in the prime
sense, except as the author is omnipresent, and knows each character she
writes about as only the artist knows the thing he has made, by first ex-
periencing it in imagination" (pp. xx–xxii). Since 1943 Welty has produced a number of works, among them a third collection of superb shorter
pieces, *The Bride of the Innisfallen,* which surely places her among the very
select company of masters of the shorter form.

Her other works, however, are novels, each distinctive in its way. *The
Robber Bridegroom* (1942) was markedly eccentric for its time. Critics
praised it for a witty and engaging handling of various kinds of folk tale
including some of the more exciting stories that had attached themselves to
Mississippi and the Natchez Trace, but they saw nothing in it indicating

things to come. For many readers Eudora Welty's first significant attempt at the novel was and is *Delta Wedding* (1946). That work, having given a sympathetic portrayal of life in the Mississippi Delta, stirred the uneasiness of liberal Northern reviewers, who because of their predisposition in matters involving race could not quite focus attention on the writer's talent and because of their lack of experience with the South in general and Mississippi in particular could not perceive her consummate mastery of observed detail. After *Delta Wedding* came *The Golden Apples* (1949), a book that some have preferred to call a volume of interrelated stories rather than a novel, then *The Ponder Heart* in 1954 and *The Optimist's Daughter* in 1968, both of which fall into the category of the novella, and finally *Losing Battles*, which appeared in 1970 and continues even now to perplex a few critics who would have preferred something on the order of *Delta Wedding* or *The Optimist's Daughter*. Yet *Losing Battles* has not lacked champions; moreover, it exhibits characteristics drawn from the whole range of her work, all working together with an ease that bespeaks integration and final maturity rather than ingenuity or virtuosity. For that reason, among others that will be discussed later, it may properly be called a masterpiece.

In subject matter, however, *Losing Battles* does pursue a side path indicated by *Delta Wedding*. Readers will recall that the wedding in the earlier novel is one between Dabney Fairchild, daughter of a proud Delta family, to her father's overseer, Troy Flavin from Tishomingo, a small town in the hilly northeast corner of the state. The Fairchilds are well aware that the yoking about to take place is unequal; but they are not entirely snobs, and they accept Troy without conspicuous protest or fuss. Nevertheless, the cultural difference between the two is there, and it is accentuated midway through the novel when Troy's mother, who has no intention of coming to a Delta wedding, sends a present of handmade quilts, one of which has been done in the highly complex and much sought-after pattern called "Delectable Mountains." The note accompanying her gift runs as follows: "A pretty bride. To Miss Dabney Fairchild. The disappointment not to be sending a dozen or make a bride's quilt in the haste. But send you mine. A long life. Manly sons, loving daughters, God willing." Troy, of course, is delighted. "My mammy made these," he says, "I've seen her do it. A thousand stitches!" Most of the Fairchilds regard the gift as inappropriate, but they politely turn the conversation to other subjects. Ellen's mother, exemplifying the charity that is her nature, says simply and without condescension, "I think they are beautiful, useful wedding presents. . . . Dabney will treasure them, I know. Dabney, you must write and thank Troy's mother tonight" (pp. 112–113). It is with the same sort of charity, again without condescension, that Eudora Welty has explored in *Losing Battles* that other Mississippi, the one which endures and continues to thrive in the hill country that surrounds such places as Tishomingo and Iuka. A much greater difference between *Delta Wedding* and *Losing Battles*, however, and one that must be confronted, lies in the area of style. The earlier novel rests comfortably in a territory that includes not only *The Ponder Heart* and *The Optimist's Daughter* but all other fiction that traces its lineage more or less exclusively from Flaubert, Maupassant, Turgenev, and James. *Losing Battles* has a somewhat different ancestry and properly belongs to another country. It shares its beginnings with *The Robber Bridegroom* and includes in its makeup characteristics and devices that have appeared infrequently in the other novels and the short stories. The resulting combination—or mixture, as some might call it—disturbs readers whose admiration for the earlier work has fixed their expectations, and particularly those who react positively to details that suggest *Delta Wedding* or *The Golden Apples* but resent seeing them in unfamiliar packaging.

Losing Battles has much in it to suggest comparison with *Delta Wedding*. For one thing both works present a family clan, unified in spite of its diversity, that has been threatened by a challenge from the outside and forced thereby to assert, reassess, or redefine itself. The clan in *Losing Battles* is that of Granny Vaughn, her Beecham grandchildren and Renfro great-grandchildren, the intermediate Beecham parents having long ago been drowned in a flood; and the home place is Granny's hill hollow house built by her grandfather Jacob Jordan in the year the stars fell, where she lives with her granddaughter Beulah Beecham Renfro, Beulah's husband Ralph, and their five children. To this spot on a hot Sunday morning during the first week of August the whole family returns to pay tribute to Granny on her ninetieth (she says hundredth) birthday, and over half of the novel is given over to the events of this day. Over the ridge and several miles away are such relatively civilized centers as Banner, Ludlow, and Alliance, and from this outside world of churches, schools, stores, and railroads come the forces that threaten the unity of the ancient family group with its fixed habits, attitudes, and customs.

Furthermore, the challenger in *Losing Battles*, as in *Delta Wedding*, is a young person who presumes to enter the clan by marriage—in this case, Gloria Renfro, the wife of Jack, the oldest of the Renfro children and a student of sorts before Judge Oscar Moody sent him to Parchman Penitentiary on an improbable charge of "aggravated assault." One difficulty with Gloria, from the clan's point of view, is that she is an orphan of local but, as it develops, uncertain parentage. The other is that she is the last in a long succession of protégées of Miss Julia Mortimer, the archetypal schoolteacher of the region, who has taught all generations of Beechams and Renfros except the present one and who has waged a lifelong and loving battle to replace the clannishness of her north Mississippi charges with enlightenment and what she considers to be a broader view of things. During Jack Renfro's absence at Parchman, Gloria has given birth to their child, Lady May Renfro, now fourteen months old; and on this day of the annual family reunion Gloria has dressed up in her wedding dress to welcome Jack home and present him with the baby, whom he has never seen. To complicate matters still further, Miss Mortimer has just died in her home at Banner several miles across the ridge, and the assembled clan of Vaughns, Beechams, and Renfros take occasion to make much of their independence of that lady's domination and loudly proclaim their indifference to her passing. Gloria, though married to a Renfro, is thus not fully a member of the clan; and in spite of her protestations to the contrary, she constitutes in their minds an extension of Miss Mortimer's presence in their midst. The resulting tensions produce much of the activity of the novel, though not all of it.

Gloria is also the center of a more comprehensive action that gives the novel its claim to significance. Anyone who has read halfway perceptively *The Golden Apples* will know that Eudora Welty is one of those rare writers whose talent may be called mythopoeic. Granted that the term can mean different things to different readers, most would agree that she has a keen, intuitive sense of the invisible forces that give direction to human activity, especially whenever such activity, whether provincial or universal, becomes or tends to become meaningful. Here in the Christian West we all know at least some of the webs that have shaped our perceptions: the fall of Adam and Eve, the story of Cain and Abel, the story of Abraham's near-sacrifice of Isaac, and Christ's crucifixion, descent into Hell, and resurrection. These are among the Judaeo-Christian myths that have shaped our history; and there are Greek myths too, many of which have proved only slightly less effective as shapers of our views of things, among them the stories of the fall of Troy, the return of Odysseus, the labors of Hercules, and the activities of such figures as Dionysus and Orpheus. For some people the Norse myths are still efficacious, to say nothing of the Irish myths. In *The Golden Apples* Eudora Welty has drawn upon all these for articulation of the human experiences that she portrays, and readers attuned to such things can be deeply moved on encountering their mysterious shapes in a modern fable. In much the same way, though perhaps not quite so conspicuously, she makes use of myth in *Losing Battles*, where two well-known stories from classical antiquity shape the action and help to answer the questions that Jack Renfro himself cannot fully articulate: First, who is this Gloria? And, second, on what terms can he or must he receive her?

The first question is included in the second, which in Greek myth is shaped and answered by the incident we call the Judgment of Paris. Although Gloria Renfro is at the center of the action of *Losing Battles*, the occasion for that action is Jack, whose return from Parchman makes everything happen for Gloria. Jack is the heir apparent of the clan, its immediate hope of continuation without a further change of name. In mythic terms he is the Paris of a Troy that may be doomed to fall, and to him comes a bride of undetermined origin, whom he is asked to receive as a prize at the hands or with the approval of any one of three donors: his mother Beulah, who is concerned about the appropriateness of Gloria as the bearer of Jack's children and her grandchildren; Miss Julia Mortimer, who would be surrendering to him (grudgingly to be sure) a tutor in wisdom and sophistication; and Granny Vaughn herself, Miss Mortimer's ancient antagonist, who knows and still feels on her pulses the erotic springs by which all human life may be renewed. Thus Jack returns from his labors at Parchman to claim fully the bride that is as yet only technically his and to choose whether he will claim her at the hands of Juno, Athena, or Aphrodite. That he chooses to take her at the hands of Aphrodite—the only choice that could possibly give the girl to him—may not be entirely his own doing. The events of the novel have an air of inevitability about them which Oscar Moody describes beautifully: "I could almost believe I'd been *maneuvered* here. . . . To the root of it all, like the roots of a bad tooth. The very pocket of ignorance" (pp. 303–304). Eventually we come to know, though Jack himself only senses, that he could not possibly have received his bride from his mother's hand as a Renfro relative: both Judge Moody and Julia Mortimer, to say nothing of the state of Mississippi, would have prevented that. Nor could he under any conceivable circumstances have received her as a gift from Athena; for Gloria has clearly repudiated Miss Julia and her influence, and Miss Julia, as we noted, would never have approved of such a marriage. The resolution of this part of the action, coming when both Beulah's power and Miss Mortimer's have been ruled out, occurs when Granny Vaughn suddenly rises from her chair, sings "in a quick, drum-beat voice" an unidentifiable song, which could be either "Frog Went A-Courting" or "Wondrous Love," and then begins to dance. When Uncle Curtis lifts her to the top of the table, she continues her dancing from that vantage point until she all but topples to the ground and Jack Renfro races in to catch her. "I've been calling ye times enough," she tells him, and then she asks his name: "He dropped to his knees there beside her and whispered to her the only answer there was, "It's Jack Jordan Renfro, Granny. Getting himself back home" (p. 308). This is the conclusion of Part IV of the novel's six parts, and it answers the question of whether Jack is really to receive Gloria as his bride and on what terms. From this point on Troy may very well fall and undoubtedly will change, but Paris will have his Helen, and the gods are temporarily appeased.

Another obvious mythic pattern is one we associate with Oedipus, the quest for identity that results in an acceptance of self in all its consequences: the right to inherit kingship (or in this case queenship) and also the responsibility for being the perpetrator of sin and ancient crime. As the novel begins, the clan is eagerly awaiting the return of Jack Renfro, but their anticipation is darkened by the uneasy thought that he will be returning as much to meet Gloria as to rejoin the group. No one doubts that the child at Gloria's feet was sired by Jack or that the dress on her back is the wedding dress she wore when Grandfather Vaughn declared them man and wife. The great question in their minds is whether she is eligible to be a member of the clan. Thereupon they initiate a search for Gloria's identity, which in the end involves everybody. Before the search is complete we learn that Gloria's existence in the world has been the occasion of great embarrassment to at least one member of the clan, the late Sam Dale Beecham, who for physical reasons could not sire a child, and of great shame to all the rest because Uncle Nathan Beecham, in an effort to save the honor of Sam Dale, murdered brutally the seducer of the young woman whom Sam Dale had presumably married, allowed a black man to take the blame for the murder, and then cut off his own right hand as an act of penance. Thus Gloria, the princess and queen to be, has also brought to her eminence seeds of destruction that threaten the whole community;

and thus the choice she helps Jack to make, or rather the choice that presents itself to her as the inevitable one, is the redemptive one—the only one that will allow the community to survive. Jack, undiscriminating, would have her on Renfro terms, or even on Miss Mortimer's, if that were necessary. He begs: "Be my cousin. . . . I want you for my cousin. My wife, and my children's mother, and my cousin, and everything." Her response participates in the love that created the universe and moves the stars: "Jack, I'll be your wife with all my heart, and that's enough for anybody, even you. I'm here to be nobody but myself, Mrs. Gloria Renfro, and have nothing to do with the old dead past. And don't ever try to change me" (p. 361). Aphrodite has done her work well, we see; and as the novel proceeds we see also that Aphrodite is still moving among them. As they settle down to sleep—Renfros, Beechams, and Moodys scattered all over the place in every conceivable corner, young Vaughn Renfro, coming late to bed, finds Granny "tiny in her bed in full lamplight": ". . . the room was as yellow and close as if he and Granny were embedded together in a bar of yellow soap. 'Take off your hat,' Granny's mouth said. 'And climb in wi' me.' He fled out of her dazzled sight. 'She didn't know who I was,' he told himself running. And then, 'She didn't care!' " (p. 366). In the end when Jack and Gloria have lost everything but the love they have for one another and can still sing a song of rejoicing, the meaning of *Losing Battles* stands clear.

The Golden Apples plays with myth in this same intriguing fashion, but the style varies unpredictably from section to section, and the unity of the work falters accordingly. The style of *Losing Battles*, by contrast, is like an intricately woven but seamless piece of cloth, and as such it contributes significantly to the unity of the novel and to the unity of our impression of it. Once we are well launched in the reading, we become aware of the dramatic quality of long stretches of it and perhaps recall the presentational style of "Lily Daw and the Three Ladies," which quickly reached an even higher level of control in "Petrified Man." Both here and in those shorter stories we have a narrative that makes its most significant advances by way of conversation and achieves credibility partly by the recognizable authenticity of the exchanges and partly by the appropriateness of casual references to such familiar tangibles as a Willys-Knight automobile, Red Bird school tablets, orange Ne-Hi, Jax beer, and Coca-Cola. Thus as talk proceeds, we readily construct faces for the characters, learn the facts that all of them know, come to suspect the existence of a few facts that only some know, and acquire the willingness to speculate about matters that are never fully revealed to any of the speakers, at least so far as we can tell. Part of our willingness to so participate in *Losing Battles* comes from the encouraging presence at our elbow of a shadowy figure who patently knows more than any of the visible speakers and could tell all if he or she only would. We are reminded of the less perceptive but considerably more visible and much more limited narrators of "Why I Live at the P.O." and *The Ponder Heart*, in which, as in Ring Lardner's celebrated "Haircut," we get demonstrably one-sided versions of the story. In *Losing Battles*, however, the narrative voice is both childlike and magisterial; and it is reinforced by the preternatural vision of a Keats and the shaping power of a Donne. It resembles, too, the authoritative voice of Tiresias in the Greek plays or of Merlin in some versions of the Arthurian romances in that it speaks from much knowledge and a long memory, both of which might permit it to tell considerably more than it does had we only the stomach to digest the truth and time to take it all in.

A similar voice appears in a very early story called "Clytie," though there the voice is tied to a personality that is considerably less distinct and well defined than the one in *Losing Battles*. "Clytie" is a story about madness, and the unfortunate woman in it runs about the small town of Farr's Gin looking for a face that she does not find until at the end she sees it reflected in a rain barrel and plunges in to her death. The narrator in the story is privy to Clytie's mind, but she also reports what she has heard others in the community say, that, for example, Mr. Tom Bate's boy had a face as "clean-blank as a watermelon seed," or that it is easier to shave a corpse or a fighting drunk field hand than it is to shave a person who has had a stroke. But the unaccountables, which are far more interesting, include observations that the clouds looked bigger than cotton fields, that four old black cedar trees smell bitter as smoke, that Clytie's hat looked like an old bonnet on a horse, that under stress Clytie began to cry and gasp "like a small child that has been pushed by the big boys into the water," and that her black-stockinged legs upended in the rain barrel "hung apart like a pair of tongs." These editorial intrusions serve to make clear what is happening in the story, underscoring for us the portrayal of a woman who is being progressively depersonalized until she passes from humanity to something purely mechanical.

A similar device in *The Robber Bridegroom* helps to hold together that novel's remarkable mixture of history, folk tale, and fantasy. The magisterial narrator there can tell us that the river is the color of blood (which is *not* particularly remarkable) and that the sky was covered with black, yellow, and green clouds the size of whales (which *is* a remarkable observation for someone presumably restricted to Mississippi). Rain fell in a downpour, we are told, "until it sounded like the quarreling of wildcats in the cane," and "the wind was shaking the house like the cat a mouse." A bit farther on, but still early in the narrative, a flatboatman jumps into a feather bed, bursts it, and "the feathers blew all around the room like the chips in a waterspout." A third of the way through the narrative we learn that the stepmother, listening intently for hidden information in her stepdaughter's story, had ears that were "opening like morning glories to the sun" (a figure that is arresting but not exactly visual). But visibility quickly returns in such figures as "birds flew up like sparks from a flint," "a foam of gold leaves," and "a flock of cardinals flew up like a fan opening out from the holly bush." In fact, this last figure occurs in a passage that illustrates the narrator's perception throughout the novel: "How beautiful it was in the wild woods! Black willow, green willow, cypress, pecan, katalpa, magnolia, persimmon, peach, dogwood, wild plum, wild cherry, pomegranate, palmetto, mimosa, and tulip trees were growing on every side, golden green in the deep last days of the Summer. Up overhead the cuckoo sang. A quail with her young walked fat as the queen across the tangled path. A flock of cardinals flew up like a fan opening out from the holly bush. The fox looked out from his hole" (p. 77). This in a tale compounded of the folklore of the Natchez Trace, Southern history generally, and Grimm's fairy tales calls to mind the mode and voice of Hans Christian Andersen. It is a voice supported by the same genius for noting detail, the same enthusiasm for reporting it in colorful catalog, the same delight in sheer ornamentation, heaped up, pressed down, and running over.

Another important characteristic of the narrator is illustrated by a passage coming early in the book: "Her father had tried scolding [Rosamond], and threatening to send her away to the Female Academy, and then marching her off without her supper, but none of it had done any good, and so he let her alone. Now and then he remarked that if a man could be found anywhere in the world who could make her tell the truth, he would turn her over to him. Salome, on the other hand, said she should be given a dose of Dr. Peachtree" (p. 39). At this point the novel has taken up scarcely forty pages and yet it has plunged us into the midst of a narrative characterized by violence, bloodshed, and death, the like of which is unequaled outside Grimm or the bloodier tales of Christian martyrs. Even so, the equanimity of the narrator is undisturbed, for it is precisely the equanimity of an elderly storyteller, perhaps a wise maiden aunt, beguiling potentially naughty children with glimpses of a world where giants are slaughtered, handsome young heroes are turned into monsters, and princesses can be captured by bandits, cut up into small pieces, and preserved in brine until such time as an enchanter can restore them to integrity and life. In short, this narrator protects her readers and enlightens them in proportion as they can adopt the childlike stance that her manner of narration requires.

In the vastly expanded panorama of *Losing Battles* the same device becomes much more complex, and the consistency of its function tends to disappear. What it does there is to establish a narrator with a clear personality and an overwhelming authority who gives us the story on her own terms. I say "her" because that narrator is pretty surely female, as indicated early in the novel in the description of Gloria: "Gloria sat down in front of them all on the top step, a long board limber as leather and warmer than the skin, her starch-whitened high-heeled shoes on the mountain stone that was the bottom step. In four yards of organdy that with scratching sounds, like frolicking mice, covered all three steps, she sat with her chin in her hand, her head ablaze. The red-gold hair, a cloud almost as big around as the top of an organ stool, nearly hid what they could peep at and see of her big hazel eyes. For a space about the size of a biscuit around the small, body points of her elbows, there were no freckles; the inner sides of her arms, too, were snowy. But everywhere else, every other visible inch of her skin, even to her ears, was freckled, as if she'd been sprinkled with nutmeg while she was still dewy and it would never brush off" (p. 15). These are details that a woman would be likely to see or know: that starch was used to whiten the high heels, that four yards of organdy had gone into the dress, that the inner sides of her arms were snowy as compared with the freckles on the outside, and that the effect of the freckles was that of nutmeg on a white surface. Yet male or female, the narrator is clearly one with a "poetic" turn of mind; that is, she sees data always as a comparison with other data, and this pervasive characteristic appears as early as the second sentence of the book when we are told that "a long thin cloud crossed [the moon] slowly, drawing itself out like a name being called."

Another arresting and totally engaging example comes scarcely seven pages later when the Renfros bow their heads at breakfast to say the blessing: "All heads were bowed. Mr. Renfro's head was bald, darkened by the sun and marked with little humped veins in the same pattern on both sides, like the shell of a terrapin. Vaughn's was silver-pink, shaved against the heat, with ears sticking out like tabs he might be picked up and shaken by. Miss Beulah and her three daughters all raked their hair straight back, cleaved it down the middle, pulled it skin-tight into plaits. Miss Beulah ran hers straight as a railroad track around her head; they were tar-black and braided down with the pins she'd been married in, now bright as a nickel. The girls skewered their braids into wreaths tight enough to last until bedtime. Elvie's hair was still pale as wax-beans, Etoyle's was darkening in stripes, Ella Fay's was already raven. Granny's braids were no longer able to reach full circle themselves; they were wound up behind in two knots tight as a baby's pair of fists" (p. 7).

One could multiply examples indefinitely. They appear throughout and call attention to themselves by their sheer ingeniousness: eyes as blue as jewels, flowers from an althea bush as pink as children's faces, little boys' shaved heads shining an albino white or silver gray, like the heads of little old men, a vaccination scar shining like a tricky little mirror, a flock of bantam chickens "like one patch quilt moving with somebody under it." Whatever the sex, this narrator is mature. She has cooked, sewed, raised children, cared for livestock, and forgotten nothing that she has seen, heard, tasted, or smelled. She is most likely a Mississippian and rarely uses figures that would not have been intelligible to the characters in her story. One exception is a reference to vehicles crossing an old cable bridge with a noise "like forty anvils making a chorus" (p. 408). Here the possible allusion to Verdi may be unintentional, but it is unmistakable for us, though we cannot be sure that anyone in the story would have recognized it. Occasionally, but only occasionally, the comparisons are so special as to be eccentric. An observation of "the jonquil smell of new pencils ground to a point for the first day" (p. 409) is a comparison of this kind, but even here we are struck with the appropriateness of the figure. Newly sharpened pencils are indeed aromatic, and they have a cedar bitterness about them that is not unlike the bitter smell of jonquils in the spring. Reading details like these is one of the delights of the novel, though some critics have found it a distraction not to be countenanced in serious contemporary fiction.

It is a distraction, certainly, if one expects fiction to be accessible directly —that is, presentationally—or through some mediator who is himself an observer of the events or a participant in them. It is a distraction also if one on principle resists ornament for ornament's sake. Unfortunately we live in an age that eschews literary gingerbread and would simplify even Christmas trees. Eudora Welty lives in that age also, but she ignores the temper of the time and in a sheer love of detail joyfully adorns her story with all the enthusiasm and generosity of an ingenious child embellishing a drawing. Even so, there is nothing childlike about her manner of dealing with that detail. It is rather the manner of a sophisticated adult using for her own purposes the *persona* of childhood—the manner of a Hans Christian Andersen, who could write in a lovely story called "The Wild Swans": "The sea transforms itself more in an hour than a lake does in a year. When the clouds above it are dark, then the sea becomes as black as they are; and yet it will put on a dress of white if the wind should suddenly come and whip the waves. In the evening when the winds sleep and the clouds have turned pink, the sea will appear like the petal of a giant rose. Blue, white, green, red: the sea contains all colors; and even when it is calm, standing at the shore's edge, you will notice that it is moving like the breast of a sleeping child."[1] It is also the manner of Homer, who ornaments after the Greek manner but nonetheless purposefully, for every simile in the *Iliad* helps extend the action described there in the direction of universality. So here; but only one character in the novel sees as much, and that is young Vaughn Renfro, who after the others are asleep rides old Bet to where the schoolbus has been stranded near Banner Top and hauls the vehicle out of the ditch: "Over and under the tired stepping of Bet, he could hear the night throb. He heard every sound going on, repeating itself, increasing, as if it were being recollected by loud night talking to itself. At times it might have been the rush of water—the Bywy on the rise in the spring; or it might have been the rains catching up after them, to mire them in. Or it might have been that the whole wheel of the sky made the sound as it kept letting fall the soft fire of its turning. . . . The night might turn into more and more voices, all telling it—bragging, lying, singing, pretending, protesting, swearing everything into being, swearing everything away—but telling it. Even after people gave up each other's company, said good-bye and went home, if there was only one left, Vaughn Renfro, the world around him was still one huge, soul-defying reunion" (p. 363).

---

[1] "The Wild Swans," trans. Erik Christian Haugaard, *The Complete Fairy Tales and Stories* (New York: Doubleday and Company, 1974), pp. 121–122.

What happens in this brief episode, however, is merely an example of what has been happening all along in Welty's remarkable novel. In her carefully contrived *persona* she has been declaring from time to time, but invariably showing in her plethora of similes, the connectedness of things. We are thus prepared to believe, or at least to entertain the possibility, that her tale of humble people in a hill-country ravine actually is the tale of Everyman and his fall, and of the fall of Priam and Paris and Achilles and Agamemnon, too, and that, moreover, to fall like any of these is to be human and in its way a victory in defeat. Vaughn Renfro sees this con- catenation of paradoxes, and in his night ride to rescue the schoolbus he meditates as follows: "Had today been all brave show, and had Jack all in secret fallen down—taking the whole day to fall, but falling, like that star he saw now, going out of sight like the scut of a rabbit? Could Jack take a fall from highest place and nobody be man enough to say so? Was falling a secret, another part of people's getting tangled up with each other, another danger to walk up on without warning—like finding them lying deep in the woods together, like one creature, some kind of cricket hatching out of the ground big enough to eat him or to rasp at him and drive him away? The world had been dosed with moonlight, it might have been poured from a bottle. Riding through the world, the little boy, moonlit, wondered" (p. 363). This is the cumulative effect of *Losing Bat- tles*: it does not so much enlighten as it makes us wonder. Regardless of what happens at any given moment in it, we are being reassured by our unidentified narrator—by her presence and manner if by nothing else— that all things are connected, or at least connectable, that wonderment is allowable and no harm will be done if we indulge in it, and that regardless of appearances nothing in Banner community or anywhere else can ever really be lost if love is allowed to perform its recreative office.

The consequence, and perhaps the intent, of Welty's distinctive method of narration in this work is to rescue modern fiction from some of the lim- itations inherent in the tradition of Flaubert and Henry James and from some of the disasters that reaction against that tradition has brought us to. The assumptions behind Flaubert's art became imperative when the les- sons of the late Renaissance finally sank into our consciousness and de- veloped in western man the laudable habit of demanding proof for any experience he would accept as valid. Flaubert and his followers lifted to a high art those techniques of making fiction credible which the Renaissance made mandatory. For most sophisticated readers in their day it appeared or could be made to appear that Plato's repudiation of poetry (or fiction) as the lie had been effectively answered. Nevertheless, the epistemological agony that followed in the wake of the Renaissance and drove the best philosophers of the Enlightenment to skepticism finally caught up with nineteenth-century aesthetics, and ultimately readers found it no longer possible to believe in any experience not actually their own. The West had demanded proof as the prelude to belief, and proof had once more proved elusive. Coleridge's easy injunction to suspend disbelief could no longer be heeded by responsible readers; and in the absence of something like faith, which had enabled the medieval Dante to shatter the impasse of human blindness and climb painfully to the point where grace could lift him to a full and transcendent knowledge, the modern desperate descent into self, in an attempt to find there at least some basis for belief, proved in the end to be only a descent into a solipsistic prison where all worlds vanish and the dream of universality becomes a trivial irrelevance. Eudora Welty is not alone among moderns in her wish to achieve an escape from this latter-day prison, but her attempt to do so has put her in rare company. In the fullness of her maturity she has developed to that end special techniques which can be compared favorably with those of both an epic poet like Homer and a writer of sophisticated fairy tales like Andersen. She has also had the daring to use those techniques in a major novel. "Faith" may be a term that disturbs modern readers but whether we call it that or "suspension of disbelief" or something else, Eudora Welty in *Losing Battles* solicits from us an attitude of acceptance commensurate with her own courage. We cannot appreciate the surface of *Losing Battles* unless we can relax our demands for proof and become as little children in the presence of a storyteller whose magic extends to all parts of her tale—figures, fable, and the web of language that holds it all together. It has always been true that the meaning of Eudora Welty's fiction is not available to the reader who cannot respond to that web of language, to the texture as well as to the rest of it; for in the end she still stands with her first mentors, Flaubert and Henry James, and requires that the tale be credible enough to meet Aristotle's criterion of probability. With Conrad she still requires that we hear, feel and, before all, see; but she also demands as she sets one of her latest and best artifacts before us that we heed the injunction of ancient Paulina in *The Winter's Tale*: "It is required you do awake your faith" (V.iii.95–

96). For those of us who put that part of our attention to sleep soon after we left the nursery or the campfire, such advice is troublesome but salutary; and it is the prerequisite to understanding any fiction worth the trouble and time, including the works of Homer and Eudora Welty and all the golden mansions in between.

JOHN
EDWARD
HARDY Marrying Down
in Eudora Welty's Novels

"PEOPLE GET MARRIED beneath them every day," Edna Earle Ponder says, "and I don't see any sign of the world coming to an end" (*PH*, p. 37). Miss Edna does not, perhaps, qualify as an expert witness on questions of eschatological evidence. To hear her tell it, great balls of fire frisking about the parlor of a country house during a thunderstorm are wonders entirely of the known and natural order. Enough to make a Negro woman run and hide under the bed, certainly, enough even to scare a flighty, sickly girl to death, it might be; but nothing so rare as to unsettle a healthy and sensible white Christian lady of mature experience. Simply on the frequency of marriages which may be regarded as somehow degrading to one or both of the partners, however, she is unquestionably right. In the world of Eudora Welty's novels, which is, after all, the world of every day, such alliances are commonplace.

The complex treatment of this theme in *The Optimist's Daughter* is anticipated in all three of the earlier works—*Delta Wedding, The Ponder Heart,* and *Losing Battles*—which I choose to call "novels" with regard not only to their length but to their basic realism as stories of domestic commonplace. The theme is present also in *The Robber Bridegroom*; but that book does not qualify as a novel on the second and more important point of my definition.

I

The ceremony uniting Dabney Fairchild and Troy Flavin, her father's bumpkin overseer, is distinctly anticlimactic in the narrative pattern of *Delta Wedding*. And the marriage of these two promises in every way to affect the fortunes of the plantation family, for good or ill, less radically than they are affected by the earlier misalliances of Dabney's two uncles, Denis and George Fairchild.

The story of the separation of George and his wife Robbie—the former Robbie Reid, sometime store clerk in the nearby town of Fairchilds—is interwoven with the account of the preparations for Dabney's wedding and of the celebrations following it. If the novel as a whole has a climax, it is in the scene of Robbie's confrontation with the Fairchild women at Shellmound plantation house after her walk out from town.

The Fairchilds are landed "aristocracy." Denis, George, and Dabney "marry beneath them" in the plain sense that their mates come from the lower social and economic classes. The question, of course, is whether class superiority assures superiority on other counts.

When Robbie attacks the Fairchilds' pretensions with the taunting remark that they are "not even rich," it is the pathetic irony of her situation that she has mistaken the best evidence that they are wealthy for signs that they are not. "Only four gates to get here, and your house needs a coat of paint! You don't even have one of those little painted wooden niggers to hitch horses to!" (p. 163).

Gate-counting aside, the references to "paint" sufficiently indicate the superficiality of poor little Robbie's judgment. People with as many houses as the Fairchilds have do not need to keep them freshly painted. And, for those who can produce a real Little Uncle to look after horses, there is hardly any need to maintain an artificial nigger.

Robbie has a point, beyond her conscious reckoning, which we will come to later. But the Fairchilds are rich, all right. They are rich in houses, rich in land. They even have plenty of ready cash. It is vulgar to talk about money; a lady shrinks even from handling it in the condition in which it is given out by the banks in these degenerate times. But however absurdly and literally "laundered" by Aunt Mac, the considerable payroll of the plantation is always met. If Dabney should decide that she does not want to get married after all, then she too can go to Europe, like her sister Shelley, or back to college. Ellen herself is charitable enough to think so (p. 237), but the chief of the Christian theological virtues is in all likelihood not what motivates the Chinese gentleman in Greenwood who opens his grocery store on Sunday for Shelley.

The nearest "cultural" center, and that too far away for real convenience, is Memphis! Yet, the Fairchilds are rich also in the life of the mind and the sensibilities. Perhaps Shelley is right in confiding to her diary that "none of the Fairchilds are smart, the way [Troy] means smart" (p. 84). But they are in varying degrees sensitive, perceptive, acutely responsive to the forms, colors, and moods of both the natural and the human environment, fanciful, witty, at their best gravely reflective, capable of a tact deeper, more sympathetic than tolerance. They have grace, style beyond manners. Over the time of a hundred years, their provincialism has become a deliberate, subtly structured mode of existence, no longer a deprivation.

It is comparatively easy, on the other hand, to comprehend the sexual interest in Dabney's and George's choices. Physical beauty is not the Fairchilds' long suit in either the female or the male line.

Troy Flavin, besides being twice as old as Dabney, is certainly a bit of a shocker for looks at close quarters, with his head of upstart red hair and tufts of it growing out of his ears. But the figure of the "dark shouting rider" in the fields, which Dabney sometimes likes to think of as appealing exclusively to her, is obviously attractive in a half sinister way even to Aunt Primrose.

Robbie is a skimpy little switch of a thing, frail, childish. Now that she is married to George and living in Memphis, she can buy her own clothes and lots of them, no longer has to make do with Shelley's hand-me-downs as she once did when she was clerking in Fairchilds. She still wears high heels in the country, a wool tam-o-shanter and a pongee dress with a sash for walking down a dusty road on a hot day. All hopelessly wrong. But at least the younger children find her very "pretty." And her waif's appeal for big George is more or less taken for granted by the whole family, if with a scattering of sighs and lifted eyebrows.

In matters of personal morality, and of the strength and integrity of personal affections, it becomes finally very difficult to demonstrate the superiority of the Fairchilds to their lower-class spouses.

Crazy Virgie Lee, Denis's widow, with her long matted hair and shapeless garments, glimpsed only now and again trudging along beside the road as Shelley and company shuttle back and forth between plantation and town on their various expeditions, is permanently beyond the pale, a merely allegorical figure of reproach to the family and their vanities. Troy is somewhat more fully developed, more humanized, in both his engaging and his sinister aspects, seen close up in several conversations and in the intimate reflections of Dabney and Shelley. But he remains, if not allegorical then semi-mythic, at least as much field-god as man. Neither Troy's consciousness nor that of any other male character in the novel is visited by the omniscient narrator. He is viewed, from outside, by the narrator, more often by other characters. He speaks a few lines. But Robbie enjoys, or suffers, much fuller exposure. We see her as described by the narrator, talked about and thought about by a number of the other characters. Her own unspoken reflections and observations, as well as her conversation, are recorded at considerable length.

The total portrait is one of a woman who is at least the equal of any of the Fairchild women in moral character, and very possibly their superior in emotional integrity and stamina. She is vulgar, "common," in taste and manners. But if one sure sign of her vulgarity is her readiness to "make a scene," she always makes it in the interest of her legitimate passions. For all her frailty, she is tenacious, tough, resourceful, and cagily independent. Unlike Troy, who thinks of his union with Dabney as "marrying into" the Fairchild family, Robbie will come to terms with the others only to the extent necessary to secure her hold on George, and she wisely avoids making common cause with Troy.

No doubt, she is to some extent motivated in her hostility to the Fairchilds by the bitterness of enforced gratitude. When she was growing up in the town, the Fairchilds not only furnished her secondhand wardrobe but paid for her high school education. (In addition to clerking, she had also briefly tried teaching the lower grades; it is one of the great disappointments of her life that she was unable to attend junior college.) But she can never be accused simply of "using" George as an instrument of retaliation against her benefactors.

It is easy to see Robbie as mean-spirited and callously selfish in preferring herself to Maureen, the retarded child of Virgie Lee and the dead Denis whom the Fairchilds have reared from infancy at Shellmound. From the Fairchilds' collective point of view, Robbie's absurd and hysterical behavior at the railroad trestle, crying out "George Fairchild, you didn't do this for *me*!" (p. 61) when George risked his life to rescue Maureen from the path of an approaching train, is just what one would expect of such a common little thing with her head turned by marriage above her station. But if Robbie's peasant cruelty is undeniable, so is the callousness of the whole Fairchild family in permitting the younger children to tell the story over and over again, laughing at their Aunt Robbie, and implicitly at Maureen, even in the presence of comparative strangers like the Reverend Mr. Rondo.

The Fairchilds' own attitude toward Maureen is morally ambiguous, to say the least, tainted with sentimental self-righteousness and family pride. Further, it appears that Robbie might have had reason to think she was pregnant at the time she saw her husband lingering on the railroad track, so that her protest was not, perhaps, quite so selfish after all.

And if the Yellow Dog, thoroughly domesticated and dependable beast that it is, was probably going to stop anyway, seeing one or more Fairchilds on the track, the irony of that consideration is clearly one that cuts both ways on the issue of Robbie's conflict with the family. It is, as Battle says of the ownership of Marmion, all rather "complicated."

But in the aftermath of the trestle incident, Robbie's leaving George in Memphis and returning to him at Shellmound, the moral issues are not so complicated. Robbie is clearly the injured party. She leaves George, it would appear, as the only way she can think of to make him take her and her concern for him seriously. George is the generally acknowledged living "hero" of the family. But the quality of his heroism is severely scrutinized, implicitly by the narrator, and more directly by Ellen both in her words and in her thoughts. Once Robbie has left him, George makes no very strenuous effort to find her. When he might be spending his time out looking for his wife he is instead picking up *another* stray girl in the woods and taking her over to the old Argyle gin for a roll in the Delta equivalent of the hay, attending to the emotional needs of sundry Fairchilds, young and old, standing about staring tragically into space, traipsing off to dinner at the Grove.

Ellen may be right in thinking that George tells her about the episode at the gin as a subtle way of comforting her in her own pity and concern for the lost girl, whom she too had briefly encountered in the woods. But for reasons that do not necessarily reflect unfavorably upon the quality of her moral intelligence, it is doubtful that Robbie could be expected to take so exquisitely charitable a view of the matter as Ellen's.

When Robbie makes her scene, launching into her hysterical diatribe against the family for their hypocrisy and vanity, she has been directly provoked to it by a series of vulgar, petulant attacks from Fairchild daughters and aunts, united in condemning her for leaving George while at the same time secretly wishing she would go away forever. " 'You almost ruined my wedding!' cried Dabney. . . . '*Why* have you treated George Fairchild the way you have?' said Tempe. . . . 'Except for Denis Fairchild, the sweetest man ever born in the Delta?' ... 'How could you?' Shelley suddenly gushed forth tears" (p. 158). " 'Of course you only married George for his money, [Aunt Mac] continued" (pp. 160–61).

Aunt Mac has the excuse and advantage of being physically deaf, so that she does not hear Robbie's devastating reply: "No ma'am. I married him because he begged me!" (p. 161). All the others, except Ellen, are impaired in the ear of mind and conscience.

Ellen is finally compelled to acknowledge forthrightly that there are things to be hated in the Fairchilds. Soothingly, tactfully, above all honestly, she persuades Robbie, however, that her fight is over things, not people—"things like the truth, and what you owe people" (p. 163)—and goes to the heart of the matter, when Robbie says that she wishes she were dead, to remind her that it is just because she does love George that she must not die. When words fail, at the moment of George's return from the Grove, she superbly faints.

The faint is superb because, again, it is above all honest. Ellen is exhausted, she is pregnant. She can say and believe all the things she has said to Robbie, say and believe what she says to returning George, "Don't let them forgive you ... you've made this child suffer" (p. 166), because she herself as a Virginian is a lifelong outsider in the Fairchild circle despite her long service as wife and childbearer. But it is to her further credit that she does not *claim* the outsider's privilege, but refers to the Fairchilds as "us" when she admits that George himself may hate some things in them; to her credit, that she can support Robbie while she herself is in love with George. Ellen, no doubt, is altogether superb.

But in the climactic "scene," Ellen's is in every sense a supporting role. When she has assisted in restoring Robbie to George, commanding him to recognize his responsibility for his wife's suffering, her essential function has been accomplished. Later, when George still rather childishly insists on his right to do as he pleases in matters such as standing on railroad tracks, and Robbie has the last word—"But you're everything on earth to me!" —we may suppose that Ellen would agree with Aunt Tempe's unspoken assessment of the declaration. "The *vulgar* thing she said!" Tempe thinks, casting her eyes upward (p. 187). But Ellen further suspects that this kind of vulgarity may be of greater service to George in the long run than "too close a divination" such as her own sympathetic insights provide.

In any event, Robbie and George are still center-stage at the night picnic on the banks of the Yazoo which closes the novel. George is doing most of the talking now. But if any one of the women present holds the key to the Fairchilds' collective future it is, through George, Robbie.

Economic considerations figure prominently in the talk and the unspoken reflections of the adults at the picnic. After letting the twenty-five room Marmion stand empty for more than thirty years, the Fairchilds are suddenly beginning to find themselves a bit cramped for living space. The decision has been made that Dabney and Troy are to move into the mansion, and the work of renovation has begun. "I could get it done in one day," Battle has remarked (p. 227), "if I could spare that many Negroes —all but the fine touches!" Little Laura McRaven, as well as Virgie Lee and Maureen, has claims to the property which might or might not be legally enforceable, if anyone were ever disposed seriously to raise the question, but which pose no immediate threat. But still another problem arises with the possibility that George and Robbie might come to live on the plantation.

Economically, the proposal is both troublesome and promising. It would add yet another family's support to the burden of an enterprise that is already showing signs of being dangerously over-extended. On the other hand, it is obvious that George's notion of diversifying, by adding orchards, horses, cattle, even gardening and truck-farming, offers the best realistic hope for continuing profitable use of the land now given over entirely to cotton.

Battle is hopelessly short-sighted in this regard. And Troy, for all his character as field-god, spirit of rejuvenation—"dat high-ridin' low-born Mr. Troy," as Partheny calls him—differs little from his father-in-law as managerial theorist. For Troy, too, the secret of survival in the Delta is "just a matter of knowing how to handle your Negroes" (p. 95). For George, who promises to "keep in touch" (p. 247), Troy is at least as doubtful an ally as he was for Robbie. But the point of final importance is that the whole idea of George and Robbie's moving back to the Delta from Memphis may or may not be realized.

Robbie has thought only: "The Grove. . . . Well, for her, it *would be* that once more they would laugh and chase by the river. Once more she and Mary Shannon, well-known as that star Venus, *would be* looking at each other in that house. Things almost never happened, almost never could be, for one time only!" (p. 244, emphasis added). (Mary Shannon was the first Fairchild wife in Mississippi. Robbie recalls the time in her childhood when she was taken into the house at the Grove after falling into the river and saw Mary Shannon's portrait on the wall.) George says to Troy only: "We'll keep in touch. . . ."

Nowhere but in the vague promise to Troy does George use even the contraction of "will." Elsewhere, it is all a matter of how he "could" plant this, "might" build or try that. Robbie, either in words or in unspoken thoughts, never strays beyond the conditional.

The condition, it seems to me, is her still ungranted agreement to the star-gazing "man talk" plan of return. (" 'Oh, foot, Tempe,' said Primrose. 'Can't you listen to man talk without getting upset?' " [p. 245].) For the moment, it is sufficient that she has her man back again, whom she knows very well how to take care of. Assuming that life as a Fairchild is a worthy aspiration, in a world that has not quite yet come to an end and could be restored on a new footing, she might in good time decide on that. Meanwhile the flat in Memphis—assuming that there too the problem of "handling your Negroes" can be worked out—remains a viable alternative.

In *The Ponder Heart*, Edna Earle is endlessly resourceful at finding ways to avoid admitting that her Uncle Daniel is not quite all there, while forewarning her guest at the hotel that the man she is about to meet at dinner is likely to behave in a somewhat alarming fashion. If he should greet the young lady by moving up beside her on the lobby sofa and giving her a little hug, it is not to be taken amiss.

Uncle Daniel is always giving things away—money, ice-cream cones, himself in marriage, pair of goats, two laying pullets, the rest of the list that beats "Twelve Days of Christmas"—but the penchant is only an expression of his "open disposition," certainly not to be mistaken by any truly reasonable person for evidence of mental incompetence. If Grandpa Ponder was finally driven to agreeing with the Clanahans that "when the brains were being handed around . . . Daniel was standing behind the door" (p. 40), that is sufficiently explained by previous references to the old man's own tendency, like his son's, to get "carried away," a native "impatience" that has grown worse with the passing years.

In his more or less adult life, Uncle Daniel twice marries beneath him, each time a step lower on the social scale. Miss (or Mrs.) Teacake Magee is merely a Baptist. The Peacocks are poor white trash on all counts. Daniel himself insists that he has been married *three* times, counting the Tom Thumb wedding at the church pageant in his childhood. We gather that this first bride, Birdie Bodkin, was of a family which at the time might have claimed near equality with the Ponders. But the Bodkins too "have gone down since" (p. 34).

Edna Earle knows that a time has come when fewer and fewer people can be trusted to see the difference between Ponders and even Peacocks, let alone Bodkins and Sistrunks. (Miss Teacake Magee was a Sistrunk before her first marriage, to "Professor" Magee.) Having been born "the smart one of the family," Edna Earle sees it as her duty to keep the grounds of distinction clear. That, of course, is why she must resort to every available euphemism in describing and accounting for Uncle Daniel's foolishness, why she must insist always that it is a flaw of the "Ponder heart," not of the mind, that gets him in trouble. She knows that it is in the area of questions about relative intellectual capacity, about mental normality and abnormality, that people who are themselves otherwise intelligent, like the hotel guest who wants to "read" rather than "listen," are most likely to go wrong in judging of social distinctions. So she simply distracts attention from the doubtful territory as much as she can. (For all sorts of reasons, what is *never* mentioned directly is the possibility that Uncle Daniel's troubles might stem from a source darker and deeper than either mind or heart.)

Describing the flighty Bonnie Dee as she first saw her—with her "baby yellow hair . . . and not a grain beneath" (p. 34)—Edna Earle goes on to add that "Uncle Daniel may not have a whole *lot* of brains, but what's there is Ponder, and no mistake about it. . . . There's a world of difference" (p. 35). She knows quite well, we may assume, that even Bonnie Dee's six-year collection of *True Love Story* and *Movie Mirror* is beyond Daniel's intellectual reach. But it is the *quality* of mind that is the precious class and family heritage she cherishes, and she will go to any lengths, even perjury and subornation, to prevent Daniel's revealing his childishness to those who are incapable of distinguishing between qualitative and quantitative capacity.

When she rises up in the courtroom to forbid Daniel's giving away the dreadful secret that he literally tickled Bonnie Dee to death during the thunderstorm, she does not yet know that he is also about to give away all his money. But it can be assumed that she would not care if she did know. The heritage is more valuable to her than the inheritance she might have hoped to receive but for Daniel's unhappy alliance with Bonnie Dee.

All of this is not to say that Edna Earle is simply an absurd snob. Of the three trials with which the novel is concerned—the trial marriage of Daniel and Bonnie Dee, the trial of Daniel for Bonnie Dee's "murder," and the lifelong trial of Edna Earle which she suffers just as a consequence of being a Ponder—Edna Earle's, of course, is the one that most engages our sympathy.

Granted that when she tells Tip Clanahan, or wishes she had told him —"People get married beneath them every day, and I don't see any sign of the world coming to an end. Don't be so small town" (p. 37)—half her motivation, as she freely acknowledges, is simply the need to squelch the smugly pretentious old lawyer and the town at large. "That held them, till Grandpa got back." But the other half, we realize, is a genuine disdain for provincial small-mindedness. She chooses not to acknowledge openly her awareness that Uncle Daniel literally bought his acquittal in the murder trial, but we know that she *is* aware. And we know, further, both that moral if not legal justice was served in the trial and that she is at least half right in condemning those who sat in the courtroom, whether whooping or fainting, and shamelessly pocketed the money Daniel scattered among them. She is at least half right in blaming the economic paralysis of the town on the people's loss of "the power to be ashamed of themselves" (p. 147).

Edna Earle does not undertake to protect Uncle Daniel simply as a vulnerable embodiment of the family honor. She protects him because she genuinely loves him, and does not want to see him hurt. She is capable of unaffected affection even for Bonnie Dee: "And you know, Bonnie Dee Peacock, ordinary as she was and trial as she was to put up with—she's the kind of person you do miss. I don't know why—deliver me from giving you the *reason*" (p. 156). And a good many readers have seen a simple pathos in the situation of this fundamentally good and much-abused, middle-aged lady at the end of the story—impoverished, neglected, burdened probably for a good many years yet to come with the care of the ruined and nitwit, much-married uncle in whose interest she has sacrificed, no doubt permanently, her own hope for marriage.

But perhaps we can sympathize with her at least as much admiringly as pityingly. She is, it seems to me, at least as much victor as victim.

It was Edna Earle, after all, who put the ad in the Memphis newspaper to lure Bonnie Dee back after she had run off from Daniel. No matter that it was not, in fact, Bonnie Dee but her sister Johnnie Ree whom Mr. Springer had seen in the city. The ad worked; that is the important thing.

It was Edna Earle who persuaded Daniel, after Bonnie Dee had kicked *him* out, to cut off her allowance, thus precipitating the fatal effort at reconciliation. She does not exactly dwell on the fact of her responsibility, but she says nothing to conceal it either. And she is clearly willing to accept the consequences of her actions. The chances are that she and Mr. Springer will never get married, although she continues to entertain herself with the idea that they might. But one suspects that she really does not want to be married, has never wanted it.

What Edna Earle wants is to talk. Marriage would seriously cramp her style as indefatigable and unchallenged narrator. She may keep on "keeping company" with Mr. Springer as occasion offers, but nothing more. Of course, if the fortunes of Clay should ever so far decline that *nobody* comes to the hotel, that would be a real pity. But, short of that eventuality, Uncle Daniel and his tale are no great burden for her. In some curious way, she has had her way.

The marriage of Jack and Gloria in *Losing Battles* involves no social disparity that anyone outside the Banner community would be in the least capable of recognizing. It is amusing, and more than amusingly relevant to the theme of identity so prominent in the novel, that Jack's family try to find grounds for looking down on foundling Gloria. But she is doubly vindicated, and the whole issue of family pride is reduced to deepest farce, when even after the ordeal of the watermelon-initiation and the trimming of her bridal gown she continues to resist not only the Vaughn-Renfros' desire to claim her as a blood-relation but any and all efforts to identify her parents.

Everyone can find his own favorite losing or already lost battle in this long book. But one of the struggles near the center of the design is the conflict of the married and the not-married. Grandpa Ponder "regarded getting married as a show of weakness of character in nearly every case but his own" (*PH*, p. 26). Grandpa reveals another kind of weakness in making the exception for himself. The notion that marriage might be in all cases a sign of weakness, that whenever two people get married they both "marry beneath them," is often hinted at in Welty's studies of the relationship. Perhaps it is best kept implicit, because novelistically if not philosophically it is pretty clearly a dead-end idea.

The idea simply that each of the partners in a marriage is the superior in one or another respect is a different proposition. As we have seen, there is quite a good deal of that in *Delta Wedding* and *The Ponder Heart*, and dealt with more or less explicitly. The other notion—that marriage is somehow a betrayal of one's deepest identity, not only personal identity but one's essential *human* identity, that it is better to burn than to marry—is kept well submerged in these novels. It comes to the surface only in *Losing Battles*, which in a good many senses is a story that takes us if not to dead-ends then to one or more jumping-off places.

Schoolteacher Julia Mortimer, who appears on-stage only at the very end, and then in her coffin, is the obvious principal champion of the dedicated single life. Her wake and funeral compete in ceremonial interest with the Vaughn-Renfro family reunion, where the central figure is the sibylline Granny Vaughn.

Miss Mortimer, doomed in her very name, is dead, worn out with her long struggle against the forces of ignorance and sloth and superstition, the imbecile, lawless pieties of a debased religious faith and tribal custom that have combined with implacable nature and a cruelly exploitative national economy to devastate the Banner community. The nature of the sinister alliance is so far beyond the comprehension of the abused people that much of the time they do not even suspect they *are* abused.

Granny Vaughn, so frail and thin that surely the next stiff breeze will carry her away, clings slyly and unaccountably to life and intermittent rationality. There is much confusion on the question of her exact age. But she is surely ancient. She may very well live forever. The embodiment of everything that Julia Mortimer feared and despised and strove to defeat, enthroned at the head of the crudely bounteous reunion table and cloaked in the pastoral majesty of Delectable Mountains, she exacts tribute and reverence from a numberless progeny.

But the final battle in the war of the married and the not-married is not between Granny and Julia Mortimer, but between Gloria and Julia. The Vaughn-Renfros collectively take the simplistic view that they have captured Gloria, successfully initiated and absorbed her into the tribe, so that she no longer threatens to take their beloved Jack away from them, whether they can make a plausible case for blood-kinship or not. If blood is not available, watermelon juice will serve—perhaps all the better, since if the consanguinity were proved Jack might have either to return to the penitentiary or to live in Alabama. But they have not been listening to Gloria. She wants that two-room house for her and Jack and their baby to live to themselves, and means to have it. And her determination finally has nothing whatever to do with the truth or untruth of the various stories of her origins.

When Judge Moody says to her, "The fact is, you could be almost any-body and have sprung up almost anywhere" (p. 315), Gloria is more than "ready" for the "strong words," as Mrs. Moody calls them. The judge has unwittingly paid Gloria what she considers the greatest of compliments. It is not, finally, that she considers any particular set of parents unworthy of her. She simply prefers that their identity remain unknown because it gives her an advantage in asserting the truth and the superior right of her unique identity, which she would argue is not in anyone defined by either the genetic or the environmental influence of parents.

Even more fiercely than Robbie Reid, Gloria believes that it is possible to marry a man without marrying his whole kin. She has not yet quite suc-ceeded in convincing Jack, and now and again she is close to despair, but the dominant and recurrent temper of her mind is hopeful. In her own mind, she is still a long way from being taken captive by the tribe.

Julia Mortimer, it is clear, did not share her protegée's own faith in her ability to keep her identity in marriage. It is for that lack of personal faith, for Julia's having *laughed* at her, presumably in bitter disappointment and scornful pity when she told the old woman of her intention to marry, that Gloria cannot forgive the person to whom she owes her education and the still-cherished example of professional pride. Gloria refuses to go to Julia's house to "pay her respects" to the dead. She does consent to accom-pany Jack to the graveside, but even in this relenting she is principally con-cerned just to keep an eye on her husband.

Julia saw herself as in every way superior to the Banner community to which she had so thanklessly dedicated herself. Actually, the people of the community do recognize their debt to her, although they make jokes about the tyranny of her determination to educate them. If under the pressures of their own poverty they neglected her material needs, and in a sense aban-doned her, in her age and infirmity, to a nurse who might have been worse than neglectful, still they pay her spiritual homage even in the jokes. But she scorned their reverence. And the presence at her funeral of all the distinguished mourners from the great outer world "proves" her superiority to the Bannerites.

Most prominent among the outsiders, and at once especially offensive and especially awe-inspiring to the locals, is the priest who says the final words, in Latin, over Julia's grave. The representative of the distant and malign majesty of the Roman Catholic Church is easily the most "foreign" of the visiting dignitaries, if that were all that is required.

But there is another significance in the priest's presence. We are not to forget what Uncle Nathan answers when Brother Bethune asks him why he did not "tell the preacher," rather than Julia Mortimer, about his terrible sin in killing Dearman and letting an innocent man hang for the crime. " 'The preacher was Grandpa,' said Uncle Nathan" (p. 345). So much for the efficacy of a married clergy. Julia Mortimer was qualified as a confessor in large part by her celibacy. And it is clear that she also regarded teaching as a priestly vocation, incompatible with marriage.

Not so Gloria. Whether she is ever to step into a classroom again or not—and it is not inconceivable that she should—she indicates again and again that she proposes to remain a teacher in her mind and spirit, which for her is all that really counts. She can no more cease to be a teacher than she can forget a word of "Abou Ben Adhem."

Gloria feels not only that she continues to be worthy of all the work and pride that Julia Mortimer invested in her, but that she is at least in one respect her mentor's superior. That is, paradoxically, in never having lowered herself to the level of the Vaughn-Renfro tribal mentality.

On the way back from the burial Jack says of Julia Mortimer: "I expect she might be the only one could have understood a word out of that man burying her. If he was a man.... She was away up over our heads, you and me." Gloria responds: "Once. But she changed. I'll never change" (p. 432).

There is nothing in the immediate context to indicate what "change" in Miss Mortimer she is talking about. But I think it most likely that she does *not* mean anything like what might have happened as a consequence of Julia's having an affair with Dearman—*if* she had one—not to speak of the inevitable and universal consequences of aging. What she probably means, as I see it, is that Julia degraded herself in contributing to the vulgar commotion over the obscurity of Gloria's origins, writing letters about what might happen if she had a baby, and so on. In this, Gloria might well see Julia as having put herself on a level with the Vaughn-Renfros at their collective worst, in a way that merely marrying one of them, and loving him and trying to teach him to live up to the best in himself, does not involve.

The Bannerites in general, not just the Vaughn-Renfros, have already confounded the law; they may well confound the church, and let both together slide into the Bywy any day. And the apparition of the old white horse in the pasture, near the end of the novel, as it were miraculously resurrected from the rendering plant, is of ambiguous significance. Education, too, with the other institutions, may soon sink into oblivion, and celibate Julia be all too cruelly vindicated. But if anyone can stay the erosion, it is Gloria, with her Jack, joke, poor potsherd of a husband.

II

In *The Ponder Heart* it is difficult, in *Losing Battles* all but impossible, to define to the outsider's satisfaction the grounds on which the husband's family assert their social superiority to the bride. But the marriage of Clinton McKelva and Wanda Fay Chisom, in *The Optimist's Daughter*, involves a disparity unequalled even in the misalliances of *Delta Wedding*.

As we have seen, Robbie Reid has strengths of character and competence, some individual and some attributable to her lower-class origins, which serve to explain and justify George Fairchild's attraction to her. Uncle Daniel Ponder's "innocence" relieves him of all accountability. Jack Renfro can hardly make matters any worse than they already are for himself and his family by marrying Gloria.

Judge McKelva's choice of a second wife seems irresponsible on any grounds. She is much younger than he, by some thirty years. But at approximately forty she is not young enough to dazzle a sensible man with the sheer radiance of youth, and McKelva shows no symptoms of senility. Not only is he incomparably better educated than she, bookish, trained in the usages of influence, prestige, a tradition of taste and manners which is beyond her reckoning, but she would not appear to have any considerable native intelligence which he might have hoped to cultivate.

Fay's family are only a slightly modernized version of the Peacocks, and all the worse for the updating. Further, if Bonnie Dee was the pick of the Peacocks, Wanda Fay is surely the best of her tribe *only* physically. Otherwise, she is the worst of a bad lot. Robbie and Gloria are obviously intelligent, and, as sometime schoolteachers, have small but legitimate pretensions to respect for learning. Robbie is justly proud of her talents in cooking and housekeeping. Fay cannot teach, cannot or will not cook or keep house. She can, or could, operate a typewriter, but even that she will probably not do again if she can avoid it. Unlike Gloria, who does not know who her parents were or are and does not want to find out, Fay knows hers but tries to deny them. Not only does she offer no hope of rejuvenation for the moribund McKelva family, but in surviving her husband she seems bent on destroying as quickly as possible all that is left to dignify his memory.

Beside Fay's grotesquely selfish outbursts against the dying Clinton in New Orleans, Robbie's "George Fairchild, you didn't do this for *me!*" (*DW*, p. 61) is as nothing. If Robbie "stood up staunch as the Bad Fairy," it might appear that Wanda Fay *is* the bad fairy. Robbie "did not seem to know whether she had let the bird in [the house] or not" (p. 160). Perhaps we need not ask what bad weather brings the bird to trouble Laurel Mc-Kelva Hand's long night in her father's house at Mount Salus.

What is to be made of all this? I do not think it will work simply to point out that in her earlier fiction Eudora Welty provided many sympathetic portraits of the lower orders, dignified their lives in the dramatization of universal themes, affectionately and subtly employed them, without condescension, to puncture the pretensions of both the petite and the haute bourgeoisie as well as the "aristocracy" of the South. Neither does the touching treatment of Grandpa Chisom in this novel serve to redeem the squalor of his family. Grandpa is at best only a melancholy reminder of Chisom past, and his greatgrandson Wendell, the most forlorn of sentimental hopes for the future. Chisom present yields Wanda Fay, whose attempt to deny her family tells us after all at least as much about them as it does about her, and whose boast to Laurel that *she* is the future is probably the most reliable prophecy.

In none of her earlier novels, works which she obviously had still in mind when she wrote this one, did Welty present a major character in whom vulgarity and viciousness seemed so nearly to coincide as they do in Fay Chisom. Moreover, the apparent change of attitude toward the lower classes is reinforced with a change of narrative technique.

In *Delta Wedding* and *Losing Battles*, where a good many different characters are studied at length, it is difficult even to define who the truly central figures are, not to speak of identifying the author's viewpoint with any single one of theirs. The use of an internal narrator in *The Ponder Heart*, one who speaks in uninterrupted monologue "in character" from beginning to end, is a transparent device for maintaining authorial detachment. In the third-person narrative of *The Optimist's Daughter*, Laurel Hand's dominant and solid middle-class, quasi-artistic consciousness—we see almost everything through her eyes—is much harder to distinguish from what we might suppose Eudora Welty's to be.

But I see the new technique as a grave challenge to the reader, to discover the common essence of humanity in a story of an era in which the breakdown of the older class structure has resulted not in an increase of tolerance but in a frightening exacerbation of social hostilities. It seems to me the last thing we should assume is that Eudora Welty, this most serenely detached of artists, has decided at last to commit herself to a mere heroine. And, once we have reserved judgment on that point, all the other all too readily "apparent" facts about the relationship of protagonist and antagonist in the novel are open to question.

I think it worthwhile to ask whether Laurel, in part from a fundamental defect of vision and in part from an instinct of self-preservation, has not overlooked certain important facts about Fay and her relationship to her old husband. We may start with the scene in Dr. Courtland's examining room.

Fay thinks that Clinton must have scratched his eye against a thorn while trimming Becky's rose bushes. Good Dr. Courtland tries patiently to explain that the problem, a slipped retina, is not the result of a superficial injury but of damage to the "inside" of the eye, "the part he sees with." But the attentive reader will not be inclined to dismiss Fay's diagnosis until all the evidence is in. No doubt the doctor is right so far as the operable condition is concerned. But McKelva dies. And there can be little doubt that the affliction of the "inner" eye which kills him, as opposed to that of the "inside" one which does not, is somehow related to his bungling solicitude for the first Mrs. McKelva's everlasting roses.

If it were only a matter of the condition of the inside eye, the slipped retina, Dr. Courtland would almost unquestionably have done better to insist on calling in Dr. Kunomoto. Courtland and McKelva are old family friends and neighbors. And McKelva, it develops, helped to pay for Courtland's medical education. But Kunomoto was Courtland's teacher, and now has a new and presumably superior technique which his former student has not yet mastered. It is not often a good idea to let ties of ancient friendship affect one's decisions in professional matters, especially when the friendship is tainted with gratitude. As primitive Fay somehow understands, the situation is only more dangerously complicated when the profession in question is one that must deal with the whole man, not exclusively with his physical parts.

It is easy to be at once vexed and amused by Fay's obstinacy in blaming the bad eye on Becky's roses, even after Courtland has explained the medical problem to her, by her vulgar insistence to the bitter end that they should have let "Nature" take care of it. But when she and Laurel leave the hospital on Mardi Gras night, after McKelva's death, Laurel hears in the noise of the carnival crowd that fills the city "the unmistakable sound of hundreds, of thousands, of people *blundering*" (p. 43). And one must wonder if even she is not reluctantly recalling the image of Dr. Courtland as she last saw him a few minutes before, "in evening clothes" (p. 41). It is not without justification, beyond her vulgarity, that Fay screams after Dr. Courtland as they drive away in the chauffeured car he has provided them: "Thank you for nothing!" (p. 43).

The coincidence of the day of Judge McKelva's death, Shrove Tuesday, and Fay's birthday—at any rate, she *says* it is her birthday—is part of a complex pattern of references to private and public ceremonials in the novel. In her grotesquely selfish complaint against her husband for choosing this particular day to die, Fay betrays herself not only as emotionally retarded but as hopelessly provincial.

As they drive away from the hospital she cries out with "the longing, or the anger, of her whole life all in her voice at one time, 'Is it the Carnival?'" (p. 43). And the chauffeur is duly scornful: "Where you come from?" he says. "This here is Mardi Gras *night*."

But there is a question whether Fay's more than naively agitated account of the things she has seen earlier on the way to the hospital—the skeleton-suited man in the company of a woman with snakes in her hair, another man dressed all in Spanish moss and vomiting in the street—is not more in keeping with the real terror of the situation than Laurel's relatively cool and sophisticated attitude. Wanda Fay, of course, does not know what "carnival" means. She thinks of it, or has thought of it, before she saw it, simply as the supreme festival of pleasure. But she is beginning to sense now something of the primitive significance of the celebration that makes it a background not at all inappropriate, in fact, to what has happened at the hospital.

The sight of the vomiting man in the suit of moss seems to have frightened Fay as deeply as if she had witnessed not simply a particularly revolting spectacle of masked abandon, but a real metamorphosis. 'Why did I have to be shown that?" she cries (p. 43). She has not merely seen something. She feels, rather, that she has suffered some terrible revelation, all the more profoundly disturbing for the fact that it is not entirely intelligible.

Of course she does not "understand" the vision. But if, to repeat, Fay does not know what "carnival" means, neither does Laurel really. Vis-à-vis the ancient Catholic tradition represented in the New Orleans Mardi Gras, she and her father, and Dr. Courtland for that matter, are all hicks.

It is also doubtful that one in a thousand of the revelers, even of the native Catholics, knows or cares very much about the Christian religious significance of the festival, not to speak of the still more ancient pagan rituals from which it probably derives. But to acknowledge the general ignorance is only to recognize the enormity of the problem of cultural disintegration which is represented in Laurel's and Fay's inability to communicate—not to minimize the central importance of the latter for the novel, but to place it in proper perspective.

If it were not for her vulgarity, her strident spitefulness on all occasions, it would be difficult not to sympathize with Fay in her disrespect for the Mount Salus sense of tradition. Why was Judge McKelva out pruning Becky's rosebush at the time he noticed he was "seeing behind" himself? Well, Dr. Courtland explains: "Because George Washington's Birthday is the time-honored day to prune roses back home" (p. 6). No matter that, as McKelva himself has pointed out a moment before, it is bad horticultural practice to prune a climber before it has bloomed. Besides being totally irrelevant to the intent of Fay's question, Dr. Courtland's answer explains absolutely nothing about the origin of the Mount Salus observance. And if he speaks with "amicable voice," the amicability is the thinnest mask of condescension.

Courtland does not give Fay a real answer because he does not really want to answer. All he wants to do is keep her quiet and in her place, tell her in effect that she cannot possibly understand about Washington and the roses, or about the Judge and Becky either, simply because she does not and never will "belong" in Mount Salus. Essentially the same spirit informs Laurel's pretensions to seeking communication with Fay.

Laurel is in a sense "forgiving" of Fay's many offenses. She does not directly accuse Fay of having caused or hastened McKelva's death when, as the nurse rather incoherently describes the episode (p. 32), she "laid hands on him" a moment before Laurel's arrival. When Fay hysterically accuses *her* of behaving unforgivably in failing to reproach Mrs. Martello for a lack of proper respect, even spits at her, Laurel does not react in anger.

She is, of course, preoccupied with her own grief for her father. Perhaps her tolerance also reflects an awareness that Fay too is under severe emotional strain. But her attitude is, after all, better described as tolerant rather than forgiving. Neither in the hospital waiting room nor anywhere else does Laurel treat Fay with a courtesy, not to speak of charity, greater than is required by her upbringing as a gentlewoman. Each time she feels the brief promptings of a deeper human sympathy, she fastidiously retreats at the first sign of Fay's easily predictable resistance to her overtures. Laurel, in her gentility, is neither more nor less true to her class than Fay is to hers in her vulgarity, her open selfishness and suspicious hostility.

In Mount Salus, after the funeral and the unexpected visit of the appalling Chisoms, Laurel tells Adele Courtland (the doctor's spinster sister) and the other ladies gathered in the McKelva garden that she hopes she will never see Fay again. Beyond the range of Laurel's candid and simple intention, the remark is involved in a number of contextual ironies.

Physically, Laurel does not get her wish. Just before she returns to Chicago, she does see Fay again. Psychologically, on the other hand, the hope is realized, and realized as a confirmation of what has already happened, or failed to happen, in their previous encounters. Laurel has never been able to "see" Fay, has not wanted or tried to see her, and still does not see her on the last day.

There is no arguing with the fact that Laurel herself thinks she has seen all there is to see in Fay, at least in their final confrontation over the breadboard, if not before. The breadboard, as an object made by Laurel's husband for her mother, both now dead, has a special and complex sanctity. Fay's casual abuse of the board as something to crack nuts on amounts almost to sacrilege in Laurel's eyes. But the sad truth is that the affair of the breadboard does simply provide final confirmation of the tendencies we have observed before in Laurel's behavior.

Throughout the long, terrifying night in the old house where she is alone except for the captive bird, and on the next day until Fay unexpectedly returns, Laurel is engaged all but exclusively in the struggle to come to terms with the fear and guilt of her memories of events prior to her father's second marriage. She is concerned only with her own marriage and with her mother's, with her father's death only as it is related in the pattern of her experience to Philip's and her mother's and her grandparents' deaths.

Taken off-guard by Fay's return from Texas, a moment after she has made the dismaying discovery of the abused breadboard, Laurel emerges from her "excited reverie" and seems on the point of recognizing the other woman as a real person, who has had some materially significant connection with the man they recently buried. For the first time, she openly charges Fay with having "desecrated" the house, quarrels with her over possession of the breadboard, exchanges boasts and insults with her on the issue of which is the better equipped by her upbringing for coping with widowhood and the hard facts of life in general. But at the crucial instant, when she is on the verge of actually striking her tormentor with the breadboard, Laurel recovers herself and gracefully settles the dispute by backing out of it.

She has thought of Fay's return as somehow inevitable, but continues to see in Fay only an ideal antagonist, conveniently provided by fate to assist her in dramatizing an argument that is essentially one with herself. The issue is one of "feeling," not of the rights of material possession, and therefore one that Fay is simply incapable of understanding. Fay, she argues, is devoid of the capacity to feel anything in a truly personal way, understand and appreciate the feelings of another person, in the same way that she is incapable of appreciating the things of the past. Both require "powers of passion [and] imagination in herself" (p. 178) which it would seem Fay was either born without or robbed of in the harsh struggles of her Chisom childhood.

When Fay boasts that the past is nothing to her, Laurel is quick to assure her, reversing the phrase, that she already knows Fay is nothing to the past. It occurs to her "that Fay might already have been faithless to [Judge McKelva's] memory." But she takes comfort in the reflection that neither Fay nor she herself can "do anything" to the past now. It is "no more open to help or hurt" than the dead. The past is "impervious." "The memory [i.e., the memory as a capacity of the living mind] can be hurt," she says to herself, "time and again—but in that may lie its final mercy. As long as it's vulnerable to the living moment, it lives for us, and while it lives, and while we are able, we can give it up its due" (p. 179).

Fay, as if sensing that her enemy has somehow slipped away from her, and detecting the nature of the tactic, tries to recover with her own gesture of contemptuous capitulation. The breadboard is not worth fighting over. " 'Take it!' said Fay. 'It'll give me one less thing to get rid of.' " But Laurel has the last word, of course, and refuses.

" 'Never mind,' said Laurel, laying the breadboard down on the table where it belonged. 'I think I can get along without that too.' "

But if all this sums things up more or less satisfactorily for Laurel, who is running late and has a plane to catch, I am not at all sure that it ought to content the unhurried reader. Laurel's resignation of the breadboard strikes me as still none too subtly challenging. Fay's previous remark is merely spiteful. Laurel's response is both spiteful and smug, nothing surely to inspire confidence in the accompanying philosophical reflections as undertaken in "calm of mind, all passion spent."

The more Laurel strives to repudiate Fay, the more curiously she comes to resemble her. We should not forget that the breadboard is only the last of many things Laurel has decided since the funeral she can "get along without." There is, to be sure, between Laurel's phrase for it and Fay's— "one less thing to get rid of"—a difference that is more than idiomatically significant of character. But the differences between the two women are readily apparent. The likenesses are harder to get at, but nonetheless essential to Welty's design.

Laurel herself from time to time, even back in Mount Salus, has with a kind of horror suffered feelings of sympathy and kinship. (See pp. 60 and 132, for example.) But each time she has, as we have noted, rejected the temptation to yield. Not since fairly early during their stay at the Hibiscus in New Orleans has she made even a perfunctory effort to "know" Fay. The questions she has put to her since then—asking her why she had lied about the existence of her family in Texas, what she had intended when she "struck" the dying McKelva—are obviously more challenge than inquiry, requiring no answer and impervious to the response that is offered. But try as she will to deny Fay human status, to put her down as something that has visited the house like a force of external nature, more or less reliably "predicted" by Becky as one predicts the weather, for the reader if not for Laurel the odious questions persist, the odious suggestions of a likeness between the two women and their situations. Both, after the trial of the death and funeral, have gone "home" for a brief visit in an effort to come to terms with the terrors of the past. Both now are lightening ship for the alien future, jettisoning ruined breadboards and whatever other worse than useless equipment is lying about.

Both are pitiable and lonely fugitives from their pasts; both the more pitiably doomed to solitude, for the fact that they cannot throw off the inherited habits of mind and emotion. If Fay's actions, in going back to Texas, the very vehemence of her tone in expressing her contempt for the breadboard, belie her words—her earlier denial, in New Orleans, that any of her family are living, her assertion during the final encounter that the past is nothing to her—Laurel is caught in disturbingly similar contradictions.

Laurel subtly argues the case for herself as true defender of the past in its inviolability that is inseparable from the vulnerability of memory. But she is uncommonly *anxious* to dispose of the material reminders of her past.

Adele Courtland, one of the many minor characters in Welty's fiction who often seem to embody the authorial presence in a way that the major figures cannot, is a crucial witness of Laurel's actions early on the day of her departure. She stops on her way to school to watch as Laurel burns the family mementoes she has collected from the house during the night: "She looked at what Laurel was doing and her face withheld judgment" (p. 169). Then, when Laurel attempts to give her the little soapstone boat that Judge McKelva had carved for Becky, Adele refuses it and kindly but firmly reproaches the younger woman for the impropriety of the offer. Laurel is duly chastened for the moment, seeing that she has intolerably "presumed." But we are left further to wonder how Adele would have looked, what she would have said, had she witnessed a bit later Laurel's surrender of the breadboard to Fay.

Only the more interestingly for the fact that she herself might have expected to be asked to succeed the first Mrs. McKelva—whether she would have accepted is another question—Adele is also the only consistent defender of Fay among the ladies of Mount Salus. Miss Tennyson tries to dismiss her with a friendly joke—"Adele has the schoolteacher's low opinion of everybody" (p. 109)—but Adele persists in countering every disparagement of Fay's and her family's behavior at the funeral with a reproach to herself and the others gathered in the McKelva garden. Most pointedly, she addresses her remarks on Fay's "emulating" her own mother to Laurel: "We can't find fault with doing that, can we, Laurel?" (p. 111).

Laurel does not answer. But, then, Miss Adele has not said that Fay *needs* no defender. For all that they are fellow Baptists, the schoolteacher has a way with words that makes her observations considerably less easy to answer than the mere typist's are.

But it is not my purpose, with or without help from Adele Courtland, to defend Fay at Laurel's expense, or to condemn or to "redeem" either one or both of them or either one or both of the rival Madrid and Mount Salus contingents at the funeral. The other conflicts are, after all, interesting principally for their relevance to Laurel's inner struggle to be reconciled to the fact of her father's death.

Most critics of the novel, I believe, have agreed that Judge McKelva's "optimism" is a euphemism for a species of moral cowardice, the inability to face unpleasant facts about human nature. Called "liar" and "Lucifer" by the dying Becky for having falsely promised that he would take her back "up home" to the mountains when he knew that it was no longer possible, he seems to have learned nothing from the experience. With his second wife, he only repeats and compounds the perfidy when he promises to take her to the Mardi Gras but instead chooses to stage his own death on the holiday.

Laurel, on the other hand, is generally regarded as a tough-minded and scrupulous realist. At her father's funeral she is outraged by the lying stories of cliché heroics his old cronies tell about the judge. It is interesting that Laurel attempts in this episode to defend her father also as a champion of unvarnished truth, insisting that he himself "hadn't any use for what he called theatrics" (p. 80). But she, in any event, will have nothing but the truth.

And yet, nothing in the novel is plainer than the fact that Laurel does not want, and will not accept when the broadest hint of it is offered to her, the whole truth about her father and Fay. She is quite evidently reluctant also to pursue certain implications of her own husband's behavior in seeking the most dangerous possible assignment in the war; but that is a question of relatively minor importance. She recalls without flinching the harsh facts of her mother's deathbed curses on both her and her father. But she repeatedly and persistently seeks to account for her father's attraction to Fay on grounds either of his physical infirmity or of his imaginative compassion, all but shutting her eyes to the evidence of his more vulgar inclinations.

When Fay's nephew Wendell starts to cry at his grandmother's stories of the Chisom family tragedies, Laurel feels an urge to take the little boy in her arms to protect and comfort him. "He was like a young, undriven, unfalsifying, unvindictive Fay. So Fay might have appeared, just at the beginning, to her aging father, with his slipping eyesight" (p. 76). Later, alone in the house and remembering the scene of Fay's "attack" on the old man in the hospital, she reflects that she, unlike her father, "cannot feel pity for Fay" (p. 131).

What actually caused McKelva's death, prompted him at last to "sneak out" as Dr. Courtland puts it, is never made clear. As plausible a guess as any is that he succumbed to despair in recognition of his inability to lay the ghost of Becky. Laurel is in a sense right that he died "worn out with both" the wives (p. 151). She does not, however, clearly see how great a part she herself must have played, as a kind of reincarnation of her mother, in bringing on the fatal exhaustion. In any event, Laurel does well to abandon the notion she briefly entertains of making any charges against Fay that would "stand up in court." For there is no disinterested living witness (Mrs. Martello is clearly prejudiced) to gainsay Fay's assertion that when she "struck" her husband she was "trying to scare him into living . . . to make him quit his old-man foolishness" (p. 175). And the judge is disqualified by death.

"Struck" is the word Laurel uses. Mrs. Martello says that Fay "laid hands on him" (p. 32). The nurse's hostile attitude to Fay is clear, but the phrase she uses is unintentionally ambiguous. One can, of course, "lay hands" on a person with a variety of intentions ranging all the way from murder to benediction. The word "hand" is elaborately played upon in the novel. Laurel herself participates to some extent consciously in the wordplay with reference to her husband's name. It is singularly interesting that she seems to have forgotten Mrs. Martello's exact words.

There is no objective evidence to support Laurel's notion that her father doted on Fay as a kind of overaged child, that his feeling for her was any species of "pity." Much of what others have told her—e.g., Miss Tennyson's reference to their "billing and cooing" over Sunday dinners at the Iona Hotel—would suggest quite different emotions. When the thought occurs to Laurel that her mother "had suffered in life every symptom of having been betrayed" (p. 174), she skips nimbly around the obvious implication to assure herself that it is only as an embodiment of "Becky's own dread," *after* her death, "that Fay had ever tripped in" on Judge McKelva's life. "Perhaps," she thinks, it was not until then that "her father himself had ever dreamed of a Fay" (p. 174). And indeed "perhaps" she is right. But there is nothing besides Laurel's own clearly self-protective thinking to support her reconstruction of the history of her father's relationship with Fay. And, whether one chooses to think that he did or did not know Fay before Becky's death, there is nothing to counter the appalling evidence of the pink-satined bed.

Mrs. Bolt, the minister's wife, refers to it not as Fay's bed but as "their bed." Even Laurel, although she prefers to think of it as now exclusively

Fay's, cannot deny that it is the same bed, obscenely transformed, in which she herself was born and in which her mother died. What she must deny, in effect, cannot help denying, is the obvious implication that her father as much as Fay was responsible for whatever "desecration" the house suffered in the judge's second marriage. It is manifestly absurd to suppose—although it is at the same time necessary that we understand Laurel's need to believe the absurd—that Fay entered the house uninvited, or changed anything in it to suit herself without her husband's approval.

There is abundant evidence to support Laurel's belief that her father was a man of "delicacy." But what Laurel cannot bring herself to believe, as even the most intelligent offspring very often cannot, is that delicacy could coexist with a gamey sexuality in the man who was her father. There is more than one irony in the senile fantasy of old Mr. Dalzell when he "adopts" Judge McKelva as his delinquent son Archie Lee, repeatedly and vainly admonishing him not to "let the fire go out." Beyond any reasonable doubt one of the qualities that the judge most appreciated in Fay was her very vulgarity, chiefly but not necessarily exclusively in the sense of the word "vulgar" as it is most often used by vulgar people.

Becky, it appears, was a many-talented person of considerable intelligence and great charm, capable of great kindness on occasion. But she seems to have been in some ways a hard woman to live with. When Fay tells Laurel the story of Becky's throwing the bell at Mr. Cheek, Laurel goes beyond her mother's own reported words that she had no "*wish* to hurt any living creature" (emphasis added) to assert flatly that she "never did hurt any living creature" (p. 174). But the assertion is clearly at variance with the facts as Laurel herself recalls them. Unless we are to restrict "hurting" to the sense of inflicting physical injury, then both Laurel and her father were most grievously hurt by Becky: the woman who never ceased to regard the "home" to which her husband brought her as inferior to the "up home" of her origins, who on her deathbed called that same husband "liar" and "coward" and then gave the final twist to the knife by taking "his hand to help him bear it" (p. 148), who in her "last remark" to Laurel deliberately passed on to her daughter the burden of her own irrational guilt in having failed to "save" her parents' lives. Such a woman surely exacted a terrible price for the privilege of loving her.

After so many years of suffering the pain of Becky's refinement, it is understandable that Clinton McKelva should find relief in Fay's candid selfishness and sensual hunger. In refusing to understand, and thus in a sense being herself "unfaithful to her father's memory," Laurel yet proves herself "the optimist's daughter" in excess even of the judge's example. In failing, or refusing, to understand Fay and the nature of Judge McKelva's attraction to her, she fails in the final analysis to understand herself, and settles for the false comfort of an insight unworthy of her moral intelligence.

I think this reading of Laurel makes her no less interesting a character, nor even less admirable, than the triumphant realist other critics have seen in her. It only makes her a tragic character—a person whose vision is tragically incomplete—rather than the heroine of a rather snobbish, and specious, moral comedy.

Eudora Welty herself is surely no "optimist." I think in the novel's dimension of social criticism it is abundantly clear that Laurel's method of dealing with Chisom, simply handing over possession of all the material remains of the McKelva tradition to Fay without a fight, does not have the author's unqualified blessing.

One hopes that Laurel has not abandoned her idea of taking up bread-making when she gets back to Chicago, even if she should have to do it only for herself. Such arts are the basis of civilization. But she will need a good breadboard. And her notion of restoring her mother's old one was sensible and frugal. Perhaps she can find something suitable in house-wares at Marshall Field. But it will be expensive, and certainly no *better* than what she has sacrificed to spite and to dubious principle in Mount Salus. The name of Chisom is legion, even in Chicago, and if Laurel's example in this matter is to be followed, there will soon be no possessions, and therefore no civilization, left to surrender.

I do not mean that Eudora Welty is a pessimist, either. If one is not disposed either to marry or brain a Chisom, the novel suggests, I believe, options other than Laurel's fastidious retreat. But the suggestions properly remain suggestions. For the novel is not primarily a novel either of manners or of social criticism. It has these dimensions. But it is first of all a novel of tragic realism. Eudora Welty, as distinguishable from Laurel McKelva Hand, is the true and complete realist.

ALBERT J.   Eudora Welty's
DEVLIN   Mississippi

BECAUSE OF HER long-standing admiration for William Faulkner, Eudora Welty must have rejoiced in 1946 when Malcolm Cowley brought him back into print and began the arduous process of elucidating his fictional domain. Faulkner, Cowley argued, was essentially "a creator of myths that he weaves together into a legend of the South," not a mere writer of discrete novels and short fiction. His work falls into cycles treating the important familial, geographic distinctions of Yoknapatawpha, but these "cycles or sagas," Cowley maintained, "are closely interconnected; it is as if each new book was a chord or segment of a total situation always existing in the author's mind."[1] Perhaps this is why Faulknerians come to resemble Quentin Compson of *Absalom, Absalom*! They too are "peopled with garrulous outraged baffled ghosts, listening, having to listen," to voices from "old ghost-times."

Eudora Welty has also created many distinctive voices, although it was not her way to locate them in such a reflexive fictional world. Certain stories may be more familiar to specialists, but others speak to a wide and responsive audience. We recall such triumphs as "Keela, The Outcast Indian Maiden," "A Worn Path," and "Powerhouse." Each story was printed periodically between 1940 and 1941 and then collected in Welty's first volume, *A Curtain of Green* (1941). Each story renders black life in rural Mississippi, but diversity in mode and tone obscures whatever bibliographical and thematic unity this group may possess. "Keela" remains essentially gothic in spirit, while "A Worn Path" embodies the pastoral impulse and "Powerhouse" explores a stratum of ritualistic comedy. Temperamentally, this group exhibits at one pole the absurdist's suspicion of meaning, at the other, the most traditional humanistic values. Perception

[1] Introduction to *The Portable Faulkner* (New York: Viking Press, 1946), p. 7.

of such diversity, expanding beyond our initial group to include the full collection, not only characterized many early assessments of *A Curtain of Green*, but has since become a staple of Welty criticism. Writing in 1942, Robert Van Gelder summarizes this attitude. "Each story is distinct, purely individual, born of its subject and a point of view that is so wide and deeply understanding that it is as though there were no brand of one mind upon the stories. Their outstanding similarity is formed of the intensity that went into their writing. They create moods as powerful as the moods developed by good poetry."[2] This is meant as high praise and usually would not prompt reservations. In Welty's case, however, acute emphasis upon the distinctiveness of each story has obscured from critical view the formation of a larger social vision. Rarely has anyone thought to accuse this superb stylist of writing "closely interconnected" stories that possess the amplitude of cultural history.

Perhaps this is the fate of any short story writer whose work has been widely anthologized, but Eudora Welty or, more properly, some of her admirers, have also had to contend with the hovering presence of William Faulkner. How, asked one anxious reader in 1953, did Welty "avoid rewriting Faulkner," when so many countrymen had already succumbed to his model? Presumably, she made a strategic decision early in her career that insured uniqueness. The critical assumption is that Faulkner's world resounds with "the clash" of mighty historical forces, but its scope and density so militate against intimate depiction of character that we can "seldom think" of his people apart from such categories as Snopes and Sartoris. Here, according to Robert Daniel, was Eudora Welty's "opportunity."[3] While Faulkner portrayed the large outer world of historical action, she would paint finer china and poetically evoke the inner world of psychological nuance. When history functioned at all in her work, it would provide atmospheric verisimilitude. Both writers are equally violated by this curious division of the house of fiction, but while the Sartoris-Snopes mythology has been tempered by more recent scholarship, early descriptions of Welty's uniqueness persist in the critical literature. In 1972 she still provided a "feminine counterpart" to Faulkner's complex world of "men and ideas and the course of history."[4]

[2] "An Interview with Eudora Welty," *Writers and Writing* (New York: Charles Scribner's Sons, 1946), p. 289.

[3] "The World of Eudora Welty," *Hopkins Review*, 6 (Winter 1953), 50, 57.

[4] Elmo Howell, "Eudora Welty and the Use of Place in Southern Fiction," *Arizona Quarterly*, 28 (Autumn 1972), 248.

Commentators speak according to their several abilities, but even the more valuable discussions of Eudora Welty have not redressed this faulty balance of inner and outer weather. Her best stories do weave a pattern of imagery around experience and precipitate "moods as powerful" as those "developed by good poetry." But these inward states ultimately reflect a solid world, governed by time and causality and beset by social pressure. The lyrical Welty can recede for a moment. My search is for a novelistic self which found enough "edges and corners" to make its native Mississippi as "treatable" as William Faulkner's. Her work has not cohered with either the frequency or the intensity needed to create a Yoknapatawpha, but in contending with the problematic relations of past and present, Eudora Welty has developed a cohesive view of historical reality. Very early in her career, she assumed what Henry James termed "the tone of the historian."

II

Perhaps one reason *A Curtain of Green* appealed to Northern reviewers is that it seemed to conform to a prevailing image of the benighted South. In 1917 H. L. Mencken had ridiculed this "Sahara of the Bozart" for its "Baptist and Methodist barbarism," its commercial boomers "inoculated with all the worst traits of the Yankee Sharper," and for its racist political economy. This "picture" gave not only Mencken "the creeps,"[5] but also the rest of the nation, while it watched a procession of Southern grotesqueries. During the 1920s this carnival stopped for the Great Monkey Trial in Dayton, Tennessee, where (as Mencken reported) "holy rollers" and other "gaping primates" battled the leviathan of modern science; and in Florida, where "the world's greatest poker game, played with building lots instead of chips," attracted hordes of eager Americans. Even the flies in this speculative Xanadu had been trained, as Will Rogers observed, not to bite "until after you'd bought." Labor violence accentuated Georgia and North Carolina in the national imagination, but during the 1930s its focus remained most steadily upon Alabama's callous indictment of the "Scottsboro Boys." When President Roosevelt asserted "that the South presents right now, in 1938, the Nation's No. 1 economic problem,"[6] he inadver-

---

[5] The revised 1920 text of "The Sahara of the Bozart" is reprinted in *Southern Writing: 1558–1920*, eds. Richard B. Davis, C. Hugh Holman, and Louis D. Rubin, Jr. (New York: Odyssey Press, 1970), pp. 971–979.

[6] For the image of a "benighted South" and for its illustrations, see George Brown Tindall, *The Ethnic Southerners* (Baton Rouge: Louisiana St. Univ. Press, 1976).

tently summarized the prevailing belief that this region daily defamed the most cherished American ideals. There was, of course, no reason for assuming that Welty's imagination had responded specifically to any of these episodes, but her Northern reviewers did find a situational excess in *A Curtain of Green* that seemed further to propound an image of the benighted South. Although they reproved her "strong taste for melodrama,"[7] these early commentators also thought they detected a satiric attitude that made Eudora Welty a reliable observer of the Southern grotesque.

What nearly every reviewer termed her preference for the odd or the grotesque was noted not only in "Keela" and "Powerhouse," but in stories that detail contemporary white experience as well. In "Petrified Man" Leota and her beauty shop patrons are known by their graceless idiom, abrupt intimacies, and shabby materialism. Because they pervert love, these modern Gorgons find their symbolic reflection in Mr. Petrie, a carnival freak who is turning to "pure stone." The simple Lily Daw worships more enthusiastically at the shrine of romantic love, but Mrs. Carson, the Baptist preacher's wife, decides that her honor can best be guarded at the Ellisville Institute for the Feeble-Minded. Everyone in Victory, Mississippi, comes to see Lily off, but when a red-haired suitor appears on the platform, her guardians cancel plans for commitment and propose a hasty wedding. If the plot of "Lily Daw and the Three Ladies" turns upon the officious, inconsistent nature of middle-class piety, then in "Clytie" we witness a lingering aristocratic order whose pathos is measured finally by suicide. The youngest daughter of a once-prominent family, Miss Clytie Farr discovers a truth-telling image in an old rain barrel. To break its hold, she slips into "the kind, featureless depth" of the water.

Perhaps the reviewer who found Welty composing her scenes "almost inch by inch" felt, as I do, her urge to encompass in these early stories a range of experience that would represent the aspirations peculiar to blacks and whites, to riffraff, to proper matrons, to a fading, if minor, aristocracy. But this same alert reviewer betrayed the dominant mood of her mind when she assumed that these deformed and defeated people could readily issue from "some broken-down medieval scene" governed by "its own obscure decomposing laws." Within this "atmosphere of decaying feudalism"[8] resides the most persistent myth of Southern life, but here the plan-

---

[7] "New Writers," *Time*, 24 Nov. 1941, p. 111.
[8] Louise Bogan, "The Gothic South," *Nation*, 6 Dec. 1941, p. 572.

tation legend of the nineteenth century has been stripped of its glamorous trappings and presented as a neo-abolitionist image of a decadent society. Presumably, Eudora Welty shares this contemporary attitude. Her habit of "detached observation," the "cool distance"[9] from which she views her grotesques in *A Curtain of Green*, would seem to assign to this artist a satiric, defensive view. It will soon be clear, I trust, that Eudora Welty's sensibility is not regulated by any facet of the plantation legend, or by any rigidly enforced thesis of decline and fall. In attempting to understand her unfortunates, she would adopt strategies more complex and compassionate than those usually employed by the satirist.

It might be helpful here to sketch a clarifying picture. In 1931 Eudora Welty completed her education in the North and returned to her native Jackson, where she wrote radio copy, reported local society for the *Memphis Commercial Appeal*, and later served as a publicist for the Works Progress Administration. Only the duration of her sojourn in Madison, Wisconsin, and New York City is known; its personal note remains guarded by an author whose aversion to biography is long standing. We can only interpret with prudence and suggest that between 1927 and 1931 Eudora Welty could observe closely the formation of a distinct Northern attitude toward the apparent excesses of her region. She retained her independence while, if Donald Davidson is correct, other prominent writers such as Ellen Glasgow capitulated to the pressure by "producing Southern versions of what New York thought was wrong with the South."[10]

For a Southern writer in the 1930s, the more intense pressures, though, were probably home grown. In *Tobacco Road* (1932) Erskine Caldwell argued that "an intelligent employment of his land . . . would have enabled" Jeeter Lester "to raise crops for food, and crops to be sold at a profit. Co-operative and corporate farming would have saved them all" in depression-scarred Georgia. Its discursive tone may offend the contemporary reader, but this is not a casual formulation. It follows the course of economic recovery advanced by Howard Odum and other well-known regional planners at the University of North Carolina. Perhaps a better measure of this liberal group's influence can be found in the persistent antagonism of a still more influential group of conservative Southerners who found a com-

[9] Bogan, p. 572, and Arthur J. Carr, "Among Recent Books," *Accent*, 2 (Spring 1942), 188.
[10] "Dilemma of the Southern Liberals," *The American Mercury*, 31 (Feb. 1934), 233.

mon voice in *I'll Take My Stand*. Published in 1930, this symposium assailed the foundations of scientific rationalism by stressing the religious character of experience. To a young writer, the Agrarians who gathered at Vanderbilt may have provided a convenient, if not seductive, vehicle for organizing manifold impressions into a coherent point of view. These various conceptualizations of Southern life understandably might distract a writer who was just beginning to gather her most vivid impressions of contemporary Mississippi. Eudora Welty's actual independence, however, can be gauged by turning briefly to "Death of a Traveling Salesman," a story that has been considered "too suggestive of an 'Agrarian' design."[11]

As John Crowe Ransom indicated, Agrarianism rests upon a series of interlocking dichotomies which culminates in the formula, "Agrarian *versus* Industrial."[12] Apparently, Welty adopts a similar tension in organizing "Death of a Traveling Salesman." R. J. Bowman hopes to reach his destination "by dark," but as the "graveled road" gives way to "a rutted dirt path," the painful admission grows that "he was simply lost." A bright winter sun seems to "push against the top of his head," intensifying the strange perspective from which Bowman views his unfamiliar world "after a long siege of influenza." When his dusty Ford falls into "a tangle of immense grapevines," he can only make the admission complete and seek help at a nearby cabin. Here he finds the same kind of traditional family life, marked by unvarying domestic patterns and lived in conformity with nature, that the Agrarians proposed as an antidote to mass culture. But soon after entering this rustic cabin, R. J. Bowman senses a "quiet, cool danger," for the fruitful ways of husband and wife heighten the futility of his own life of relentless travel and brief encounters. When he traces Sonny's "old military coat" to a more distant campaign than World War I, we may suspect that Welty's imagination has been thoroughly captivated by an Agrarian design. With characteristic boldness, Allen Tate declared that "all European history since the Reformation was concentrated in the war between the North and the South."[13] By asserting its progressive temper, America had deflected the old South from its agrarian ideal. The "precious thing" that was lost apparently moved Welty to pic-

---

[11] Frederick J. Hoffman, *The Art of Southern Fiction* (Carbondale, Ill.: Southern Illinois Univ. Press, 1967), p. 59.
[12] Introduction: A Statement of Principles, *I'll Take My Stand*, ed. Louis D. Rubin, Jr. (1930; rpt. New York: Harper & Row, 1962), p. xix.
[13] *Jefferson Davis: His Rise and Fall* (New York: Minton, Balch, 1929), p. 301.

ture "an alien commercial drive" still assaulting the last reserves of provincialism.[14]

For all its echoing of Agrarian themes and motifs, the final accent falls differently in "Death of a Traveling Salesman." R. J. Bowman's destination is Beulah, a hamlet in Bolivar County in northwestern Mississippi, but also a state of repose that evokes the journey of Bunyan's pilgrim and countless other legendary antecedents. Sonny and his wife rehearse the same round of domestic chores described by Andrew Lytle in *I'll Take My Stand*, but with a gravity that elevates the commonplace and gives it the portentous aspect of ritual. They are not merely attuned to nature; its creative principle imbues Sonny's "hot, red face" and illuminates the shining eyes that reveal to Bowman the miracle of an unborn child. If Welty's Northern reviewers approached the plantation legend from its reverse side, then the Agrarians simply turned this historic image over and found reflected in classical form an antebellum society based upon European standards of establishment. "The organic culture of the Middle Ages had been reborn in the Cotton Kingdom."[15] In "Death of a Traveling Salesman," Welty's symbolic pattern leads beyond this vision of bounty into a more primitive heritage. The Agrarians' pursuit of a fixed order, rich in social attainment, is contested by the "soft, continuous" sound of a stream—the Mississippi, I am sure—that passes by Sonny's isolated cabin. "Death of a Traveling Salesman" lacks the stiffness of Agrarian ideology. In her first published story, Eudora Welty discovered the unique perspective from which she would continue to observe contemporary Southern culture. The reconciliation of past and present fails here because the protagonist, R.J. Bowman, wants imaginative energy; but in projecting his current dilemma against the background of myth, Eudora Welty made the exploration of Mississippi's legendary past an inevitable next step.

III

Kurt Opitz once used a brilliant image to describe the elusive quality of *A Curtain of Green*. "From the surface, fine threads seem to run to a hidden center, suggesting by their trace rather than demonstrating in obvious display a secret core in life. There is a precise and particular face

---

[14] See Alexander Karanikas, *Tillers of a Myth* (Madison: Univ. of Wisconsin Press, 1966), p. 46.
[15] Karanikas, p. 60.

value to everything Eudora Welty writes in those early years, but however active, this face value is also and mainly simile of a vaguely irrational purport."[16] After briefly discussing "The Key," Opitz veers erratically through several later works, abandoning his image of "fine threads" running to "a hidden center." Curiosity should lead us back to "the remote little station" near Yellow Leaf, Mississippi, where Albert and Ellie Morgan reenact the most basic search in *A Curtain of Green*.

To the sleepers, the "fierce metallic sound" of a dropped key seems an insult, hurled by a curious stranger who watches with amusement their "startled" faces. But to the Morgans, both without speech and hearing, the key is an apparition which causes "strange joy." "You could see memory seize his face" (p. 59). "It means something," Albert says "on his hands" to Ellie. "Maybe when we reach Niagara Falls we will even fall in love, the way other people have done" (p. 60). There "you listen with your arms and your legs and your whole body. You'll never forget what hearing is, after that" (p. 67). But Albert and Ellie Morgan do not reach this "hidden center" where human contingencies are subsumed into nature's vast articulation. The appointed train comes and goes, its reverberations undetected. The portentous key, tucked away in Albert's pocket, now seems trivial, for the curious young man places another bearing the legend "Star Hotel, Room 2" in Ellie's "red palm." To return to the language of Opitz, hearing has become a simile of remembering, but in "The Key" the filaments of memory prove too brittle to recover either the hum of the Falls or, more closely at hand, the "tenuous voice" of insects "telling a story" in the night. Its walls "dirty with time," the tiny station constricts to "a nutshell." Patterns of spatial, natural, and temporal imagery converge with remarkable subtlety in "The Key." They are the fine tracings that typify the stories of *A Curtain of Green*.

Often Welty will endow simple objects with the pathos of diminished personal space—Keela's cage, Lily's hope chest, Ruby Fisher's imaginary coffin, the falling tree in "A Curtain of Green," the guitar box which focuses a random murder in "The Hitch-Hikers," the "little old window" through which Sister protests her happiness in "Why I Live at the P.O.," and, most pathetically, the rain barrel from which Clytie's legs protrude "like a pair of tongs." To Clytie, "the most moving sight in the whole world must be a face" (p. 159). But her preoccupation with the hundred or so faces that appear in Farr's Gin is less a product of sheer aberration,

[16] "Eudora Welty: The Ordeal of a Captive Soul," *Critique*, 7 (Winter 1964–65), 82.

as the ladies opine, than a search designed to recall the image of a lost countenance. When had she first seen it? Perhaps as a child. "Yes, in a sort of arbor, hadn't she laughed, leaned forward . . . and that vision of a face . . . had been very close to hers" (p. 163). But Clytie's search for love and self-esteem is thwarted by other faces "thrust between," demanding that she uphold the local preeminence of her family, that in its decline she serve a paralytic father, an imperious sister, and a neurasthenic brother. As Robert Penn Warren has observed, Clytie is trapped in a "house of pride"[17] whose locked doors and windows forbid intercourse with man or nature. The narrow confines of the rain barrel evoke these years "of waiting" by giving back to Clytie an image which bespeaks her deprivation. "Too late, she recognized the face" and realized that "the poor, half-remembered vision had finally betrayed her" (p. 171). Although utterly personal, Clytie's vision of diminished space assumes historical significance when measured by the impressions of an early traveler in the Mississippi Territory. "The shores of the Mississippi," Governor Claiborne wrote in 1801, "are fertile beyond description. . . . Its future . . . is beyond the wildest imagination to calculate. This great delta is almost entirely unoccupied."[18] Here apparently was space commensurate with even the most immoderate of dreams.

To Howard Odum, this Southland was still potentially a garden, possessing the "optimum quartette of temperature, moisture, surface and soil." But when Odum and his colleagues at the Institute for Research in Social Science began to inventory the Southeast, they documented an immense gap between this potential and the actualities of technical deficiency, waste, and outmoded institutions. In 1930 Mississippi was the poorest of the poor. Fifty percent of its population lived on tenant farms that produced an average annual income of $604. To alleviate such conditions, Odum called for a diverse, carefully planned economy that would effect "a working balance between nature's endowment and its use."[19] If we listen closely to another of Welty's early stories, we may hear a faint demur, for in "The Whistle" man and nature enter an equation that challenges the dictates of scientific optimism.

In the dramatic foreground are the tomato farmers, Sara and Jason

[17] "The Love and the Separateness in Miss Welty," *Kenyon Review*, 6 (Spring 1944), 255.

[18] *Mississippi as a Province, Territory and State* (1880; rpt. Baton Rouge: Louisiana St. Univ. Press, 1964), p. 221.

[19] *Southern Regions of the United States* (Chapel Hill: Univ. of North Carolina Press, 1936), pp. 23–25.

Morton; in the historical background is a model experiment that anticipated by sixty years the methodology of Odum's "new regionalism." Progressive farmers living on the Jackson prairie realized that cotton was poorly suited to local conditions and introduced in the mid 1870s the "scientific cultivation of tomato plants." By 1927 the area around Crystal Springs shipped annually some 1500 carloads of the staple. As described in *A Guide to the Magnolia State*, a volume to which Eudora Welty contributed several photographs in 1938, these farmers had turned to diversification and were among "the most prosperous in the State."[20] To Sara and Jason, this must have seemed a phantom wealth, for over the last thirty years they had slipped into irremediable poverty. A local entrepreneur owns their farm, and as tenants they illustrate the fixity of old economic patterns. But nature proves a still more inscrutable force than economic necessity. As the title of the story indicates, the threat of a sudden frost can be announced confidently, but its scope and intensity lead finally to meditations upon our contingency.

The eyes of both Sara and Clytie are "strained" with waiting, but Sara more nearly recovers a time of "legendary festivity" that relieves "the chill" of the present. Her mind becomes "a theater," a "place of pleasure" in which joyful farmers, raucous children, and "a perfect parade" of exotic Florida packers savor the "heady, sweet smell" of a triumphant harvest. "Let the packers rest," Sara thinks. Let them talk to the "girl wrappers," whose faces remain "forever sleepy and flushed" (p. 110). But the cold obtrudes, annulling the perfection of the harvest vision, calling both Sara and Jason to witness a scene of spectral desolation. Outside "everything looked vast and extensive to them," but this frozen land, illuminated by "the intense whiteness" of a distant moon, hardly resembles the illimitable space perceived by Governor Claiborne more than a century ago. This has become empty space, a strange, silent world that not only eludes technical mastery but also seems to extend tragically beyond our capacity to understand. At a similar juncture, Erskine Caldwell claimed that the people of *Tobacco Road* "had so much faith in nature . . . that they could not understand how the earth could fail them."[21] This is not Welty's focus at all, for the earth

[20] Federal Writers' Project of the Works Progress Administration, *Mississippi: A Guide to the Magnolia State*, American Guide Series (New York: Viking Press, 1938), pp. 100, 393.
[21] "After Ten Years," Introduction to *Tobacco Road* (New York: Modern Library, 1940), pp. viii–ix.

has not failed anyone in *A Curtain of Green*. As Sara and Jason stare "idly" at the sky, they dramatize their alienation from each other and from a natural world that continues to live a mysterious seasonal life. In the title story, "A Curtain of Green," Mrs. Larkin also stares "without understanding at the sky," but her "unknowing face" is touched by a summer rain that imbues nature with "inexhaustible" force. Those who can reconcile its different phases will experience the tranquility that Sonny and his wife naturally inherit. Welty probably encountered the success story of Crystal Springs during her tenure as a W.P.A. publicist, but what attracted her to this obscure bit of Mississippiana was its innate historical character. What began as a brave venture in diversification had narrowed to deprive Sara and Jason Morton of a future.

Time in the ruins is finally a measure of tedium. Among Sister's recovered possessions in "Why I Live at the P.O." is a kitchen clock that will reiterate endlessly her loss of Mr. Whitaker, "the only man [who] ever dropped down in China Grove." Marian detects "a smell . . . like the interior of a clock" when she enters the Old Ladies' Home in "A Visit of Charity." "How old are you?" she asks the "face on the pillow," but it only "gathered and collapsed," appalled that still another birthday had arrived. It remains, however, for old Mr. Marblehall, the most enigmatic figure in *A Curtain of Green*, to demonstrate the full tyranny of time abstracted from the flow of history.

There has been a Mr. Marblehall in Natchez since the earliest days, when this outpost on the Mississippi assumed its dual character. High on the bluffs, elegant homes and gardens displayed the aspirations of Mississippi's first native aristocracy. Natchez-Under-the-Hill attracted thieves, gamblers, prostitutes, and all the hardy young men who traveled the river and the nearby Trace. Philosophically considered, the present Mr. Marblehall may seek to fill what Robert Detweiler calls "an existential void," but the terms of his bizarre double life are quintessentially historic. By maintaining two establishments, replete with patrician and common wives and heirs, he attempts to recapitulate the duality of his heritage. Either in actuality or in dream, Mr. Marblehall or Mr. Bird pursues both space and abundance, "shuttling . . . back and forth" between his "ancestral home" and the little galleried house "under the hills." His is the most fertile historical imagination in *A Curtain of Green*, but it is also the most pathetic. Old Mr. Marblehall's secret bigamy reflects both a personal dilemma and the dilemma of a culture that can no longer "assure one a place within a physical or spiritual community."[22] For all the grandeur of his vision, it cannot redeem the time allotted to old Mr. Marblehall. He will continue to lie abed, reading pulp *Terror Tales*, in order to "get through the clocking nights." "He is killing time" (p. 182), not unifying it.

A Curtain of Green demonstrates the truth of Paul Tillich's observation that a "mythical element," encompassing "original epochs and final epochs," penetrates all serious historical writing. Welty's unfortunates not only bear the weight of "successive stages of finiteness,"[23] but they also sense an imminent ending in the collapse of familiar social, economic, and domestic institutions. Like Howard, the young husband in "Flowers for Marjorie," they fear that everything in the world has stopped. Such futility does not, however, prevent strenuous efforts to extend personal space, to recover nature, or to give chronology its full body. Welty's people continue to dream of "original epochs," but as we have seen, memories of these abundant, youthful times recede all too abruptly into a distant past. Whatever aesthetic distance finally separates these characters from Eudora Welty is less a measure of satiric intent than an index to her comprehensive view of historical process. For all the subtlety of her vision, the patterns of spatial, natural, and temporal imagery which dominate *A Curtain of Green* announce starkly that the Southern frontier has closed some fifty years after Frederick Jackson Turner made a similar report on the western line of expansion. Open space has given way to "the solid wall"[24] and with it an inevitable internalization of conflict. Perhaps the lyrical Welty, banished at the outset, can safely reappear, for the acute inwardness of her unfortunates has now assumed a historical as well as an aesthetic rationale. She has assimilated the ruinous statistical profile which Mississippi presented in the official census of 1930 and has reprojected it as intimate personal experience.

Like her unfortunates, Eudora Welty cannot contemplate ends without considering beginnings as well. She possessed the resources needed, however, to follow the historical tracings of *A Curtain of Green* back to their

---

[22] Robert Detweiler, "Eudora Welty's Blazing Butterfly: The Dynamics of Response," *Language and Style*, 6 (Winter 1973), 59–61.

[23] *The Interpretation of History* (New York: Charles Scribner's Sons, 1936), pp. 96–97.

[24] See Harold P. Simonson, *The Closed Frontier* (New York: Holt, Rinehart and Winston, 1970), p. 38.

ultimate source, to Mississippi's original epoch of frontier exuberance. In *The Robber Bridegroom* she tested the notion of a "hidden center" by imagining spacious contours and by resuming her meditations upon nature and time. I suspect that she also turned to the past with a certain scepticism for epochal theories of history that would impress watershed dates upon our collective memory. Part of the groundwork for this counterview had already been established in the one story from *A Curtain of Green* which remains to be discussed. Its title and strategic positioning in the volume suggest that "A Memory" can help to mend some of the broken circuits we have observed. The vantage point will be improved, however, if we first consider *The Robber Bridegroom* of 1942, the one work by Welty for which Faulkner revealed a strong affinity.

IV

With perfect insouciance, Eudora Welty grafted the remote world of the Brothers Grimm onto the local brag of Mike Fink, producing a multi-layered impression of life in the Natchez country during the 1790s. In particular, Faulkner probably admired this daring blend of European fantasy, Mississippi lore, and frontier humor, but other early readers were less sure of their bearings and frequently temporized. *The Robber Bridegroom* became as "playful" a book as the gossamer forest in which Rosamond, a beautiful Rodney heiress, and Jamie Lockhart, the bandit of the Trace, consummate their love. Apparently, even Welty herself did not know "what she [had] concocted." [25] Several years ago, Welty emphasized the deliberate character of this book, explaining that she sought to make "working equivalents" [26] of local history, legend, and fairy tale; but in the meanwhile this curious novella had been orphaned by critics who either exaggerated its uniqueness, or who failed to pursue an intuition that *The Robber Bridegroom*, for all its capering, did not necessarily break the pattern of Welty's thought. Earlier, in describing her turn to the past as an "inevitable next step," I undoubtedly gave the impression of sequential relationship. What scant bibliographical data we have suggest that a text of *The Robber Bridegroom* was complete and in circulation by 1938. So dated, it becomes a still more integral part of the search which Eudora

[25] Reviews by Charles Shattuck in *Accent*, 3 (Winter 1943), 124, and Henry Harrison Kroll in the *Memphis Commercial Appeal*, 25 Oct. 1942, Sec. 4, p. 10.
[26] *Fairy Tale of the Natchez Trace* (Jackson: Mississippi Historical Society, 1975), p. 13.

Welty was conducting in *A Curtain of Green*. Even her earliest work seems tinctured by the sense of "a total situation" guiding choice and treatment of subject matter.

In 1938 the town of Rodney, as well as China Grove, was designated "extinct" by Mississippi's official *Guide to the Magnolia State*. Perhaps this was provocation enough for Welty to restore the old river town to its heyday as the scene of many festive landings. After disembarking, Rosamond's father Clement is borne on waves of light and sound to a crowded traveler's inn where the same spirit of commotion reigns. Never before has Clement Musgrove encountered such awesome bedfellows as Mike Fink and Jamie Lockhart, whose swaggering manner and prodigious libations astound the unassuming planter. His way home may lie through a wilderness "beset with dangers," but Clement will hear no fiercer cry than Jamie's assertion of independence. "Guilt is a burdensome thing to carry about in the heart. . . . I would never bother with it." A more thoughtful Clement attributes these sentiments to "a man of the times, a pioneer and a free agent" (p. 27), who has neither recoiled in self-consciousness nor identified time and space as dreadful adversaries.

The Robber Bridegroom is most eloquent when it crosses broad fields, passes through fragrant groves of locust, and follows Rosamond into the forest where a dark lover brings her dreams to womanly fruition. "Red as blood" Jamie's horse "rode the ridge," accomplishing "the fastest kidnaping" ever recorded in "that part of the country." Their steep ascent follows the course of the sun which "mounted the morning cloud, and lighted the bluff" from which Jamie and Rosamond view a resplendent Mississippi. If R. J. Bowman could only hear distantly its "soft, continuous" sound, then these lovers not only see its coiled form but also bring its winding motion into close accord with their own sexual expression. An abundant nature continues to support their idyll in the weeks that follow. At first, Jamie "was only with her in the hours of night, and rode away before the dawn" (p. 82) to do his robbing, but once he "did not ride away with the others, and then the day was night and the woods were the roof over their heads." Of course, in a world that "had just begun," there was no reason to "feel deadly faint" and to stagger with Melville's Ahab "beneath the piled centuries since Paradise." Lacking absolute value, the day and the night derive their character from the disposition of Jamie and Rosamond, who both dominate time and claim the vast forest as a personal domain. *The Robber Bridegroom* "sprawls" as a consequence, the action covering a year and wandering almost to Zanzibar. It seems to defy the extreme concentration of *A Curtain of Green* by inhabiting a "fairyland" where the line separating physical and human nature remains indistinct. But there are ominous signs too. A wicked stepmother, Salome, vengeful Indians, and the vicissitudes of history threaten to wake Jamie and Rosamond from their "dream of time passing."

The time of *The Robber Bridegroom* is summer, when "myths of apotheosis, of the sacred marriage, and of entering into Paradise" prevail,[27] but as Clement Musgrove realizes, these are "the deep last days of the Summer." He foresees the triumph of a new era, the same "Age of Brass" that Joseph Baldwin described in *The Flush Times of Alabama and Mississippi* (1853). Once dislodged from Spanish control, Mississippi passed rapidly through its territorial phase, achieved statehood in 1817, and entered the "hurly-burly" times which Baldwin, as frontier lawyer and politician, relished and which, as an informal historian, he skillfully described. "Avarice and hope joined partnership" in this new country. Emigrants from every part of the nation sought to mend tattered fortunes or to imagine themselves anew by amassing extensive property. "The times were out of joint," prowled by "unclean beasts of adventure" that affrighted such "retiring men of worth and character"[28] as Clement Musgrove. For him "the journey down" is a bitter trip, culminating in the murder of wife and child. Even the reason for coming "is forgotten now," he tells Jamie. "I know I am not a seeker after anything, and ambition in this world never stirred my heart once" (p. 20). Yet at the urging of his second wife Salome, Clement becomes a wealthy planter. "We must cut down more of the forest," she counsels, "and stretch away the fields until we grow twice as much of everything. . . . the land is there for the taking, and I say, if it can be taken, take it" (p. 99). Here in this extractive economy is the origin not only of Baldwin's "flush times" but also of the progressive alienation from nature which comes to full effect in *A Curtain of Green*.

So far my description of *The Robber Bridegroom* suggests that Eudora Welty has evoked a golden time—a "hidden center" of natural fulfillment —only to begin the long downward path to disillusion. She shares with Robert Frost the knowledge that "nothing gold can stay," and realizes that as "original epochs" beget "final epochs," historical patterns emerge which

[27] Northrop Frye, "The Archetypes of Literature," in *Twentieth Century Criticism*, eds. William J. Handy and Max Westbrook (New York: Macmillan, 1974), p. 240.

[28] *The Flush Times of Alabama and Mississippi* (1853; rpt. New York: Hill and Wang, 1957), pp. 59–66.

cannot be swayed from their course. But in the speculative temper of Clement Musgrove, she begins to affirm a counterforce, perhaps not unlike the "strange resistance" to "the stream of everything" that Robert Frost also detected in "West-Running Brook." Clement's meditation is extended and complex, but it follows closely an important development in the relation of Jamie and Rosamond.

A rather fanciful plot demands that Rosamond wash the berry stains from his sleeping face and discover that Jamie Lockhart, her father's new friend, is also the king of the bandits. "Good-by," he tells her, for "you did not trust me," but his violation of Clement's trust, although inadvertent, proves a more serious offense. When Clement learns that the man commissioned to find his daughter is also her abductor, he takes to the forest, encloses himself in a circle of stones, and studies "the lateness of the age." Nature appears complex and manifold to Clement, for "here are all possible trees" and "upon each limb is a singing bird," but it reflects order as well, following the discipline of the seasons. That, Clement muses, "was the way the years went by" when he lived "in the peaceful hills" with his first wife. But "what kind of time is this," when change is so rapid that "wrath and love burn only like campfires." For all his brilliance, even the hero is "but a wandering fire soon lost" (p. 143), a subtle reference on Welty's part to "First Love" and "A Still Moment," stories also published in 1942 and based upon the historical aspirations of Aaron Burr and John James Audubon. Their experience in the Natchez country would lead them to ask with Clement, "What will the seasons be, when we are lost and dead? The dreadful heat and cold—no more than the shooting star" (p. 144). Apparently, "the time of cunning" has frustrated Clement's wish for order and simplicity in nature, but before he can rediscover permanence in change, he is dragged to his feet by those who know best "the lateness of the age."

Eudora Welty's use of the Natchez Indians involved a solecism that she both recognized and exploited. Virtually annihilated by the French in 1732, the ghostly Natchez could roam the forest and poignantly reaffirm its spirit. When Salome, a captive with Jamie, Clement, and Rosamond, defies "the elements," she is commanded by the Natchez to dance "until the dance was raveled out and she could dance no more." But "still the sun went on as well as ever," confirming the faith of the Indian in the midst of his historic desolation. *The Robber Bridegroom* moves briskly to shape this vision into a future for those who survive the present ordeal.

In the following spring, Clement returns to New Orleans and finds a daughter whom he thought dead. Rosamond points to a new life with her husband, Jamie Lockhart, rich merchant and father of "beautiful twins." Perhaps Rosamond "did sometimes miss ... the rough-and-tumble of their old life," but the city, she trills, "was splendid ... it was the place to live" (p. 184). Eudora Welty has positioned herself along the Mississippi and viewed the same "procession of civilization" that Frederick Jackson Turner found at the Cumberland Gap. As Clement realizes, "the planter will go after the hunter, and the merchant after the planter, all having their day" (p. 161). Each in his time and place is worthy, even the nation-builder Salome, at whose Faustian vigor we marvel. But *The Robber Bridegroom* also moves decisively to restore its comic phrasing. A child named for Clement not only tempers the bitter loss of the past but also instills a cyclic sense of life perpetually renewing itself. "God bless you," Clement says, before returning to Rodney and what remains of the planter's life. Should he again enter the forest and occupy a circle of stones, Clement will speak as one who has descended into time and wrestled with change only to find permanence. According to Michael Kreyling, he "has won an integrating vision"[29] that binds past and present into a moment of full perception. In the process, Eudora Welty has assured herself that wrenching historical developments occur within larger patterns of cyclic duration.

In the present age, Sonny and his wife and old Phoenix Jackson most nearly approximate the pastoral condition that briefly obtains in *The Robber Bridegroom*. A "little tree" is etched in the "numberless branching wrinkles" of Phoenix's forehead, suggesting the same sympathy with nature that underlies the intimacy of Sonny and his wife. As they hear the "soft, continuous" sound of the stream, they are transported metaphorically to the same bluff where earlier lovers consummated their relations. But these are essentially simple characters whose wholeness precludes the kind of vigorous striving that Clement Musgrove demonstrates. For his modern counterpart in *A Curtain of Green*, we must turn finally to "A Memory," the most personal of all Welty's stories.

V

The time again is summer and the place, although not directly identified, is Livingston Park, a popular resort in Jackson. The "sun, sand, water, a

---

[29] I am indebted to Kreyling's discussion of *The Robber Bridegroom* in "The Novels of Eudora Welty," Diss. Cornell University 1975, p. 47.

little pavilion, a few solitary people in fixed attitudes" are enclosed within a "brightly lit" rectangle, no larger than the framing fingers of the young girl who habitually adopts this controlling perspective. It is her need to judge "every person and every event," to anticipate "grimly and possessively" the revelation of "a secret of life." She is in love "for the first time." Later, she will realize how "hopelessly unexpressed" this passion for an unknowing schoolmate remained, but now the memory of their "brief encounter" can expand with "overwhelming beauty, like a rose forced into premature bloom." The simile jars ever so slightly and prepares the reader to follow the course of this memory when a family of bathers, as gross as they are energetic, suddenly enters the illuminated rectangle. They not only objectify the young girl's fear of the unknown, "the untoward," but also penetrate the "retarded, dilated, timeless" quality that confines her dream of love. "Sprawled close to where" she was lying, these "loud, squirming, ill-assorted people" cannot be blinked; their images are retained visually even with her eyes "pressed shut." If it is not too fanciful to superimpose the young girl's spot of sand upon Clement's circle of stones, then we may sense that both characters have been confronted by "beasts of adventure" that challenge static, sentimental views of human experience.

"A Memory" confirms Walker Percy's surmise that Jackson "bears more than an accidental relation"[30] to Welty's writing. Livingston Park opened in 1920 and immediately provoked a controversy. Mayor Walter Scott decreed that bathing suits must be of opaque cloth and that the "women folks," in traveling to and fro, must cover their "bare limbs"! Churchmen were not reassured and criticized the city for allowing "bathing on Sunday" and "indiscriminate public dancing." One "well-known Jackson woman" wrote to the *Daily News* and expressed her inexpressible shock upon seeing women in "one-piece bathing suits, minus stockings," parading before "the public gaze. We ought to have a crusade against this thing,"[31] she concluded.

Traces of "this thing" appear, perhaps with some unspoken wryness, in Welty's portrait of the family. "They wore old and faded bathing suits which did not hide either the energy or the fatigue of their bodies, but showed it exactly." The older brother "protruded from his costume at every

---

[30] "Eudora Welty in Jackson," *Shenandoah*, 20 (Spring 1969), 37.
[31] See the *Jackson Daily News*, 30 May, 1 June, and 29 July 1921.

turn," while the younger girl threatened to burst from her "bright green" suit and go up "in a rage of churning smoke" (p. 148). For the girl of memory, "a peak of horror" is reached when the older woman loosens the front of her suit, "so that the lumps of mashed and folded sand came emptying out" (p. 151). Both the editor of the *Jackson Daily News* and, in retrospect, Eudora Welty realized that the underlying issue was the threat of modernity to a small provincial capital. The "well-known" woman who visited Livingston Park undoubtedly sensed that this public scene challenged more traditional, exclusive patterns of Jackson society. She may also have guessed that its daring, innovative quality foreshadowed a decade of extraordinary growth when much of the city's "nineteenth-century flavor" would be lost.[32] The young girl of "A Memory" (and Eudora Welty, too, I suspect) moves just as uneasily between these poles. Her sensibility has been formed in the matrix of a traditional family but is assaulted by insistent, vulgar forces which change "the appearance of the beach like the ravages of a storm." She can only feel pity for the "worn white pavilion" and confess that her dream, as vulnerable as Clement's untested view of nature, "had vanished."

Clement and the young girl of "A Memory" are separated by more than a century of cultural experience. The ease with which Jamie and Rosamond adapt to a mercantile existence could not be repeated in Welty's more complex modern world. For R.J. Bowman and for Harris of "The Hitch-Hikers," commercial life has become an exercise in futility. But these two periods also produce constants which have the effect of abridging time. Each character has been positioned at an identical juncture where change seems to accelerate and present the human imagination with nearly insuperable difficulty. If Clement's "way" lies through meditation, then the girl of memory formalizes this impulse by assuming the guise of an artist. She is abetted by Eudora Welty who has infused the structure of "A Memory" with dual perspective. In recording the facts of experience, the "I" of the story speaks from a point in time that implies personal growth and maturity. She can gauge the disproportion of her dream to its trivial source, but this retrospective gaze does not dissipate the original intensity. ". . . even now, I remember unadulteratedly a certain morning when I touched my friend's wrist . . . as we passed on the stairs in school" (p. 145).

[32] Gwen Ann Mills, "A Social History of Jackson, Mississippi, 1920–1929," M.A. Thesis University of Mississippi 1966, p. 66.

Even now, "I still would not care to say which was more real—the dream
. . . or the sight of the bathers. I am presenting them, you see, only as
simultaneous" (pp. 146–47). Within this unification of time rests an
authority which is not granted to any other story in *A Curtain of Green.*
Strategically placed as the ninth of seventeen stories, it renders, aesthetical-
ly and psychologically, the condition of temporal wholeness sought by
each of Welty's protagonists. The blond boy on the stairs is a perennial
vision. Aesthetic memory has not only restored the past but also transformed it into a timeless order of experience. Involvement and detachment, dream and actuality, permanence and change exist as simultaneously
within the frame of "A Memory" as they do in Clement's heart. To look
ahead to *The Optimist's Daughter*, this same "precipitous moment" serves
as the base for a renewed social experience as well.

During the 1960s Eudora Welty lived through such "humiliating" local
events as the ambush of Medgar Evers and its aftermath of violent demonstration. In "Must the Novelist Crusade?" she tells of midnight phone
calls challenging the writer to open her mouth and "do [something] about
it," but Welty answers that the writer, even in these "relentless" days,
"works neither to correct nor to condone, not at all to comfort, but to make
what's told alive." This "is the continuing job, and it's no harder now
than it ever was. . . . Every writer, like everybody else, thinks he's living
through the crisis of the ages" (*ES*, p. 157). What may seem indifference
actually reveals a more intense commitment, for Welty continues to be
guided by a historical attitude that emerged in her first two books. With
the Civil Rights movement, Mississippi entered a phase of historic change
which promised to many still another Age of Brass. Those who panicked
failed both morally and imaginatively. As one epoch begets another, "ex-
ternals" change "dramatically," but the girl of memory confronted by
social and sexual change and contemporary Mississippians facing the pros-
pect of a multi-racial society were responding to the same beast that
Clement Musgrove discovered in the forest, "slowly and softly and forever
moving into profile" (p. 141). Welty's people are immersed in their time
and their place, but in her imagination they also occupy an extratemporal
moment of mysterious relationship.

In the 1930s the writing of Southern history reached a "take-off point."
Older histories that were "unscholarly, romanticized treatments" had encouraged H. L. Mencken's kind of South-baiting. A more rigorous his-

toriography, emboldened by the examples of Virginius Dabney and others, moved to reexamine "many hypotheses" once "regarded as axiomatic."[33] The work of Faulkner coincides conspicuously with this effort. In the life of the plantation legend, there is no sharper moment of exegesis than one which occurs in *Absalom, Absalom!* When Charles Bon, the dispossessed son, appears on the gallery at Sutpen's Hundred, he brings down the grand design—"house, position, posterity and all"—as if "it had been built out of smoke." Eudora Welty's critique tends to be more implicit. Too often, her readers have assumed that the unsettled contemporary life in *A Curtain of Green* reflects some kind of latter-day allegiance to the plantation myth of order and stability. Undoubtedly, a part of Welty's imagination could not avoid hearing the "long, withdrawing roar" of a lost tradition, but a far more important part rejected ideological demands of the past that would force human experience into narrow, progressive patterns. When Welty snapped at William Buckley on *Firing Line* (24 December 1972) that she was "not a bit interested in preserving the home of Jefferson Davis," she was only reasserting her view of history as a fluid, continuous phenomenon, shaped, as Allen Tate says, by "the doings of specific men who acted their parts in a rich and contemporaneous setting which bewildered them."[34]

William Faulkner underlined this attitude in editorial correspondence with Malcolm Cowley. While preparing *The Portable Faulkner*, Cowley had found the characters and events of *Absalom, Absalom!* composing themselves into "a tragic fable of Southern history." Without specifically rejecting this reading, Faulkner told Cowley that "art is simpler than people think because there is so little to write about." He wrote that "life is a phenomenon but not a novelty, the same frantic steeplechase toward nothing everywhere and man stinks the same stink no matter where in time."[35] In his brief foray into Southern literature, Leslie Fiedler described two lines of Faulknerian descent: "the masculine Faulknerians," chiefly Warren, who treat "complex moral and social problems"; and such

[33] See James P. Hendrix, "From Romance to Scholarship: Southern History at the Take-Off Point," *Mississippi Quarterly*, 30 (Spring 1977), 193–211, and F. Garvin Davenport, *The Myth of Southern History* (Nashville: Vanderbilt Univ. Press, 1967), pp. 106–115.

[34] "Religion and the Old South," *Collected Essays* (Denver: Alan Swallow, 1959), p. 310.

[35] *The Faulkner-Cowley File*, ed. Malcolm Cowley (New York: Viking Press, 1966), pp. 13–16.

"distaff Faulknerians" as Eudora Welty, in whose work the "masculine vigor of Faulkner" tends "to disappear among the more delicate nuances of sensibility."[36] This is only to repeat, with added pomp, that Faulkner and Welty divided the fictional resources of Mississippi along lines of gender. The truth is that both have unified their work and infused it with social significance by embracing the only view of historical reality that can produce intense human drama.

[36] *Love and Death in the American Novel* (New York: Criterion Books, 1960), pp. 449–450.

WARREN   "All Things Are Double":
FRENCH   Eudora Welty
         as a Civilized Writer

NOTHING ELSE in American literature is quite like *The Robber Bridegroom*—even among Eudora Welty's other writings; and, as with many unique gifts, we recipients haven't known quite what to make of it. Because of its fairy-tale qualities, a tendency has been to display it on the bric-a-brac shelf with the Hummel figures; whereas, it ought to find its place with such rare attempts to find archetypal patterns an American home as "Rip Van Winkle" and Thomas Cole's magnificent canvases of "The Voyage of Life."

The relatively little attention that the tale has attracted has been dominated since the original reviews by observations about its relationship to European fairy tales, especially the Grimm Brothers' story of the same title. Most commentators have, if not echoed, at least paralleled John Peale Bishop's remarks in the *New Republic* (16 November 1942), "If Miss Welty meant to establish that our tall tale is the equivalent of the European folk tale she fails to do so." Bishop was the most subtly perceptive of the early judges of the tale, however, for he recognized the transformation that gave the narrative its direction and observed, "All bridegrooms, she seems to be saying, are robbers," who steal a woman's love; "but in time, the hurt is healed and at last the robber bridegroom is seen as a prosperous gentleman of the world . . . . nothing is easier than the transfer of a bandit into a merchant."

Although Bishop was too exclusively preoccupied with the sexual aspects of the tale, many subsequent critics have not followed the plot as far as he did (for plot there is, despite some reviewers' doubts). Generally the tale has been treated as a delightful, but dubiously successful tour de force. Even one of its most impressed readers, Alfred Appel, Jr., after describing *The Robber Bridegroom* as "a joyful wedding of the European fairy tale and the lore of the American frontier," concludes that it is an example of "the comic spirit," in which "Miss Welty succeeds in capturing the lost fabulous innocence of the American frontier, its poetry and comedy."[1]

Innocence, however, is far from the principal concern of the tale, in which innocence is, if anything, doomed or at least relegated to the subservient role of a force of vanishing authority. John Peale Bishop did not quite get the point, either, when he speculated that Welty's "deepest interest would seem to be in the question of identity" and that "nothing is what it seems," for her point cannot be so tidily resolved in terms of Aristotelian categories. Eudora Welty is concerned rather with the quite non-Aristotelian notion that people are two things at once and that their "identity" at any given moment is determined by the context in which they are discovered. Although Bishop comments early in his review on the ominous setting in the "violent country" of the old Natchez Trace, he fails to read this fable of identities against the background of the specific time and place in which it is set. He was working without the benefit of some of the author's strictures on the significance of setting, but today we need to consider her observation in "Place in Fiction" that "every story would be another story and unrecognizable as art, if it took up its characters and plot and happened somewhere else" (*ES*, p. 122). Fantasy must be grounded in the concrete facts of place, she advises. Although "all bridegrooms" may be robbers, a particular robber/bridegroom's behavior may be modified by circumstances of time and place that Bishop does not take into account.

J. A. Bryant, Jr. comes closer than other commentators to getting at the grounding of the story. He first establishes the worlds of difference in time and place that separate Eudora Welty's *The Robber Bridegroom* from the Grimm Brothers' story with the same title, in which a girl has "two suitors, a bad one to outwit and a good one to live with happily ever after." If the European tale had put the two together as Miss Welty does, Bryant argues, it "would have spoiled all the 'fabulous innocence' and made a solution impossible."[2] Bryant perceives, further, the importance of wanderer/planter Clement Musgrove's speech to his daughter Rosamond about "doubles" as the pivotal point in this tale of transformations: ". . . all things are double, and this should keep us from taking liberties with the outside world, and acting too quickly to finish things off. All things are divided in half—night and day, the soul and body, and sorrow and joy and youth and

---

[1] *A Season of Dreams* (Baton Rouge: Louisiana St. Univ. Press, 1965), pp. 69, 72.
[2] *Eudora Welty* (Minneapolis: Univ. of Minnesota Press, 1968), p. 19.

age . . ." (p. 126). The principal embodiment of this doubling comes in *The Robber Bridegroom* in the recognition scene in which Rosamond wipes berry stain from her robber/bridegroom's face and learns that he is also the Jamie Lockhart who has been her father's respected dinner guest (p. 134). Even before this revelation, however, Musgrove has worked out through the case of the mysterious bridegroom the practical application of his principle about a person's double nature: "If being a bandit were his breadth and scope, I should find him and kill him for sure. . . . But since in addition he loves my daughter, he must be not the one man, but two, and I should be afraid of killing the second" (p. 126).

As a result of Musgrove's caution, he ultimately sees Jamie and Rosamond rewarded "with a fine mansion, a hundred slaves, and rich merchants to go boating with" and himself rewarded "with the knowledge that his children have such things."[3] Curiously, however, having perceived the importance of the embodiment of robber and bridegroom in the same person, Bryant misses the very sentence that John Peale Bishop had spied as the key to the denouement of the tale, "the outward transfer from bandit to merchant had been almost too easy to count it a change at all, and [Jamie] was enjoying all the same success he had ever had" (pp. 184–85). By bringing these two readings together—in a fashion peculiarly appropriate to a tale of doubling—we can perhaps perceive the significance of Eudora Welty's choice of the "concrete facts of place" for *The Robber Bridegroom*.

Although Clement Musgrove meditates on several manifestations of doubleness (all of which play a role in the tale), Welty is most concretely concerned with a particular set of doubles in both character and situation. Rosamond is not the first to discover Jamie Lockhart's secret. Earlier in the novel, Jamie has on one occasion "just started to stain his face with the berry juice" (p. 107) that transforms him into the bandit of the violent Trace when he is interrupted by "sounds of screaming out of a cave in the hillside." He comes upon the bandit Little Harp and a kidnapped girl and, as a result of becoming involved in this episode, compromises himself; for Little Harp recognizes him: "Your name is Jamie Lockhart and you are the bandit in the woods, for you have your two faces on together and I see you both."

"At that," the narrator explains, "Jamie staggered back indeed, for he allowed no one who had seen him as a gentleman to see him as a robber,

---

[3] Bryant, p. 20.

and no one who knew him as a robber to see him without the dark-stained face, even his bride." He pulls out his dirk to kill Little Harp, but is restrained when something seems to speak to him and say, "This is to be your burden, and so you might as well take it" (p. 112). This moment when the two Jamies are recognized by the actual physical division of his face into differing halves is also the psychological dividing point of the tale. From here forward the behavior of the two Jamies, hitherto entirely at odds with one another, merges more and more into a single pattern until Jamie discovers at last that he need not conceal his doubleness since it proves really no burden at all to his success within the law. He can abandon the refuge of masks; the berry juice can be left in the forest.

Nathaniel Hawthorne knew well the doubleness that Eudora Welty explores through Jamie. At a late point in *The Scarlet Letter*, after Hester, Dimmesdale and Pearl have met in the woods, they meet again in the city on a great holiday and Pearl asks her mother, "Was that the same minister that kissed me by the brook?" "Hold thy peace, dear little Pearl!" whispers Hester. "We must not always talk in the market-place of what happened to us in the forest."

Much of the history of what has happened to the New World Columbus discovered can be brought into focus through examining events in relation to this dichotomy of "the market-place" and "the forest." When this continent was discovered by (and for) the Europeans, it was entirely "forest" and much of its subsequent history has been of its transformation into "market-place." Jamie Lockhart is only one of the many implicated in the consequences of this transformation.

Our mythmakers have been of at least two minds about this phenomenon. Some would preserve the forest, while others would further the market-place. As Hester's caution suggests, the forest is the place of greater freedom, spontaneity, naturalness, but also of greater dangers from the robbers who operate under cover of its darkness; behavior in the market-place must be conventional, controlled, artificial—one must respect established codes—but one receives in exchange for a loss in one's freedom the seeming security and safety of the community.

William Faulkner stands as the outstanding spokesman for the vanishing forest. In "The Bear," Ike McCaslin traces the corruption of our culture back to the division of the unbounded woods to serve the needs of self-aggrandizing men of the market-place. Ike tells his cousin that he cannot "repudiate" his inheritance because: "It was never mine to repudiate. . . . Because it was never Ikkemotubbe's fathers' fathers' to bequeath Ikkemotubbe to sell to Grandfather or any man because on the instant when Ikkemotubbe discovered, realized, that he could sell it for money, on that instant it ceased ever to have been his forever. . . ." In a companion story, "Delta Autumn," some final words of this last man of the forest render a verdict on the triumph of the market-place: "No wonder the ruined woods I used to know don't cry for retribution! . . . The people who have destroyed it will accomplish its revenge." By breaking his mystical tie to nature to exploit the forest, man at last destroys himself.

Scott Fitzgerald's Nick Carraway stands poised precariously as middle-man in this generally wistful debate, as spokesman for those who lament the destruction of the forest but see it—as Hawthorne himself did in "Earth's Holocaust"—as the inevitable consequence of man's inadequacy to match the potential of the unspoiled natural world. At the end of *The Great Gatsby*, Carraway describes the early visitors: "for a transitory enchanted moment man must have held his breath in the presence of this continent, compelled into an aesthetic contemplation he neither understood nor desired, face to face for the last time in history with something commensurate to his capacity for wonder." But at the very beginning of Nick's account, we have discovered that he wants "no more riotous excursions with privileged glimpses into the human heart," but rather "the world to be in uniform and at a sort of moral attention forever." Men must congregate in the market-place because of their incapacity to cope with the aesthetic challenge of the forest. Faulkner's stories present—along with Mark Twain's *The Adventures of Huckleberry Finn*, for example— the anti-civilized position, while Fitzgerald's novel presents—as Melville had even more forbiddingly—the reluctantly civilized.

Faulkner's fellow Mississippian Eudora Welty stands, however, at the farthest end of the spectrum from him; and recognition of *The Robber Bridegroom*'s place in our fiction can restore a balance that often seems missing. While I dislike digressing into personalities in literary criticism, I do think it appropriate to mention here Victor H. Thompson's pointing out that "the newspapers present Miss Welty as perhaps the most amiable and inoffensive writer that America has ever produced."[4] What this statement suggests is that she is a thoroughly "civilized" person, some-

---

[4] *Eudora Welty: A Reference Guide* (Boston: G. K. Hall, 1976), p. ix.

thing that, for whatever reasons, few of our writers have been. Many of her contemporaries have proved as wild and flighty as the talking raven in *The Robber Bridegroom.*

We have been slow to perceive Eudora Welty for the civilized writer she is, because we haven't especially been seeking fictionists of this temperament. Lately literate Americans—reacting against their genteel forebears—tend toward nostalgia and fancy themselves sons of the pioneers, so that they equate being civilized—much as Huck Finn did—with being effete, prissy and overly inhibited. Most of the proponents of civilization in our fiction—like William Dean Howells and Willa Cather—have come from frontiers and have had serious misgivings about civilized society that have increased as they have aged and withdrawn into their private forests. Hardly anyone among our writers before Welty had been able to find more enjoyment than displeasure in the products of civilization, and most of the few that did—like Henry James and Gertrude Stein—felt compelled to spend most of their lives abroad. I think that the reason why critics have scarcely known what to make of Eudora Welty's work is that most of them, like the writers with whom they identify, can flourish only on denunciations of the very civilization that makes their trade possible. (In the forest, they see themselves, of course, "called" as shamans.)

This is not to say that Welty is naively unaware of the discontents and displeasures of urban society (for we are here in a necessarily limiting way equating "civilization" with "the market-place"). Scarcely a wide-eyed innocent in an adolescent success story, she is able to maintain her stance because she has an adequate sense of irony to perceive that our choices are not usually between the better or best of alternatives but between the lesser of evils—a stance that manifests itself as early in her work as *The Robber Bridegroom.*

The forest is really never given much of a chance in this tale. The "innocence" that Welty ascribes at the beginning of the narrative to the only thoughtful character, Clement Musgrove—with a first name wonderfully symbolic of merciful judgment—has been misconstrued. He is hardly, as John Peale Bishop would have it, "guileless," for he is often wary in his dealings; nor is he *innocent* in the sense that crops up so often in discussions of Faulkner's egomaniacs, that of being unaware of the conventions of society and thus uninhibited in one's actions. Rather, Musgrove is innocent in the simple sense of "guiltless." He wishes no one ill, nor does he scheme or connive against anyone; he strives only to make the land productive and to please his loved ones with presents. "My time is over," he observes after a long meditation on the cycle of the seasons, "for cunning is of a world I will have no part in" (p. 142).

The Indians in this tale are even more clearly doomed, for they do not, like the white characters, have two faces; and this lack of doubleness works to their disadvantage. Early in the novel Musgrove muses that despite the redmen's success in one raid that killed most of his loved ones, "The Indians know their time has come. . . . They are sure of the future growing smaller always, and that lets them be infinitely gay and cruel" (p. 21). Near the end of the book, after another Indian uprising that claims Musgrove's duplicitous second wife, he muses again, "The savages have only come the sooner to their end; we will come to ours too. Why have I built my house, and added to it? The planter will go after the hunter, and the merchant after the planter, all having their day" (p. 161).

This meditation carries us beyond the point that we have reached in this argument and hints of its end; but, as in the sequential process described here, we must dispose of the forest before moving to town, because if the day of the merchant will at last end, it has now arrived—"the time of cunning has come," as Musgrove recognizes (p. 142). He himself has led a double life and has been torn between the forest and the cultivated field: "he was an innocent of the wilderness, and a planter of Rodney's Landing, and this was his good" (p. 182). With what time is left to him, after having seen his child settled and refusing to stay with her, he returns to the plantation, feeling that it grows smaller as he grows older. Finally even for Jamie Lockhart, who has been divided by his two faces between the forest and the market-place, it is the forest visage that has been the affectation. He has had to stain his face with berry juice to maintain his standing as a robber of the Trace and to keep his genteel identity entirely separate; but, when he realizes that "the bandit's life is done with" (p. 166), he has only to remove his mask to claim his place in the city—unlike the Harps who are not cunning enough to survive the transition.

By setting her story thus on the already vanishing Natchez Trace just at that time early in the nineteenth century when the American economy was shifting from one dominated by the trailblazers of the forest and tillers of the fields to one dominated by city merchants, Welty has grounded her fantasy in "the concrete facts of place." *The Robber Bridegroom* is, paradoxically, a legend of civilization, a fantastic representation of a very real movement as the nineteenth century began of the United States from a primarily wild country to the international market-place it had become by the time the century ended.

Eudora Welty does not, however, like the ebullient boosters of our "go-getter" tradition, equate change with progress. In *The Robber Bridegroom*, a shift in the controlling elements of society brings into power not a new class of persons but the most resourceful figures from the older order of things, wearing new guises. The observation that binds together the wandering threads of the tale is, as already pointed out, that for Jamie "the outward transfer from bandit to merchant had been almost too easy to count it a change at all." The implications of this wry summary is that no *inner* change has been required by the transformation—merchants are quite like bandits operating within legal sanctions in a civilized community. The further comment that Jamie "was enjoying all the same success he had ever had" indicates that the same talents are required for the two callings.

This putdown of mercantile probity reveals also that the tale itself partakes of an as yet unmentioned double identity as part of two literary traditions, although its origins in primitive folktale only have usually been observed. Although I have maintained earlier that there is nothing else like *The Robber Bridegroom* in American literature, it finds a kindred spirit elsewhere in one of the wellsprings of "civilized" urban literature, John Gay's *The Beggar's Opera* (1728), which created much of its enduring impact with such ironic statements as merchant Peachum's: "A rich rogue now-a-days is fit company for any gentleman; and the world, my dear, hath not such a contempt for roguery as you imagine," and again, "In one respect, indeed, our employment may be reckon'd dishonest, because, like great Statesmen, we encourage those who betray their friends." The most marked similarity occurs at the end of the pieces: the ostensible beggar-author of Gay's play observes, in a statement that matches Welty's about Jamie Lockhart, that "it is difficult to determine whether (in the fashionable vices) the fine gentlemen imitate the gentlemen of the road or the gentlemen of the road the fine gentlemen." (For Eudora Welty, of course, no dilemma exists, for the two are one, imitating none, but turning only toward differing situations the appropriate face. Macheath's final revelation after his fantastic reprieve that he is married to Polly Peachum may hint as well that this robber/bridegroom, too, may find the transition to inheritor of Peachum's mercantile empire scarcely a change at all.)

The Robber Bridegroom thus weds two traditions of fantasy—the primitive fairy tale of ancient rural cultures with the "Newgate pastoral" of the bourgeois ascendancy in England.

A further evidence of cultural transition is afforded by Welty's handling of the loose frame story of the legendary American riverboatman Mike Fink. He appears at the beginning of the tale as the third lodger with whom Clement Musgrove and Jamie Lockhart must share a bed for the night. Despite his physical prowess, Fink is outwitted by the cunning Jamie and, as we learn later, loses his standing in his own community because of the way he has been gulled by apparent spooks. Rosamond encounters him near the end of the story come "down in the world" from his former splendor to be a mail rider, though still a gifted teller of tall tales. Fink flourished during the days of the conquest of the forest through his physical strength; but in the new era of mercantile princes, physical force is no match for cunning, and he becomes a servant rather than a master of a culture that depends upon communication rather than confrontation. He thus shares the fate of a similar character in a story that Eudora Welty herself has commented upon in a much different context, Stephen Crane's "The Bride Comes to Yellow Sky" (*ES*, pp. 86–87). In Crane's story, Scratchy Wilson, "the last one of the old gang that used to hang out along the river here," continues to terrorize a Western community as in frontier days until the coming of Marshal Potter's bride emblemizes the triumph of civilization. Scratchy even turns up later in a too much neglected counterpart story, "Moonlight on the Snow," as Marshal Potter's deputy. Although we are assured in *The Robber Bridegroom* that Mike Fink's name was "restored to its original glory" (p. 180), he must return to a life already fading into legend; whereas Jamie Lockhart can abandon his stealthy life on the Trace to take an honored place in the rising city.

Jamie can make the transition, among other reasons, because he is unburdened by guilt. He is not, like Musgrove, guiltless; but he finds guilt "a burdensome thing to carry about in the heart.... I would never bother with it." After this announcement, Musgrove salutes Jamie as "a man of the times" (p. 27). Jamie has found also a useful wife in Rosamond, a talented liar. Yet despite the gain in luxury and security that the pair enjoy, something is lost—even this tale acknowledges—in the transition from forest to market-place. The talking raven that once rode on Mike Fink's finger as emblem of man's affinity with wild and wise things is caged and neglected after Jamie acquires it; and, at last, after the Indians during a final outbreak burn the robbers' hideout, it "flew out over the treetops and was never seen again" (p. 148). The mystical tie with the forest is gone.

In the course of these speculations I have not just idly linked *The Robber Bridegroom* with such acclaimed works as "The Bear" and *The Great Gatsby* and "The Bride Comes to Yellow Sky," for it seems to me that this usually too lightly dismissed tale (let us not quarrel about "novels" and "novellas" when the important antecedents are evident) deserves to take its place beside these others as the unflaggingly beguiling embodiment of one of several points of view toward the experience central to American culture of the transformation of "the forest" into a patchwork of "trading districts" centered around "the market-place." Perhaps because like Faulkner's Ike McCaslin our heart is in the forest or like Fitzgerald's Nick Carraway we feel defeated by our possession of capacities we cannot manage, we are more impressed by these works than by Eudora Welty's delicate polishing of the cutting cynicism of the tradition of *The Beggar's Opera*; but it is no small achievement to have fashioned from scraps of tradition the fitting vehicle for any position toward an inescapable aspect of man's experience.

What Welty meant to "establish," if John Peale Bishop's rather pompous term fits her storytelling at all, is not our tall tale "as the equivalent of the European folk tale," but the contribution that both this ancient vehicle and the later fantasies of city wits can make to the fictional embodiment of a stage in the development of a culture that moved with unprecedented suddenness from forest to market-place. She subsumes both fairy tale and "Newgate pastoral" within her own peculiarly original form to suggest the continuation of the past in a present beyond which most people's consciousnesses do not extend. "Yet no one can laugh or cry so savagely in this wilderness as to be heard by the nearest traveler or remembered the next year. A fiddle played in a finished hut in a clearing is as vagrant as the swamp breeze. What will the seasons be, when we are lost and dead?" muses Clement Musgrove, losing himself so deeply in his reverie that the Indians are able to seize him once more (p. 144). What indeed would be remembered next year but for the intervention of the artist whose words fix the fleeting seasons?

It may be useful to view what—as Eudora Welty suggests—may be the passing triumph of the market-place through the detached consciousness of a civilized writer rather than the claims of its celebrators and detractors, who, whether they are impetuously guileless or deliberately duplicitous, produce more outrageous fantasies than *The Robber Bridegroom*.

JULIA DEMMIN
AND
DANIEL
CURLEY

Golden Apples
and Silver Apples

> And pluck till time and times are done
> The silver apples of the moon,
> The golden apples of the sun.
> "The Song of the Wandering Aengus"—Yeats

A NUMBER OF CLASSIC myths help to give *The Golden Apples* its richness, but neither any one of them nor any combination of them in their classic form gives anything like a satisfactory shape to the book as a whole. In fact, the shape of the book can be understood only if one examines Eudora Welty's use of the old material for the creation of her own myth of human wholeness, a myth that will finally transcend not only the ancient myths of the male godhead but also the even more ancient myths of the female mysteries.

We must always be aware, however, that Welty's handling of myth is very tricky. She turns it on and she turns it off. There is nothing like a systematic development of the whole story, nothing approaching the rigidity of allegory. Rather, the myth remains something in the background, a note to be struck in some complex harmony of her own. She uses it. She abandons it. She extemporizes on it. She invents new elements. The reader must be very watchful not to be led to carry the parallel of the myth too far or on the other hand to forget the pervasive effect of its undertone.

The identification of King MacLain with Zeus is obvious and has been well documented, but King's godlike power is nowhere more important than in its limitations and its failures and in its conflict with the opposing female power, so much less clearly developed and so much more mysterious. King appears in the role of Zeus in the first story, "Shower of Gold." In this story Snowdie can easily be assigned the role of Danae, because King's effect on her is to leave her looking as if "a shower of something had struck her, like she'd been caught out in something bright." But it is difficult and dangerous to try to make out that the twins must therefore be Perseus or, since they are twins, Caster and Pollux or even Hercules and

Iphicles. What is of more importance, however, is that the twins are clearly King's heirs and the inheritors of his power.

The inheritance is shown when King returns home after one of his frequent and mysterious absences and is frightened off by the boys, who are wearing Halloween masks. Welty is at great pains to make the event mysterious—did it or did it not actually happen? Mrs. Rainey says more than once that the event doesn't seem ever to have happened at all, although she also says that it happened only a week before. But real or not, what we have at one level is a funny story of a man trying to come home and being frightened by his little boys—surely a shock to any man's nerves—and at another level, the little boys as Halloween demons do ward off the booger, which is precisely the function of Halloween masks. The fact that the boys scare off King does not necessarily mean, however, that they are antipathetic to him. They are dressed as boogers and recognize him as one immediately—it takes one to know one. The fact that he is frightened by them may only mean that he recognizes his own power in them. Uranus was dethroned by his son Cronus, and Cronus was dethroned by his son Zeus. Must not Zeus then fear his sons in turn?

In "Sir Rabbit" also, King's power is clearly shown to have been passed to his sons. The sunlight imagery leaves no doubt as to the identification: "at moments the sun would take hold of their arms with a bold dart of light, or rest on their wetted, shaken hair, or splash over their pretty clothes like the torn petals of a sunflower" (p. 87). Later the playing light comes down on them "like a fountain."

It seems that in making a provisional statement about King we must consider two things: one, that King MacLain is a man who has treated his wife and other women so shamefully as to be a person of great fascination and, the other, that King represents a natural force, strength and regeneration, a pure elemental state of being. This, of course, is fully consistent with Welty's belief in forces that are quite indifferent to individual values —or at least to what individuals believe to be their values—so that however he has treated Snowdie, the result is that she appears to be transformed.

The Kingly power as defined in the early stories manifests itself once more in "Moon Lake" when Ran arrives to witness the rebirth (or resurrection) of Easter after drowning, but from this point on the power is lost or in eclipse, for a new power dominates the book. Before we turn to a consideration of this power, however, we would do well to remember that the

Kingly power is always seen from the outside, from the point of view of women and as it affects women. It descends on Snowdie and Mattie Will as shining gold and is viewed by a variety of characters, Katie Rainey, Mattie Will, and the child Loch Morrison. The result is that even in that part of the book where the Kingly power is strong it is at a certain remove from the center of importance. It is seen from the male point of view only in its failure in the case of Ran ("The Whole World Knows") and in a rare moment in which it is transcended in the case of Eugene ("Music from Spain"). It resists, however, the efforts of Miss Lizzie Stark to reduce it to the importance of a "mosquito, with a mosquito's proboscis" (p. 131).

Miss Lizzie, for her part, suggests the equal failure of the female power in isolation. To be sure, she "hates all men and is very important," but she is forced to admit "You men. You got us beat in the end. . . . We'd know you through and through except we never know what ails you" (p. 151). Consistent with her usual practice, Welty assigns knowledge to Miss Lizzie and identifies her as an anti-life figure. Much more hopeful is the case of Miss Eckhart, who in her great moment is able to get out of self, out of knowledge, out of reliance on verbal communication, to roam free in the world of music: "in playing it Miss Eckhart assumed an entirely different face. Her skin flattened and drew across her cheeks, her lips changed. The face could have belonged to someone else—not even a woman, necessarily. It was the face a mountain could have, or what might be seen behind the veil of a waterfall" (p. 49). This is the direction in which our inquiry must take us.

II

It is much more difficult to elucidate that aspect of the book relating to female magical power, for that power is not expressed in the form of clearly developed myths but in symbols, familiar enough but still mysterious. We move now from the ancient elaborate intellectual constructions of a male-oriented society in the direction of even more ancient female mysteries, intuitive and powerful. This transition exactly reflects the structure of The Golden Apples, for it is with "Moon Lake," the middle story, that the power of Zeus wanes and the symbols of female power begin to come into prominence.

Before examining the new order of things, however, it might be well to observe that these symbols which are here designated as belonging to the female area are by no means exclusively limited to women but must also be understood as having "no slight or trivial influence / on that best portion of a good man's life." Since, however, symbols are not amenable to the same kind of explication as myth but must be developed in situ, it is now necessary to go directly to the stories themselves.

"Moon Lake" is a female mystery story. Such males as do appear are exiles and pariahs with the exception of Ran, who is indispensable. Exum is not only a boy but black. Mr. Holifield, the camp caretaker, demonstrated his ineffectiveness in "June Recital" when he slept through love and fire and madness. Even Loch Morrison, the Boy Scout lifesaver, is scorned and despised by the girls and is beginning a life of isolation and wretchedness, a legacy, as will be seen, from his having once seen King MacLain and taken some of his knowledge but none of his power—he cannot even save Easter's life without the direct intervention of King's surrogate, Ran.

Nina Carmichael, the viewpoint character in "Moon Lake," is a familiar kind of Welty character. Consciousness is her difficulty. We cannot put consciousness very low in the scale of grace, but it is distinctly below the instinctive acceptance seen in Easter. Easter, on the other hand, is perhaps one of Welty's clearest statements of the virtue of acceptance. Easter's open hand, both in sleep and in "death," indicates her acceptance of life as it is offered; and the face of the night looking into the tent indicates the harmony with life which such an attitude brings about. Nina is able to open her hand to be sure, but she must will it to be open, and she recognizes that will is inferior to instinct. This is probably Welty's view also, although in the work of other writers the judgment might easily go the other way. And we must remember that Nina is seeing Easter from the outside and must be ignorant of inner processes she is well aware of in herself. We must also remember that the night looks thoughtfully at Nina, although it chooses Easter, and that Easter is in the nature of an ideal whereas Nina is more vulnerable, terrified—more human and perhaps therefore more heroic: "Nina let her own arm stretch forward opposite Easter's. Her hand too opened, of itself. She lay there a long time motionless, under the night's gaze, its black cheek, looking immovably at her hand, the only part of her now which was not asleep. Its gesture was like Easter's, but Easter's hand slept and her own hand knew—shrank and knew, yet offered still" (p. 123). Nina wakes up with her hand under her. In other words, when her consciousness is not in control, she withdraws her hand.

The scene is ambiguous, however, for when Nina sleeps, her hand sleeps too, and the virtue in Easter's hand is its sleep. But Nina dreams that her hand is "helpless to the tearing of wild beasts." Perhaps this is to say that the ideal is not without its dangers and terrors, a common dilemma in Welty's work. Still, when Nina wakes up, she must force her hand back to life by hitting and biting it, and even then it bites back ("like a cluster of bees") before it will return to normal waking life. This experience of Nina's may furnish some insight into the back of Easter's sleep, but it cannot be denied that Easter is able both to sleep and to offer, whereas Nina can do only one at a time. Nor does Nina observe that when Easter is lying on the table, presumably dead and still making the gesture of offering, her *other* hand is clenched under her. This gesture, however, has its own ambiguity in Welty's world, for there is more to life than offering: there is also withholding.

It is at this point that Ran MacLain arrives on the scene and stands in deep opposition to Miss Lizzie Stark, the presiding female power. " 'Get away from me, Ran MacLain,' Miss Lizzie called toward him. 'You and dogs and guns, keep away. We've already got all we can put up with out here' " (p. 132). She is not actually sending him away, however, and may even want to keep him there as an adult male presence; but for Welty's purposes, the significant fact is that in the previous story ("Sir Rabbit") Ran and Eugene were established as emissaries of their father, and King has been standing for Zeus, procreator and source of life and vitality. So it might be suggested that Ran has in fact come to bear witness to the resurrection that is implicit in Easter's name.

The revival comes on page 135, and it can be bracketed in less than a page between the fact that Jinny Love says "I give up" and the later fact that, just after the revival, Miss Lizzie says to Ran, "Why don't you go home—now." Jinny's self-important giving up is followed by the event she gives up about, and the event itself is followed by Miss Lizzie's dismissing Ran. He is no longer needed, either as a useful male or as a necessary source of power.

Although male power now passes into eclipse, it has established itself as a magical presence in the heart of the female mystery. At each phase of the initiation male presence is required. Easter is precipitated into the lake by the lightest touch of Exum's switch, a touch neither more nor less significant than the black rapist's touch on Miss Eckhart; for it is observed of Miss Eckhart that she did not die of shame because she "considered one thing not so much more terrifying than another" (p. 50) and of Easter "one little touch could smirch her, make her fall so far, so deep" (p. 132). Easter is then worked on by Loch Morrison with his explicitly sexual artificial respiration and is actually restored to life by the power inherent in Ran MacLain.

Easter is now fully launched, complete in knowledge and power. The girls may sing "When all the ships come sailing home," but the experience of Mattie Will in "Sir Rabbit" tells us that once the boat is launched it never comes back: "she felt at that moment as though somewhere a little boat was going out on a lake, never to come back" (p. 87). The same boat imagery is used earlier in "Moon Lake" when the three girls get into an old boat only to find it still chained to the shore and again when Miss Moody, the counselor, goes out by moonlight with her lover. So the girls may sing about sailing home; but once the ritual is complete, the process of knowledge is irreversible, as we see in all the stories. And no boat can ever return. The message is passed to the girls in one of Welty's amazing wordless communications. This time the medium is blood.

While Easter is apparently dead, the girls watch her: "was there danger that Easter, turned in on herself, might call out to them after all, from the other, worse, side of it? Her secret voice, if soundless, then possibly visible, might work out of her terrible mouth like a vine, preening and sprung with flowers. Or a snake would come out." Then when the blood does appear, "for them all, it was like being spoken to" (p. 133). At a female initiation rite, the message scarcely needs elaboration, but it is reinforced by Mrs. Gruenwald's comment and Welty's addition: " 'Oh, my child, Moon Lakes are all over the world,' Mrs. Gruenwald had interrupted. 'I know of one in Austria.' " And Welty adds, "And into each fell a girl, they dared, now, to think" (p. 137).

III

At this point it is interesting to speculate on the failure of King's heirs. After "Moon Lake" King's sons come into focus. Each has a story of his own, Ran in "The Whole World Knows" and Eugene in "Music from Spain." Ran has stayed in Morgana and is unhappily married. Eugene has lived a long time in San Francisco and is also unhappily married. Ran tries to live as the image of his father. Eugene rejects his father entirely. Both are obvious failures, although Eugene is given a moment outside himself, a moment of the true Welty harmony.

Clearly King is able to transmit his power to his sons, as proved by their power over him in "Shower of Gold" and by Ran's role in "Moon

Lake." It is equally clear, however, that the power is lost after a certain point. Since the stories relating to Ran and Eugene are both marriage stories, it is easy to suppose that the failure of each twin is a sexual failure, not, however, in an ordinary sense of impotence or sterility but more basically of magic. The twins started with the power but never achieved the knowledge to make the power meaningful. The very title of Ran's story, "The Whole World Knows," suggests the source of Ran's failure. There *is* something the whole world knows, something denied to Ran. This is what is meant in "Death of a Traveling Salesman" when Bowman discovers the wonderful secret of the house: "He was shocked with knowing what was really in this house. A marriage, a fruitful marriage. That simple thing. Anyone could have had that. . . . There was nothing remote or mysterious here—only something private. The only secret was the ancient communication between two people" (*CG*, p. 248). Ran, "the bad twin," tries to imitate his father and fails wretchedly. The girl he seduces kills herself: this is Ran's knowledge she puts on, no shower of gold for her.

In this story there is no glimmering of hope, no stance however stoic to encourage the reader. There is only Ran's prayer to his Father or to God— or perhaps they are the same after all: "Father! Dear God wipe it clean. Wipe it clean, wipe it out. Don't let it be" (p. 152). Ironically, he is immediately met by his landlady with a similar prayer. He is asked to wipe out what she can't bear, the suffering of her dog Bella. We do not ever learn whether Ran does this or not. Since he would clearly rather kill himself than Maideen, we may doubt it perhaps. Nor is there any clear indication in the story whether killing the dog would be a good or an evil act. All we can say is that Ran anxiously desires good but that he is powerless to bring it about or even decide what it is. Deserted by both Maideen and Jinny, he can lavish his tenderness only where it can be accepted, on the dog Bella, who for him tries to drink water she can only vomit in pain, another ironic metaphor for love.

It is extremely interesting that while Ran MacLain prays to find his father and talk with him, Eugene MacLain says, "God forbid [I] find him! Old Papa King MacLain was an old goat, a black name he had" (p. 178). Probably it is to show this contrast that the two stories are paired, and we can also observe that the son who rejects the father is in some important way closer to the old King than the one who, in the Maideen episode at least, seems to be trying to carry on the Kingly tradition. It is basic to this view that Eugene gets out of Morgana and that Ran not only stays but even returns to the old house and lives in a rented room there. Nor can we lose sight of the fact that it was Eugene who happened to take the free music lessons as a child, for even if he never did get past "The Stubborn Rocking Horse," some mark seems to have been made on him. We must by no means take seriously his wife's objection that he doesn't "respect music." There is no indication anywhere that what you are supposed to do with music is respect it. Further, we must not be afraid of making too much of the connection between Eugene's music lessons and his present employment as a watchmaker. The beat of time is the same: the metronome is to Miss Eckhart's breaking out into music during the tempest as the watches are to Eugene's playing hooky from the shop. Both episodes represent moments in which the rigid and mechanical notion of time is transcended and life reveals a possibility not before suspected.

The end, however, is much the same for King and Ran and Eugene. King is a frightened old man at Katie Rainey's funeral, sticking his tongue out at life and at death. Eugene is dead. He came back to die at home, spiteful, ambiguous, never speaking of what happened to him "away." Ran is now fat, mayor of Morgana, probably a bad sign. He is even linked at one point with Miss Lizzie Stark, his mother-in-law now. Ran, then, has come the farthest down. The others have managed to hold on to some part of their terror, a quick pink tongue like a child's or even spite and secrecy.

There is something else at large in the stories, however, and that is music. Music first appears as a force in "June Recital" where it is clearly in opposition to the power inherent in King MacLain and is identified with Miss Eckhart and Virgie Rainey. Thus it stands with the female virtues of accepting and offering, although it also represents transcendence of the conflict in the case of the guitar player ("Music from Spain") and of Miss Eckhart's impromptu concert during the storm. In fact, finally it becomes the very music of the spheres.

In addition to those already mentioned there are various minor heirs of Miss Eckhart. Eugene is one, Cassie Morrison is one, and Loch, her brother, is a failed heir just as Ran MacLain is a failed heir of King. These parallel dynasties represent the real tensions of the book, and it is in terms of them that the real resolution must be sought.

Although Miss Eckhart lives a baffled life and dies mad, she has within her something that we recognize and, more important, even the godlike King recognizes. She has a power that balances his own, although it is not clear that he understands what her power is. This is not surprising, however, for she has two aspects. One aspect is associated with the metronome, the rigid notion of time, which terrifies King, and the other is something beyond time, something timeless, something like what King himself is seeking. Her students believe she worships the metronome, but perhaps she values it as the boundary, marking a point the true hero must be able to pass. The power Virgie Rainey acquires over her by refusing to play to the metronome strongly indicates this. Miss Eckhart's own spontaneous music during the tempest is further indication. Here she not only abandons the metronome, but she doesn't even play the music Jinny Love turns for her so carefully—poor officious Jinny Love, missing the point as always, even so young.

Early in "June Recital" Cassie Morrison understands that Miss Eckhart is not afraid of King MacLain. She explains it to herself in this manner: "they always passed without touching, like two stars, perhaps they had some kind of eclipse-effect on each other" (p. 44). The one time we see them actually face to face the effect is quite different, however. This is at the end of "June Recital," when King is already old and Miss Eckhart mad. The scene should be examined at length because of the importance of the implications.

In the first place, this encounter—in Part III of "June Recital"—is observed by Loch Morrison, who alternates with his sister Cassie as viewpoint character. In all probability, his idiosyncratic perceptions are intended to be suggestive. Loch makes two important mistakes in identifying the actors in the scene he is observing. He first thinks of Miss Eckhart as the sailor's mother. In a sense she is, for we are later told that the sailor is just beginning a journey to which Miss Eckhart and Virgie have long been committed, but in a more important sense she is Virgie's mother. Through music she has brought Virgie through time and beyond, and for what Virgie is now, Miss Eckhart is largely responsible. The other mistake Loch makes is thinking King MacLain is Mr. Voight, the exhibitionist who roomed in Snowdie MacLain's house and who manifested himself during the music lessons. He was politely ignored by everyone because they didn't know what to do about him; but this appearance of degenerate sex in conjunction with the music ceremony is meaningful, and the confusion of King MacLain with Mr. Voight indicates a degeneration of King's power. The association can perhaps best be seen in Loch's expectation of a gift from Mr. Voight. When we learn that the gift was to be a bird that can say "rabbits," we have no doubt it was actually King who made the promise

—a glance ahead to "Sir Rabbit" makes the connection between King's vitality and rabbits. This gift does not materialize, however, but another one does: Loch gets the metronome. That is, he does not get from King the gift of power, and from Miss Eckhart he gets only the sense of time, not that which transcends time. Perhaps it is this limitation in Loch—knowledge without power, always disastrous in Welty—that explains Virgie's thought about him at the end of the book: "But he's not dead! she thought —it's something else" (p. 230). Quite simply his life has gone wrong.

When King MacLain gets into the old MacLain house, he is finally at ease. Loch sees him gaze "serenely about the walls, pausing for a moment first, as though something had happened to them not that very hour but a long time ago" (p. 73). As so often happens in the work of Eudora Welty, another passage in quite another place helps illuminate obscurity. In "Music from Spain" Eugene has a meditation on walls that will help us see what King MacLain sees when he looks at the walls of his own house. Eugene's marvelous Spaniard has given Eugene insight into the possibilities of his own city, San Francisco. But Eugene knows that the insight is, in complicated ways, both real and illusory; and, as elsewhere, Welty is careful to underline the fact that if freedom has its joys and its terrors, then isolation has equally its terrors and its joys: "He supposed he had a horror of closed-in places and of being shut in, but in late afternoon he had seen Alcatraz light as a lady's hat afloat on the water, looking inviting, and he would almost wish to go to that island himself, and say to people, 'Convicts are Christ,' or the like" (p. 192).

Now it should be possible to return to King, looking serenely at his walls and to guess that long ago the walls let him out and that he feels he has mastered them. Then Miss Eckhart comes forward, clutching her metronome, and he sees that he has, in fact, never got away at all. He sees that the great wide world he has wandered can, like San Francisco, be any man's walls still. Both King MacLain and Miss Eckhart are now mastered by time, and the story passes into the hands of their heirs. How it fares in the hands of Ran and Eugene has already been seen. Mattie Will, who put on King's knowledge with his power, has disappeared from the story after her apotheosis. The same is true of Easter, after her rebirth in Moon Lake. Snowdie MacLain, after being showered with gold, disappears until the end of the book almost as completely as Mattie Will and Easter. When she does appear, however, she is associated only with positive values: the music of Miss Eckhart's passionate outburst evokes her; she stands in opposition to the marriage of Ran to Jinny Love of the anti-life Starks, and at the end she appears as a kind of priestess with supervision of the living (King) and the dead (Katie Rainey). But the most important heir of all is Virgie Rainey, who may now be proposed as the heir not only of Miss Eckhart but of King MacLain as well.

IV

Virgie first appears in "Shower of Gold" as a baby. The only thing we know that Virgie did on that occasion was to wake up and swallow a button. Swallowing the button led to choking, and choking led to being upended and spanked to dislodge the button. All this is in the context of the visit in which the twins scared off King MacLain, and the spanking thus easily becomes a birth ritual. Whether or not this suggestion is acceptable, there can be little doubt of kinship in the later stories. However, in telling the story of King's visit, Virgie's mother says, "I bet my little Jersey calf King tarried long enough to get him a child somewhere" (p. 17). Again, it is possible to suggest that the child he did get was Virgie in this mystic rebirth. More than this, there is even a possibility that Virgie really was King's child. Mrs. Rainey enters with very vivid imagination into Snowdie's walk into the woods to meet King—had she herself met him in the same place? Further, Snowdie forms an instinctive dislike for both Mrs. Rainey and Virgie after King runs away, rather in the manner of Hera disliking Alcmena and Hercules. And, finally, years later Katie Rainey, when she is dying, confuses Virgie's life and her own in a number of ways suggesting that she too had a lover once, a lover her husband might have had to shoot—King, of course.

Nor is it probably irrelevant that King himself has something slip up on him when he is at Katie's funeral. In thinking about her, he confuses her with Nellie Loomis, who used to set fire to her stockings as an act of bravado. The confusion results in some such statement as: Katie Blazes was such a hot number she burned up her stockings. And one last thing, Snowdie's dislike of Katie continues to the end of Katie's life and is, furthermore, known in some form to the townspeople, who are uneasy about Snowdie's laying Katie out. "There was something about it nobody liked, perhaps a break in custom" (p. 210). A sentence like that often indicates that the writer is trying to help the reader by suggesting that whatever might be the truth it is certainly not a break in custom that nobody likes. In this case they are perhaps remembering the past rivalry and not quite liking the fact that Snowdie, of all people, should have at least the triumph of survival—Snowdie was too much of a lady to dance on anybody's grave. The townspeople do not know, as we do, that Snowdie herself has said, "I'd want *her* to lay *me* out" (p. 216).

Noted above is another line of descent through Mrs. Stark and Jinny Love. Mrs. Stark is a thoroughly anti-life figure. "Moon Lake" reveals that she really does hate men. She does loathe sex. It is no wonder that she has only one child. Her attitude about artificial respiration, which she confuses with sex, is that if that is the way a girl is to be brought back to life, then she had better be left dead. However, she cannot stop life no matter how much she would like to. Nor can Jinny Love.

When Jinny Love comes to Katie Rainey's funeral, she says to Virgie, "I don't have to see her—do I, Virgie? . . . I don't have to see anybody" (p. 215). The fact is she has never seen anybody, and she is frightened to death of seeing anybody. She is afraid of seeing what King MacLain saw in that moment when he confronted Miss Eckhart in the old house: what can happen to people. The fact that she wants to get everyone married off is extremely revealing. "It appeared urgent with her to drive everybody, even Virgie for whom she cared nothing, into the state of marriage along with her. Only then could she resume as Jinny Love Stark, her true self" (p. 225). The business of married people wanting to get everyone into the same boat with them is nothing new, of course, but there is a hint that if everyone is equal then she can again become herself, whereas if there are holdouts, an alternative way of life is suggested, an alternative that casts great doubt on the wisdom of the choice already made. If everyone marries, then Jinny never had a choice, but if there is a choice, then perhaps she made the wrong one.

In *The Golden Apples* Virgie is the exemplar of the choice. King MacLain represents the blind quest, pure power, but he is not able to get beyond the reflex act of the quest and is finally trapped by time. He is able to bring great moments to Snowdie and Mattie Will and to transmit his power in many directions, but we can find scattered throughout the book other great moments of a very different nature. These moments are often associated with music and are often marked by the appearance of butterflies and hummingbirds and cats as symbols of the secret and mysterious world. They are sudden manifestations, epiphanies. They almost seem to say as Katherine Mansfield has a character say at the end of "The Prelude": "Life is rich and mysterious and good, and I am rich and mysterious and good, too." It is not for nothing that Eugene and his Spaniard have only one word in common, mariposa, a common flower but also the Spanish word for butterfly. With this shared word, however, they are able to go on up the hill past the farthest point Eugene and Emma ever reached. Beyond this point it is the Spaniard who leads: "It was he who took the choice of paths, and the choice was always a clever and difficult one" (p. 194). This is exactly like the music he plays: "Were the difficulties and challenges what he had sought for most?" (p. 183). But the limits of verbal communication are soon reached, and it is precisely at the word mariposa that Eugene despairs of communication and grapples with the Spaniard, nearly causing the death of both of them. He has been led through the day from the butterfly tattoo on the boy's wrist, "an intimate place, the wrist appeared to be" (p. 169), to the mysteriously beautiful woman, "marked as a butterfly is, over all her visible skin" (p. 174), to this frustrating moment of communication and to the touch beyond words. What Eugene fails to understand about butterflies is symbolized by a pin Miss Eckhart gave to Virgie long ago. It was a butterfly pin but the clasp was broken: there is no security, no guarantee in the epiphany (p. 57).

Still, although these moments seem to disappear as if they had never been, although there is nothing at the end of Eugene's life to suggest that the Spaniard had ever appeared, although Mattie Will vanishes from the story, the moments do remain for us—and, we must assume, even in mysterious ways for the characters themselves. Eugene felt it: "it was positively there and as defined at the edges as a spot or stain, and it affected him like a secret" (p. 174). But it is with Virgie that the book ends, and the ending fixes forever the moment of her triumph, her choice, her love and recognition.

Virgie's section is entitled "The Wanderers." This title obviously picks up the Wandering Aengus theme, but even more important it picks up and unites significant aspects of the book as a whole. Elsewhere Welty writes, "the life of an artist, or a foreigner, or a wanderer, all the same thing" (p. 180). If these people are all the same, they are the same through their enforced recognition of their isolation, that "secret and proper separation" between even the closest of individuals. Their condition of artist, foreigner, or wanderer forces this awareness on them, although their reactions to the awareness may be different. Nevertheless the wanderer King is the same as the foreigner Miss Eckhart. The wanderer Eugene is the same as the artist Spaniard. The orphan Easter is the same as the showered-on

Mattie Will. And Virgie is the same as all of them, including the old black thief with whom she listens to what may be called for simplicity the music of the spheres.

The first day of "The Wanderers" ends with Virgie alone in a lovely harmony with the natural world. When all the people go away, they drag gates and barriers from her sight and open the distant view of the country-side. She walks into this view, into the river where "all was one warmth, air, water, and her own body . . . the river, herself, the sky all vessels which the sun filled" (p. 219). This is the moment of inner peace, the still moment, we have seen so often in the work of Eudora Welty as the foundation of the integrated human being. Opposed to this inner serenity is the problem of otherness, the mystery of the other as exemplified by King MacLain's restless search. On page 233 begins a series of contrasts between Virgie's reaction and King's, between her opaque assertion of the private self and his attack on all secrets: "Virgie had often felt herself at some moment callous over, go opaque; she had known it to happen to others; not only when her mother changed on the bed while she was fanning her. Virgie had felt a moment in her life after which nobody could see through her, into her—felt it young. But Mr. King MacLain, an old man, had butted like a goat against the wall he wouldn't agree to himself or recognize. What fortress indeed would ever come down, except before hard little horns, a rush and a stampede of the pure wish to live?" (p. 233). That pure wish to live is quite in contrast with the passage of pure living that we have just seen Virgie enjoy. It does look as if finally that aimless vitality of King MacLain is being put in a new perspective, but there is more. Virgie goes so far as to recognize the twinship of these apparently opposite needs. "Virgie never saw it differently, never doubted that all the opposites on earth were close together, love close to hate, living to dying; but of them all, hope and despair were the closest blood—unrecognizable one from the other sometimes, making moments double on themselves, and in the doubling double again, amending but never taking back" (p. 234).

That, of course, is the true complexity of Eudora Welty's world, both the illumination and the mystery. That is why the night-blooming cereus so upsets Virgie. It reminds her of the shortness of beauty, life, herself: "to-morrow it'll look like a wrung chicken's neck" (p. 235). It was to avoid this kind of confrontation that she abandoned music and attached herself to the cows to find "the most real stupidity of flesh, a mindless and careless and calling body, to respond flesh for flesh, anguish for anguish. And if, as she dreamed one winter night, a new piano she touched had turned, after the one pristine moment, into a calling cow, it was by her own desire" (p. 235). That disturbing sequence fades at the end of the day into another lovely nature piece, and we see Virgie enjoying cigarettes in her car with her pistol snugly in the pocket of the door.

At the end, Virgie in going off by herself is justifying herself to herself and casting herself in the heroic role of Perseus. She could have Mr. Mabry if she wished, and there is always Mr. Nesbitt, but she would have to come a long way back in order to settle for mere protection—as it is called. Instead, she makes the choice that is so terrible to Jinny Love's view of herself, and as she does so she has a vision of the picture of Perseus in Miss Eckhart's studio.

All Virgie remembers is the triumphant lift of the hero's arm, holding up the head of Medusa:

> Cutting off the Medusa's head was the heroic act, perhaps, that made visible a horror in life, that was at once the horror in love, Virgie thought—the separateness. . . . Miss Eckhart, whom Virgie had not, after all, hated—had come near to loving, for she had taken Miss Eckhart's hate, and then her love, extracted them, the thorn and then the overflow—had hung the picture on the wall for herself. She had absorbed the hero and the victim and then, stoutly, could sit down with all of Beethoven ahead of her. With her hate, with her love, and with the small gnawing feelings that ate them, she offered Virgie her Beethoven. She offered, offered, offered—and when Virgie was young, in the strange wisdom of youth that is accepting of more than is given, she had accepted *the* Beethoven, as with the dragon's blood. That was the gift she had touched with her fingers that had drifted and left her.
>
> In Virgie's reach of memory a melody softly lifted, lifted of itself. Every time the Perseus struck off the Medusa's head, there was a beat of time, and the melody. Endless the Medusa, and Perseus endless. (p. 243)

Having inherited King MacLain's power and Miss Eckhart's music, Virgie accepts the beat and accepts the melody, accepts the act and accepts the act in time, and thus floats buoyant in time, transcending time by submitting to it. This is the pattern of the integrated Welty character, and the imagery is the same here as elsewhere: harmony with nature as in the case of Audubon, Old Phoenix, William Wallace Jamieson; nonverbal communication through music as in the case of Eugene's Spaniard, Mrs. Blennerhassett, Powerhouse. It is at this point when power and knowledge come together in a moment of choice that Eudora Welty chooses to stop her story. It is the moment of triumph, the moment of something touched, not the long process of drifting and leaving. Virgie sits under a tree in the rain, "listening to the magical percussion, the world beating in [her] ears. [She] heard through falling rain the running of the horse and bear, the stroke of the leopard, the dragon's crusty slither, and the glimmer and the trumpet of the swan" (p. 244).

DANIELE   Technique as Myth:

PITAVY-   The Structure of

SOUQUES   *The Golden Apples*

"Tu remarquas, on n'écrit pas, lumineusement, sur champ obscur, l'alphabet des astres, seul, ainsi s'indique, ébauché ou interrompu; l'homme poursuit noir sur blanc."

Mallarmé

BECAUSE EUDORA WELTY herself has suggested that *The Golden Apples* was more than just another collection of short stories,[1] the structural unity of the book has puzzled critics over the years. Nearly all the articles dealing with *The Golden Apples* as a whole tackle the problem and attempt to solve it by establishing close parallels between (mostly) Greek mythology and the various characters and incidents in the book.[2] Whether they underline the recurrent myths that can be traced in the different stories or organize all mythical allusions into echoes and leitmotiv that weave a symphonic web in the book, these critical approaches remain at the surface of the work. No doubt, the task is not easy, perhaps chiefly because of the looseness of the book. It is composed of seven stories, each a brilliant experiment in technique, and of several different myths—Celtic as well as Greek—col-

---

[1] When Charles T. Bunting asked Eudora Welty about the genesis of *The Golden Apples*, and suggested that this book, like her novels, began as short stories, she made this fine point: "In *The Golden Apples* they exist on their own as short stories; they have independent lives. They don't have to be connected, but I think by being connected there's something additional coming from them as a group with a meaning of its own." Earlier in the same interview, she had said: "I mostly loved working on the connected stories, finding the way things emerged in my mind and the way one thing led to another; the interconnections of the book fascinated me." Charles T. Bunting, "'The Interior World': An Interview with Eudora Welty," *Southern Review*, 8 (Autumn 1972), 715, 714.

[2] For a discussion of the criticism see Thomas L. McHaney, "Eudora Welty and the Multitudinous Golden Apples," *Mississippi Quarterly*, 26 (Fall 1973), 589–624, especially n. 3, pp. 590–91. For a discussion of mythology see Harry C. Morris, "Eudora Welty's Use of Mythology," *Shenandoah*, 6 (Spring 1955), 34–40 and Thomas McHaney.

lected under a title that seems to introduce yet another myth. The very multiplicity of these mythic readings and the lack of a strong unifying device, such as one finds in *Ulysses*, have marred all attempts at finding a satisfactory structure. Could not then a different approach be used that would do full justice not only to this complex work but to the artist herself, who of her generation is perhaps the most deeply aware of her art?

Content cannot be dissociated from form; the text should be analyzed as a whole. Indeed, its narrative functioning deserves the closest attention since alone it shows the author's intentions. Just as important is the examination of any infraction of the norms established by the work itself, as these infractions help evaluate the esthetic success of the book and give clues that indicate the presence of a less obvious narrative system. The study of the structure of *The Golden Apples* should thus be based on the narration as well as the fiction, and take into account the apparent infractions of its narrative code. Only through such study can one perceive the essential function of myth in the book, thence the deeper meaning of Welty's work.

In *The Golden Apples* Welty very deliberately used what T.S. Eliot called "the mythical method" in his 1923 *Dial* review of *Ulysses*: "It is simply a way of controlling, of ordering, of giving a shape and a significance to the immense panorama of futility and anarchy which is contemporary history. It is a method already adumbrated by Mr. Yeats, and of the need for which I believe Mr. Yeats to have been the first contemporary to be conscious. It is a method for which the horoscope is auspicious." Myth here is technique, imposed on the world of action, shaping our perception and reaction to it. Eliot's comment is further relevant because he gives credit to Yeats for adumbrating this technique and also mentions the horoscope. Both are directly related to the technique used in *The Golden Apples*. That Eudora Welty intended to experiment with the mythical method in a sustained and deliberate way is indicated by the genesis of her work. The first story of the cycle, "June Recital," was originally called "The Golden Apples,"[3] and appeared in *Harper's Bazaar* under this title, partly inspired by "The Song of the Wandering Aengus." Yeats's poem was extensively quoted in the first version. This nucleus story was thus under the double parentage of Yeats and Greek myth. Later, it was renamed and the mythical title transferred to designate the collection

---

[3] In a conversation, 18 January 1978, Eudora Welty herself confirmed to me that "June Recital" was the nucleus of *The Golden Apples* and the story she had written first.

as a whole—a unique instance in Welty's work, for the three other collections bear the name of one story. As she worked on the various stories of *The Golden Apples*, she realized, as she said, she was "writing about the same people."[4]

The futility of decoding the characters and events of the book according to a strict mythological system becomes evident from the first story. The warning is there, in the title itself, which functions as a signal to indicate a reality beyond the events in the story. "Shower of Gold" heralds the birth of Perseus to any cultivated reader. But on what level? If we remain on the purely factual level, we read in the story nothing more than the birth of the MacLain twins, Randall and Eugene, not the clandestine birth of an only son. And the "quotation" in the text is scant; the word *gold* is not even mentioned: "She looked like more than only the news had come over her. It was like a shower of something had struck her, like she'd been caught out in something bright" (*GA*, p. 6). Moreover, this title appears as an infraction of the functioning of the story, which rests entirely on the "truth" of King MacLain's visit to his wife on Halloween. Indeed, this title has nothing to do with the fiction if we except the incomplete allusion. (It functions, of course, as a mythical clue for King MacLain, whom we are thus invited to see as the modern counterpart of Zeus. But this belongs to the surface level of the book; story after story, we are told of the amorous exploits of the character.) We must therefore look elsewhere for the function of the title, beyond the single short story, considering this first piece of narrative as part of a whole, and see whether other allusions to Perseus occur in the book.

The hero reappears, again without being named, in the fourth story, "Moon Lake." The parallel is explicit enough never to have left critics in doubt as to the equation of Loch Morrison's bringing Easter back to life after she has fallen into the lake with Perseus' rescuing Andromeda from the sea monster. The reference is quite precise, developed at length and confirmed, so to speak, by the vision of Loch, alone and enjoying his triumph outside his tent as Perseus did after his first victory. But here again, Perseus and Andromeda and their love affair have no part in the plot of the story. What is most impressive is the strong sexual coloration of the lifesaving process. We are once more aware that the significance of this episode is on a second level of reality.

Finally, Perseus' slaying Medusa is the object of Virgie Rainey's long

4 Bunting, p. 714.

meditation in "The Wanderers." The meditation functions no more directly in this narrative than in the other two stories. It should be noted, however, that Virgie's interpretation is rather unorthodox and shakes the commonly accepted views of the myth: "Miss Eckhart had had among the pictures from Europe on her walls a certain threatening one. It hung over the dictionary, dark as that book. It showed Perseus with the head of the Medusa. 'The same thing as Siegfried and the Dragon,' Miss Eckhart had occasionally said, as if explaining second-best. . . . [Virgie] saw the stroke of the sword in three moments, not one. In the three was the damnation—no, only the secret, unhurting because not caring in itself—beyond the beauty and the sword's stroke and the terror lay their existence in time —far out and endless, a constellation which the heart could read over many a night" (pp. 242–43). At this stage we can draw two conclusions. The myth of Perseus is undoubtedly present in *The Golden Apples*, and Welty's use of this myth is highly deliberate, creative. There is another technical difficulty to solve before examining more closely the function of the myth of Perseus: the title of the collection itself.

The quest for the golden apples is very distantly linked to the myth of Perseus—some late accretions, which critics bent on finding thematic unity have hunted for and made the most of. But generally speaking, no one connects Perseus with the golden apples (though he is Heracles' ancestor). Since the title "Shower of Gold" functions symbolically, we may infer that the only other title with a mythical connotation, the general title of the collection, functions in the same way: it would thus refer not to a definite search but to *any* search. The text corroborates this hypothesis. The title was at first given to "June Recital," which originally included the full last stanza of Yeats's poem, with the reference to "the silver apples of the moon, / The golden apples of the sun." When Eudora Welty revised she eliminated the too explicit lines, favoring indirectness to pedantry, the more refined method of distant allusion to a labored exercise in name dropping. In fact, she kept the spirit rather than the letter of the poem. And what quest had Yeats in mind? Several times he pointed out the duality in the myth and legends about those who live in the waters and can take any shape like "the little silver trout" which became "a glimmering girl": "The people of the waters have been in all ages beautiful and changeable and lascivious, or beautiful and wise and lonely, for water is everywhere the signature of the fruitfulness of the body and of the fruitfulness of dreams."[5]

[5] William Butler Yeats, *The Variorum Edition of the Poems of W. B. Yeats*, ed.

Indeed, the search for the apples provides a loose thematic link between the different short stories. By their Greek and Celtic parentage the golden fruit represent the artist's attempt at showing the universality of myth—human desire and longing, at bringing about a new awareness of the fundamental ambivalence of man through a comparison between several worlds.[6] The brilliant fabric of mythological names and echoes that adorns the surface of the text functions in this same way. Welty's use of this technical device is quite original; it is not coincidence or influence but technique. She uses mythology as deliberate "quotations" from Yeats, Joyce, or T.S. Eliot, with the resulting effect of implying that she is writing about universal passions as eternal as *art*, and the created world itself. (Another way of doing it is to project what takes place on earth into the stars and constellations, whose names are derived from the myth, what T.S. Eliot implied when he mentioned the horoscope.) This effect of quotation is a means of guaranteeing the truth of her fiction, just as, paradoxically, this truth is warranted at the other end, the realistic end, by the list of the characters printed at the beginning of the book. What is more, these highly sophisticated literary "quotations" are a means of suggesting that literature is itself the endless repetition of the same stories. Welty's attitude becomes reflexive, just as literature, she seems to suggest, is a mirror. She questions her art in the very moment she is creating it. Somehow, those "quotations" are the play within the play, contesting the story and the genre while functioning within it. They constitute the mirror that Welty holds to her fiction. Perseus does nothing else: the writer *is* Perseus. To the point here is Reynolds Price's superb definition of the artist—not unconnected with *The Golden Apples*, it seems, as it appears in an essay significantly entitled "Dodging Apples": "The central myth of the artist is surely not Narcissus but Perseus—with the artist in all roles, Perseus, Medusa and the mirror-shield."[7] Here, brilliantly summed up, are indeed the elements of the myth —Perseus, Medusa and the mirror-shield.

Peter Allt and Russell K. Alspach (New York: Macmillan, 1957), p. 802. This is part of the long note to the first poem of *The Wind Among the Reeds*. Here, as in "The Song of Wandering Aengus," Yeats is speaking of the same "tribes of the Goddess Danu that are in the waters."

[6] In the note on "The Song of Wandering Aengus" Yeats wrote: "The poem was suggested to me by a Greek folk song; but the folk belief of Greece is very like that of Ireland, and I certainly thought, when I wrote it, of Ireland, and of the spirits that are in Ireland," in *Variorum Edition*, p. 806.

[7] Reynolds Price, *Things Themselves* (New York: Atheneum, 1972), p. 8.

The centre of this trinity is fascination—Medusa's deadly gaze, or rather fascination defeated, overcome by another gaze—Perseus' in the mirror. At the mythic as well as the symbolic level, fascination means death. At the level of human relations, it refers to that spell, that *abus de pouvoir* by which we tend to objectify the other, to make him lose his identity and become a thing, an object. In his phenomenological study of gaze in *L'Etre et le Néant*,[8] Sartre was perhaps the first to show that fascination is central to the problem of the gaze and to the relation of one being to another. Nearly every form of meaningful relation to the other derives from fascination. Prestige likewise reverses the relation of subject-object. It forces the admirer to lose his identity and wish to identify with the object of his admiration. Emptied of his substance, drained of his blood, the contemplator dies, so to speak. There is also the reverse form of fascination, shame, which is self-loathing. Sartre concludes at the end of his chapter on gaze that, beyond the inconciliable duality of our relation to the other, there is the body, apprehended as the purely contingent presence of the other. This apprehension is a particular type of nausea. We can see how seduction and the wish to possess the body of the other are, eventually, another form of fascination with one's own death, what Sartre calls the obscene. That the myth has strong sexual connotation is evident when we look at its development. Originally, Gorgo was an ugly creature with hissing snakes as hair; she later became a once beautiful woman turned ugly by Hera's jealousy; at the Hellenistic period, she was simply a beautiful young maid whose gaze was deadly.

All the complexities of feelings based on fascination, tearing man between attraction and repulsion, loving and loathing, fulfillment and destruction inform the treatment of human relations in *The Golden Apples*. There is the fascination for an unworthy type—King MacLain, a rascal who brazenly defies all the social and moral conventions in "Shower of Gold" and "The Wanderers." The nausea linked to the flesh and the self as experienced in sex is central to "Sir Rabbit" and "The Whole World Knows." Death also provides a perilous allure in "Moon Lake." In the more complex stories the theme of fascination shapes with infinite subtlety the projection of the self onto the idealized alter-ego, as in "Music from Spain" and "June Recital," which present the most devastating picture of feelings related to this theme.

[8] See Jean-Paul Sartre, *L'Etre et le Néant* (Paris: Gallimard, 1943), pp. 310–364, 410.

Perseus is not a "culture hero" in the sense Prometheus and Heracles are culture heroes, that is, the saviors of mankind, the transgressors, the "transformers" who by their heroic action help civilization progress. Perseus' victory is of a more private kind and concerns the terrors of the soul and the agony of the heart rather than the ordering of chaos.

Even if to the painters Perseus must have been the triumphant hero ("The vaunting was what she remembered, that lifted arm"), even if Loch's victory over death swells him with too much pride in the eyes of Nina Carmichael and Jinny Love, Perseus in *The Golden Apples* is above all that most complex character who alone was able to conceive the full horror of Medusa, since he overcame it: "Because Virgie saw things in their time, like hearing them—and perhaps because she must believe in the Medusa equally with Perseus—she saw the stroke of the sword in three moments, not one" (p. 243). Those three moments in one represent the utmost fascination and the awareness of it; somehow it is the fascination of the artist himself, as Malraux, before Price, suggested in the preface he wrote for the French translation of *Sanctuary* in 1932: "The deepest fascination, the artist's, draws its strength from its being both the horror and the possibility to conceive it." [9] To this fascination, Eudora Welty gives a personal coloring: "Cutting off the Medusa's head was the heroic act, perhaps, that made visible a horror in life, that was at once the horror in love, Virgie thought —the separateness" (p. 243). Perseus stands for the fascinated become fascinator, the slaying of Medusa for the lover who could grasp the full essence of his beloved only by killing her. The severed head is not only the visible sign of that permanent scandal—death; it is also the visible sign of that other scandal—the destructive power of love, any form of love (of fascination). For it is the essence of fascination, the utmost form of gaze, to become annihilated in the very accomplishment of the transgression it implies. This failed epiphany Eudora Welty calls "separateness." In "A Still Moment" Lorenzo the watcher and Audubon, seer and voyeur, slayer and lover, knew already that fascination is a knowledge and a love that contains in itself the death of all knowledge and love.

The agony of separateness is what most married characters in *The Golden Apples* experience. Whether it be an unfaithful husband ("Shower of Gold"), an unfaithful wife ("The Whole World Knows"), or an inadequate spouse ("Sir Rabbit," "Music from Spain," Mrs. Morrison in "June Recital"), they all feel the unbreachable gulf between what they

[9] Reprinted in *Sanctuaire* (Paris: Gallimard, Le Livre de Poche, 1949), p. 9.

dream or hope for and the reality that makes their lives. In "The Wanderers," Virgie Rainey's long chain of lovers shows that she too has not been able to find fulfillment in love. Just as excruciating can be the loneliness of thwarted affection, whether born of unrequited devotion—a maternal love transfer, Miss Eckhart's feelings for Virgie Rainey in "June Recital"—or the result of death, the scandalous distress of the orphaned child ("Moon Lake"), or of the hundred smaller sorrows daily experienced.

The third constituent of the myth, the mirror, points to the fascination of Perseus—his awareness of horror and its fascination for him. The place of desire, the mirror becomes the door to death. A reflection, it is the sign of the near identity of opposites: "Virgie never saw it differently, never doubted that all the opposites on earth were close together, love close to hate, living to dying; but of them all, hope and despair were the closest blood—unrecognizable one from the other sometimes, making moments double upon themselves, and in the doubling double again, amending but never taking back" (p. 234).

This endless doubling upon oneself is fascination—again. And this is true not only of "moments," but of the short stories themselves as structures. They are built on this endless reflection, which doubles and doubles again. There are two parts or two movements in each story that are based on the ambiguity between a real experience and a dreamed one, between asserted reality and hypothetical reality. (Interestingly, some of Virginia Woolf's finest stories, like those of Welty, follow this pattern.) [10] In "The Wanderers" the axis is "the feeling of the double coming-back," as Virgie Rainey experiences it (or the double departure, which is just its reverse, its reflection in the mirror). Starting from that evident dichotomy, Eudora Welty elaborates on a most sophisticated play on reflections. Two examples will illustrate the technique and stress the duality in the composition of the book itself, since it rests on two major trends, a comic one based on the celebration of the word—the art of telling—and a tragic one based on vision—the fascination of the *spectacle*.

The reflection at times functions as the proof of the authenticity of the object, as in "Shower of Gold." The narrative problem here is the "truth" of King's visit on Halloween. In the first part, Mrs. Rainey draws a portrait

[10] Very significant is Welty's review of *A Haunted House*: *"Mirrors for Reality,"* *New York Times Book Review*, 16 April 1944, p. 3. Most of what she writes about reflections and dream effects in Virginia Woolf's stories could apply to her own fiction. Besides stressing the affinity between these two writers, the review shows how much aware of her own technical research Eudora Welty was early in her career.

of King MacLain, a rogue pursuing his amorous career all over the South, and through her we hear the adoring voice of the community. In the second part, she tells at length how he was seen at the door of his house on a surprise visit to his wife, how he thought better of it when circled by his two young sons disguised for the day, and ran away once more. But these facts cannot be proved. Apparently, part two illustrates the gossips told in part one and corroborates them. However, a close study of the narration shows that it is just the reverse: the legend surrounding King MacLain is what makes the aborted visit credible—in the narrative system of the story.

With a more refined composition, based on the alternating voices of Loch Morrison and his sister Cassie, "June Recital" sends back and forth a series of reflections that contribute to the most scathing criticism of human relations in society. The overall effect is that of the play within the play, since for each witness the *spectacle* he sees constitutes the epitome of his vision—a reflected microcosm of his world. To this mirror-effect within each narrative, a more subtle one is added, which provides the structural link between the two parts. The grey dull picture of what seems the preparation for a celebration is followed by the brilliantly-colored image of the celebration itself—the recital. We hesitate over the true nature of what we see (which is the reflection? which is the object?), and a new awareness of the tragedy of human relations is born as the second mirror-effect begins to dawn on us. Until we realize we should superimpose the two scenes so as to see the complete picture, we do not fully apprehend the structure—hence the subject of "June Recital." In Loch's narrative, Miss Eckhart's lavish decoration of her studio with "maypole ribbons of newspaper and tissue paper" reads like a black and white snapshot of the June recital narrated in Cassie's part, its negative rather. The relation between the two scenes provides the key to the understanding of the story; in spite of appearances they are very much alike. Just as we see a proliferation of stage properties in part one, part two presents a proliferation of visual elements to the prejudice of musical ones. The empty stage in part one represents a distortion of the spectacle, produced for its sole end without any audience, just as the June recital deprived of its musical end is similarly distorted. The finality of both spectacles is elsewhere. For that one night in the year the ladies of Morgana cooperate with Miss Eckhart to celebrate themselves, in the end, under the pretense of honoring their daughters. Staged by a narcissistic town enamored of its own image, the brilliantly colorful recital derives its deceptive splendor from success and power. It represents the supreme illusion of the town contemplating its social achievement therein. In the other scene, stripped of its false appearances, the studio looks what it is really—an empty stage for a demented puppet. Likewise, Miss Eckhart's loneliness is made visible together with the destructive effect of her love for Virgie; she has been drained of her vital flux by the dazzled gaze she gave her idol-pupil. Thus the two scenes function like Medusa's head and its reflection in the mirror. The reflected head loses its power to fascinate because it is deprived of the deadly glamour. Vulnerability becomes apparent with the emptiness that fascination implies. The reflection is "truer" than the object, and cannot be dissociated from it. When superimposed, the two pictures give an image in relief, so to speak, suggesting the depth of the tragedy of human relations behind the brilliant surface.

The three elements of the myth of Perseus thus correspond to the major themes and techniques of the book: they are present in every story, and each element functions in the same way as it does in the myth. This structure suggests three organizing principles: all the short stories have a plot based on fascination, they are all constructed with a mirror-effect, and the theme of separateness runs throughout the volume. In other words, the narratives that constitute *The Golden Apples* are dramatizations of the functioning of the myth of Perseus—the essential theme of the book, which was discussed at the beginning of this analysis. *The Golden Apples* illustrates what Jean Ricardou called a "theorem" in his study of the critical problems of the Nouveau Roman: "Great narratives can be recognized in that the story they tell is nothing but the dramatization of their own functioning."[11]

The Golden Apples can be read at the ordinary level of dramatic action. It offers then the picture of a microcosm with its passions and frustrations, hate and prejudice, heroes and scapegoats. At a more significant level, it is concerned with the kinds of awareness various minds have of death, which it is man's fate to fear, fight and fool as much and as long as he can. As the protean figure of Death makes his insidious way into every passion, great or small, that seethes in the heart of man, there are thousands of encounters before the final destruction. Man's dignity or heroism is this endless fight against death and all forms of evil, which are forms of death. For this, he has "the pure wish to live." He has love or art: Miss Eckhart "had hung the picture on the wall for herself. She had absorbed the hero and

11 Jean Ricardou, *Problèmes du nouveau roman* (Paris: Seuil, 1967), p. 178.

the victim and then, stoutly, could sit down to the piano with all Beethoven ahead of her. With her hate, with her love, and with the small gnawing feelings that ate them, she offered Virgie her Beethoven" (p. 243).

The myth of Perseus is central to Welty's thought from "A Curtain of Green" to *The Optimist's Daughter*. Only in *The Golden Apples*, of which she said that "in a way it is closest to my heart of all my books,"[12] has she fully developed it. The mythic method, which she uses again in *Losing Battles*, though quite differently, leaves the fight endless and somewhat unresolved, except by art. "In Virgie's reach of memory a melody softly lifted, lifted of itself. Every time Perseus struck off the Medusa's head, there was the beat of time, and the melody. Endless the Medusa, and Perseus endless" (p. 243). Pursuing her own ceaseless war with time and death, the artist comes to a different compromise in a more classical novel like *The Optimist's Daughter*. The answer is no longer determined by the fixed revolutions of the heavenly bodies, but is inscribed in human time, and relies on that best of man's weapons, memory. A crucible in which man's heart and spirit are purified of desire and remorse, memory becomes the privileged place where the patterns of our lives—any lives—are written and disclosed to the artist, whose creative vision can thus dominate chaos. In *The Golden Apples* the stars are not alone in transcending time in their eternal movement; so do myths, becoming as fixed in their revolving through centuries and cultures as the constellations which bear their names. And so does the work of art, which first explores the depth of the human heart, then stands in black letters against the white page. Gaining immortality the work of art thus gives the reverse picture of the luminous stars against the black sky, as Mallarmé once wrote. "You noticed, one does not write with light on a dark background; the alphabet of the stars, alone, is marked in this way, uncompleted or interrupted; man pursues black against white."

[12] Bunting, p. 714.

ROBERT B.   *Losing Battles*

HEILMAN   and Winning the War

I

ON THE FACE of it reading the long *Losing Battles* is like taking an extended ramble through a lush, variegated natural and human landscape in which there are many paths and so many enticements that one is constantly led off in new and unforeseen directions, always fascinated, often uncertain amid apparent aimlessness, and yet constantly suspecting the unclear presence of a controlling route, however camouflaged by the rich growths, vivid scenes, and surprising roadside attractions. Or it is like traveling in a canoe or boat moved and steered only by the current of a stream that is now an all-but-passive pool allowing plenty of time to look at tropical banks and multicolored bottom, now a languid eddy that turns us about rather than pushes us forward, now a short stretch of whitewater that brings on a tumultuous dash, now a sturdy little creek with a great deal of push, but most often a meandering flow that brings the craft to a succession of little stops and visits at dozens of logs, beaver dams, islets, gravelly promontories, sandbanks, coves, and inlets. No stop may seem to have much to do with where you're going, but then you aren't sure about the where, either; once a where begins to shape up, you may see the relevance of the stops in retrospect, or perhaps decide that some of them are there just for the fun of it. Occasionally what you sense as the prevalent drift may tighten up in a millrace drive taking you to a desperate pitch over a deep waterfall wave. But Welty may somehow slip around a danger spot hastily, or settle for an anticlimactic splash in an unforeseen pond, or just let motion die away strangely. Or the voyage through *Losing Battles* may be like listening to a perpetual-motion raconteur—drawling on breathless but always commanding, too full of stories even to stop for applause or a drink, dashing as if driven from one to another, knowing what their connection is but rarely bothering to make the connection explicit, seeming less to manipulate what is told than to be charmed by it as by an independent entity that the narrator barely touches on its way to an audience; getting from one episode to another by such devices (implicit only, never overt) as "You'd never guess what happened next," "I tell you, it was just one crazy thing after another," "Oh, I forgot to tell you what happened before that," "You see, there was this little thing in the past," "And by the way, that reminds me of another story," or "Now is as good a time as any to let Billy have his say," and so on. The surface impression, in other words, is one of haste, casualness, haphazardness, movement rather than direction, scattershot unselectiveness, of rushing ahead rather than rounding out, or of stopping short rather than keeping on, of ringing in the new before the old has been wrung out and hung clearly on the line of the finished and understood, of madcap tumbleweed hop-skip-jumping rather than of steady advance on a marked public route. This impression needs to be mentioned (a) because readers are hardly likely to escape it and (b) because the storytelling surface does not truly reflect the narrative substance. In brief, *Losing Battles* is a highly ordered book, but it does not wear its order on its sleeve. Perhaps Welty did what Sterne did in the parts of *Tristram Shandy* that he had time to polish: strove for an outer air of the accidental, the interrupted, and the inconsecutive (in Sterne, a formal mimesis of psychological disorderliness in humanity; in Welty, a capturing of diversionary tendencies inevitable in a multitude of individuals even when they are seen as a group with a purpose). Perhaps she was simply the compulsive raconteur driven to transmit episode after episode, tale after tale, as they welled up in her imagination, and yet somehow mastering them with an instinctive grasp of their potential coherence. Perhaps she is basically a designer who worked out a governing pattern with great care, instituting a relationship of parts subtle enough, or letting them have enough of an air of spontaneity, to stir up a sense of the chancy, the lively but unselected, or even the wilful. Whatever comes first, this is true: Welty digs deep enough to bring in a gusher, but she has an excellent supply of caps, valves, and piping.

The numerous ebullient parts are held together by personal and thematic relationships that I will try to spell out. A more visible kind of form is provided by typographic breaks: Welty divides the book into six uncaptioned parts and establishes most of these as logical divisions by providing them with conspicuous "closers." Jack and Gloria Renfro, the young couple just getting their married life under way, end Part 1 by leaving a family reunion to go on a family mission; the mission having taken a wholly ironic turn, they end Part 2 by returning to the reunion. Parts 3 and 4 end identifiable phases of the reunion, the latter involving Jack's startling return from another mission. Part 5 ends the reunion day: departures, bedding down, and several private excursions that look ahead to the next day. Part 6 includes the events of the next morning; again Jack and Gloria occupy the closing pages, affectionate but not unanimous about plans for the future. Jack is everybody's hero, and Gloria the hopeful young wife; still they are less a full counterpoint to the older generation than they are an accent. The central business is the revelation of patterns of living (feelings, values, attitudes) that are firmly established in the older reunionists. Jack and Gloria may alter, conform to, or even fall short of the family and village patterns gradually revealed through crowding episodes.

In each part we can discover an ordering of the materials that come at us through apparently rambling, scrambling, scurrying segments of conversational action. We can do this by the rather academic exercise of outlining the contents: thus we can see how Welty, through the surging hullabaloo of reunion talk, gradually introduces and identifies characters and issues, skillfully weaves in past events that generate emotions and speculations in the present, makes random chatter—greetings, cracks, claims or putdowns, in-house allusions, brief flytings—hover about major thematic concerns, and canvasses these concerns in a surrogate, a Chekhovian one carried to ultimate limits, for the linear plot or the special situation evolving toward a terminal point. I will simply assert this congruence instead of making the longish demonstration needed to describe fully the underlying order of any of the six parts.[1]

II

The "terminal point" is arbitrary: the ending of the reunion, and the picking up of some of the pieces scattered by the windfall events of the occasion. The compacting of various lifetimes into a single day (this one of about thirty hours, from Sunday sunrise to Monday noon, with due time out for sleeping) is less of a tour de force than it was when Frank Swinnerton did

---

[1] To detect an order, of course, is not to get at some ultimate essence of the novel. One keeps on and on describing constituent elements and their relationships, and still there is much that is elusive. The critic is only too well aware of the residual "mystery" that Eudora Welty has more than once said is lost sight of by reductive criticism. One hopes to be inclusive enough not to be reductive, but even great inclusiveness cannot give one the sense of having got it all or of having got the right things.

it in *Nocturne* (1917) and Joyce in *Ulysses* (1922). The center of the reunion is Granny Vaughn's ninetieth birthday. Since her daughter and son-
in-law are dead, the chief reunionists are half a dozen middle-aged grandchildren, the five Beecham men and their sister Beulah Beecham Renfro,
plus many spouses and offspring. "Beechams' Day," to borrow a phrase
from the Joycist world, is the first Sunday in August sometime in the 1930s.
Welty gets the essential past into the picture through many flashbacks.
These are rarely arbitrary moves of her own: they are rather stories told by
reunionists who want, or have some good reason, to tell them (the old epic
tradition of the inset story that covers more time without breaking unity
of time). Welty manages these stories with great variety and verve: they
may be long or short, the speaker may be called on or seize stage or struggle
to hold it, he may repeat a twice-told tale ("Oh why does he have to go into
that again?"), he will always face interruptions (questions, objections, pure
irrelevancies, reactions to the history narrated), and at times a story comes
as a group composition. If Welty is calling on a speaker only because the
time has come to get some facts before us, she conceals the fact well; the
narrated pasts seem to flow easily out of ongoing talk into present time.

What is told, like what goes on in the present, is not always clear; we
may have to live with some fuzziness about the edge of motive, intention,
relationship and even historical or physical fact. Ultimately this may be
due to Welty's conviction that all mystery and ambiguity cannot be washed
out in the water of logical explanation; its immediate source is her basic
technique of thrusting us plumb into the life of the reunion, submerging
us in the flood of domestic doings and family feelings—partisan, predic-
tive, philosophical, fluctuating between the casual and the intense. This is
Joycean of course: the artist as distant divinity, electing an air of Olympian
independence from all the scrabble and pother and sound effects he has
plunged his readers into. He interprets nothing; readers intuit reality from
its direct impact on their senses. They have no help from a Jamesian recording consciousness. But Joyce's management of our total immersion in
actuality, his all-around-the-town odyssey, has an air of cool calculation in
the library; Welty's is more like a flashing succession of on-the-spot inter-
views, a village neighborhood odyssey dashed off by a Dickens with Mark
Twain as co-author here and there. But unlike these lively recorders of community doings and spirit—mostly comic, frequently farcical, sometimes
edging on the grotesque or the pathetic, and implicitly and in held-down
ways, on effects rooted in still deeper feelings—Welty does no emceeing,

no open steering of actors or audience; she provides no overt introductions, explanations, or transitions. She is directly present in only one way: she sets up scenes with marvelous fullness and concreteness of detail, naming with utmost ease all kinds of flowers, fruits, vegetables, weeds, trees, animals, soils, terrains, articles of clothing, household objects, dinner dishes, parts and shapes of bodies. At gifts-for-Granny time she lists and gives quick reality to sixteen presents (p. 287). Perhaps no other modern novel would yield so massive a concordance of nouns and adjectives. Yet there is nothing of the relentlessly encyclopedic; Welty never lingers, caressing a scene or a detail of it (as George Eliot does at times); she seems always in haste, sensory images pouring out as from an overturned cornucopia, yet giving life rather than making a mess. Her pictures flash by with a cinematic fluency that makes them almost elusive.

Dialogue must occupy ninety percent of over four hundred pages. It looks uncontrolled, uncentered, and often irrelevant. Yet through it we have to learn virtually everything significant—identities, moral and mental natures, the feelings and ideas that inform life in the town of Banner, old events that influence life now. In other words, far more than most novelists Welty is using the techniques of drama. A dialogue that must be plausible in itself must effect an immense exposition of past and present for a reader who has none of the information possessed by the speakers, and must produce and sustain a tension about what is going to happen in two hours or two weeks or two years. The writer of novel-as-drama has one advantage over the writer of drama-as-stage-play: he is not bedeviled by limits of time. Hence Welty can let go on anyone who wants to talk, whether to get attention, to defend or attack or correct, to yield to a compulsion, or just to let us know what we need to know (in a very effective scene Miss Lexie Renfro, kneeling or squatting, repairs damage to Gloria's skirt while telling us about what she did as companion or nurse to a key figure, Miss Julia Mortimer, the school teacher who has just died; what with interruptions, Miss Lexie goes on for fifteen pages [pp. 271–86]). Welty makes excellent use of the figure convenient to both dramatists and novelists, the newcomer who must learn what others know. This is Uncle Noah Webster's new wife Cleo, who not only comes from away but, in an endless itch of curiosity, never stops probing with questions that we too need to have answered. Yet Cleo is more than a prop, for Welty colors her questioning with something of a prosecutor's drive; Cleo comes in on a narrow line between an itch to puncture and put down, and the candor of

a nonpartisan inquisitor whose quest for the complete and probably dis-
creditable record surpasses her tact. Thus she contributes to dramatic tension; there are many little needlings between her and Beulah Beecham
Renfro, hostess to the reunion and a lively-tongued defender of Beechams.
"Well, what's he got to hide?" asks Cleo about a Beecham urged not to
"jabber," and Beulah replies, "Sister Cleo, I don't know what in the world
ever guides your tongue into asking the questions it does! ... By now you
ought to know this is a strict, law-abiding, God-fearing, close-knit family"
(pp. 343–44). But a moment's sharpness seems never to generate an hour's
antagonism.

While she keeps clashes constantly going in the foreground, Welty is
skilled in focusing on events to come and making the most of the characters' and our expectations: notably his mother's faith that Jack Renfro,
the young hero of the family, will make it home for the reunion, and at
length his striking leap into the scene. Meanwhile we have had to wait to
find out where he would make it home from (the state "pen" at Parchman), how he got there in the first place, and how he got out and traveled
home. All that done, we look ahead again: Jack's handling of a mission
—to embarrass Judge Moody, who had sentenced him to the pen, and who
is known to be in the Banner area. Meanwhile various questions needing
answers crystallize gradually from misty hints in the family talk: why
Uncle Nathan's artificial hand, why his wandering life (Beechams stay put),
why the Biblical texts he plants about the country? What is Judge Moody's
mission, once or twice mentioned quickly by the judge or his wife, in these
parts? Who are the parents of Jack's wife Gloria, an orphan who was the
local teacher before her marriage? What, above all, was the community
role of Miss Julia, the legendary retired teacher who chooses reunion day
to die? So the constant drama of questions awaiting answer joins the dominant dialogue to commit the novel to a theater way of doing things. It is
still novel, for it aspires no whit to the stringent selectiveness of drama;
instead it clings to all the extrinsic constituents of full daily life that stage-
life cuts back ruthlessly.

Losing Battles periodically reminds us of several dramas of family life
—Eliot's *Family Reunion* and Albee's *The American Dream* and *All Over*.
Though the novel, like Eliot's play, explores some unclear but serious history that has an impact on the present, it vastly expands Eliot's farcical
elements and cuts back and underplays the notes of pain and grief; and
though it in no way minimizes rifts and tensions, the novel perceives re-

union as a symbol of residual unity among country kinfolk rather than as an ironic recorder of disunity in a country family. Some resemblances to the Albee plays help set in relief the sharply different Welty mode. In *All Over* a family and various appendages await the imminent death of a father-and-husband, and they reveal themselves through their interchanges; in *Losing Battles* the death of the teacher releases a flux of commentary that is a principal means of characterizing the Beecham way of life. Otherwise all is different, notably the tone. In Albee everybody wields a hatchet of hostility or a stiletto of self-pity; aggression and self-defense or self-serving are everywhere; the scene is harsh, and the tone falls little short of disgust. Welty's people have a comparable candor, and it can be combative; but the various selfhoods are mostly held in check by a sense of the fitting, an unspoken acceptance of limited role, and even a talent for sympathy. Welty feels friendly amusement; Albee sneers bitterly. The contrast is made sharper by *The American Dream*, since major characters match: needle-tongued Grandma is paralleled by tart Granny, domineering Mommy by competently managerial Beulah Renfro, downtrodden Daddy by misadventure-and-miscalculation-prone Mr. Renfro, and "The American Dream" Young Man by Jack Renfro. One brief look at the Albee monsters, their nastiness a filtrate of the author's malice, and we see the relative fullness of Welty's people, neither whittled down to allegories of human unlovableness nor without shortcomings; limited enough, but their limitations set off by saving spurts of energy, good will, good nature, devotion, or endurance. Albee is narrow-eyed satirist, Welty broad-gauge humorist.

III

Banner people are often feckless, foolish, parochial, prejudiced, thoughtless, thickskinned, and rich in other frailties, and they can be petty, suspicious, tactless, or calculating; but we have little sense that their less glorious moments are seriously hurtful to others. Welty does not focus on the sly, the underhanded, the devious, or the malicious; and there is not a neurotic in the carloads of reunionists that come from away. Welty rarely makes us take sides between virtue and vice. I would almost bet, knowing as I do how such generalizations can ricochet against the maker, that the only truly satirical passages are brief ones near the end. At Miss Julia's funeral several people, who sound exactly like Hardy conventionalists, sneer audibly at Jack and Gloria as a sorry pair, whose failings include not being properly dressed for cemetery rites. Here is the complacent snobbery that is an old target of satire. The pressure on the reader to reject false values is stronger when the sinner is known and acts as well as talks crassly. On each of two days Jack has spent laborious hours at the task of getting Judge Moody's Buick, which had leaped to a precarious perch high above road and river, put back on the road, towed into town, and restored to running condition. It is now funeral time, a long rain keeps up, and the road to the cemetery is all mud. The judge suggests giving Jack and Gloria a ride to the cemetery. Jack demurs; all muddied up, he may soil the Buick velvet. Mrs. Moody settles the matter: "They're young. . . . They can walk" (p. 422). Here the priority of things over people, and people who have our sympathy, makes the passage strongly satirical. The episode lacks the sheer laughableness of a little earlier when, during the risky Buick-rescue process, the car door swings open, something pops out and is gobbled by wild pigs, and Mrs. Moody mourns, "My cake!" (p. 394); when a runaway truck crashes into a ditch and makes Miss Lexie cry out that it "splashed my dress" (p. 395); and when, after drastic steps get the Buick almost miraculously down on the road again, Mrs. Moody complains, "You bring it to me covered with mud!" (p. 396). Here are not the grossnesses that catch the eye of the censor, but the irrelevancies and anticlimaxes that appeal to the humorist. There are dozens of these.

The comic range is very wide: it extends from the ironic to the farcical. In a central irony Jack sets out to discomfit the judge by causing his car to go off the road; instead Judge Moody causes himself much greater trouble by driving his car off the road to avoid running down Jack's wife and baby. Welty often credits people with epigrams that we hardly expect of them, e.g., Mrs. Moody's "Your real secrets are the ones you don't know you've got" (p. 306). Numerous comic moments hinge on replies that suddenly veer away from created expectation (a traditional mode), as when Gloria reports that Miss Julia warned her against marrying into the Beecham family, and Beulah exclaims, "For mercy's sakes! Only one of the biggest families there is!" (p. 251). Miss Julia rescues Rachel Sojourner from an apparent suicide attempt; since Rachel is cold and stockingless, Miss Julia strips off her own stockings, puts them on Rachel, and rushes Rachel to a doctor. Rachel gets the stockings off again, telling the doctor, "I don't care if it kills me, I wouldn't be caught dead in Miss Julia's old yarn stockings" (p. 258). Brother Bethune, the aged parson, speaks defensively of his lack of descendants, "I ain't got a one. Now I *have* killed me a fairly large number of snakes. . . . The grand sum total is four hundred and twenty six"

(p. 213). Such incongruities in thought and values pour out from the Welty imagination. Parts of verbal games can be scattered over several pages. Jack fought Curly Stovall because Curly was "aggravating"; Jack then carried off Curly's safe, not to "rob" him but "just to aggravate him." At Jack's trial Judge Moody scorns Jack's plea that Curly was "aggravating" and finds Jack guilty of "aggravated battery."

Welty is brilliant in farce—in scenes where intentions are defeated by accidents, where coincidence and mishap crowd in to upset plans, where helter-skelter events keep up a dizzy pace, where people are prone to collisions and pratfalls but don't really get hurt, where objects themselves seem to conspire against order. She may describe an episode with the hyperbole natural to farce: "a crowd of his sons and their jumping children and their wives ... poured out of the car," and then comes a "pick-up riding on a flat tire, packed in behind with people too crowded in to wave" (p. 9)— reminiscences of old dizzy movie scenes of dozens of people in a single car. Aunt Nanny seemed to have been "harnessed into her print dress along with six or seven watermelons" (p. 10). In their "aggravated battery" brawl Jack hit Curly Stovall with a sack of cottonseed meal; it "busted" and "covered that booger from head to foot with enough fertilize to last him the rest of his life" (p. 26). Next thing, Jack ties Curly up in a coffin made for Curly and lying inconveniently on his store floor. Curly later complains that he has been "pulled on by a hundred and seventy-five pound woman [his sister]" and "talked back to by a eight-ounce schoolteacher [Gloria]" (p. 37). Jack lugs off Curly's safe like a farcical Hercules; it comes open and scatters contents all over the road; Curly never locked it because it was too hard to get open again. When it is brought into court at Jack's trial, it has a nesting bird in it.

When Judge Moody drives his car off the road to avoid hitting Gloria and her baby Lady May, Welty could play for the melodrama of near-disaster. She does nothing of the kind. Lady May got on the road when Jack slid down a bank and fell into a ditch, and then failed to get to her because he ran into Gloria and fell into the ditch again—the pratfall series of the two-reeler. A moment later Jack whispers to Gloria, "Face 'em, from now on. Your dress is tore behind" (p. 121). The car has stopped at a Chaplinesquely precarious spot on the edge of a small cliff, its motor still running. Its wheels are off the ground, for it is resting on a sign recently planted by evangelical Uncle Nathan, "Destruction Is At Hand," the balance that saves it depending on the weight of Jack's friend Aycock

Comfort, who chased the careening car with his banjo and somehow got into it when it stopped, and who now has to stay there for nearly twenty-four hours. For half of a very hot and dusty Sunday, and several hours on a rainy and very muddy Monday, efforts to deal with the car produce round after round of farce, genuine risk though there is: everybody has contradictory ideas, advice and commentary are endless, potential helpers drive away, plans go wrong, towlines break and bodies pop in various directions, tires blow out, a dozen dogs bark assistance, Jack's baby kicks him in the eye, and then he is badly stretched in a tug-of-war with the escaping Buick (it gets away over the cliff and lands on a ledge on its "nose"), Jack's father makes a mess by dynamiting a partially obstructing tree ("with all its yesterdays tangled up in it now" [p. 391]), and an unexpected secondary explosion not only tosses people and things about but brings forth Beulah's ironic observation on her husband's work: "Some folks' dynamite blows up once and gets through with it, but you don't reckon on that little from Mr. Renfro" (p. 392). In this marvelous long-continuing zany struggle it is as if fictional life in the '30s were imitating the great two-reelers of the '20s.

Yet superabundant farce—and one could go on for pages describing it —does not supplant the comedy of events that come out of differences and inconsistencies of personality, or obscure the recurrent flickering presence of noncomic materials. There is much wit, ranging, as we have seen, from jeers to epigrams. The comedy that reflects humanity, in contrast with the farce that runs roughshod over it, usually has some share even in the most boisterous physical scenes. Some matters are wholly comic—for instance, the forgiveness theme. An annual reunion feature is a preacher's discourse which traditionally combines family history, humor, and homily—a task long carried out by the late Grandpa Vaughn, evidently a Mosaic figure, and this year committed to Brother Bethune, who is, Beulah says, "a come-down after Grandpa" and of whom Granny Vaughn asks, "Who went so far as to let him through the bars?" (p. 175). The reunion alternately ignores him, interrupts him, helps him get things straight, and cheers him on as if he were the day's floorshow—a comic medley of attitudes. Various Beechams express the hope that he will officially "forgive" Jack, apparently for doing time in the pen, and discuss styles of forgiving; Jack feels that "Nobody . . . would have forgiven" him for not making it from pen to reunion. As in drama, these quick references build up to a scene in which everything then goes quite unexpectedly. Brother Bethune suddenly directs

his discourse to Judge Moody and declares, "We're going to forgive you."
The judge is nonplussed; his wife says that they can't be forgiven for coming to the reunion, since Jack invited them. Uncle Noah Webster comments wittily that "hospitality . . . ain't no guarantee you ain't going to
be forgiven when you get there," and the judge's growing annoyance cat-.
alyzes further forgivings of him—"for bringing your wife" (Aunt Nanny),
"for livin'" (Aunt Birdie), "for calling me 'old man'" (Brother Bethune).
Brother Bethune urges him to "do like the majority begs and *be* forgiven."
The comic irony of it is that the Beechams have unconsciously used "forgive" to mean "condemn" and hence have happily had it both ways. Moody
is enraged at being "forgiven" for "being a fair judge at a trial." Beulah,
politely passing cake to the judge, assails him with a lovely non sequitur,
"Don't tell me, sir, you've nothing to be forgiven for, I'm his mother."
Three good ironies follow. The first is that Jack, who was sentenced by the
judge, strongly opposes all the forgiving; now immensely grateful to the
judge for "saving" his wife and baby (by diverting the Buick), he seems to
be apologizing for the family's tactlessness in practicing a needless and
needling absolution. The second irony is that in thus seeming to draw away
from his family, Jack is actually allying himself with them more strongly,
but by a novel tactic: he springs a surprise by declaring openly that he will
not forgive the judge, because the judge's unforgivable act was depriving
the family of Jack's indispensable labors for eighteen months. The third
irony is that the judge approves Jack's nonforgiveness, and judge and erst-
while defendant shake hands on it, each cherishing his own interpretation
of the rite of concord. Beulah ends things by lamenting "this headlong
forgiving" and helpfully suggesting to Mrs. Moody that she use a spoon to
eat the "tender" coconut cake. This substantial scene (pp. 208–13) is not
only prepared for, as we have seen, but is followed up by a number of brief
variations on the forgiveness theme (pp. 321, 372, 427), the best of them
the judge's witty "Forgiving seems the besetting sin of this house" (p. 319).

Peeping through the regular crevices in the dominant farce and comedy
are diverse touches of the somber, the pathetic, the disastrous, and even
the tragic. Since she has a many-toned sense of reality, Welty is equally
spontaneous in these noncomic notes, but she never, never holds them. Her
rich sense of the wry does not diminish her sense of what goes awry, goes
wrong, wreaks injury, but she does not linger over these; whether from
stoicism or an instinct that does not crystallize as formal choice, she so
manages human troubles that the reader may escape a solid sense of the

real difficulties faced by the characters. The very energy of the tireless dialogue somehow denies the power of events over the characters, singular in apparent hopefulness or gift for survival. The Renfros say little of their poverty, of their losses during the time when Jack, in jail, could not help them; it is from the cracks of others that we learn that their farm has become almost a wasteland (drought now, against dangerous floods in the past). It is never called so overtly, but the new tin roof is a pathetic disclaimer of defeat, a chin-up welcome to Jack as he returns to serious farm problems. Miss Julia's death makes a picnic excursion for other teachers, but at the news "Gloria stood as if she had been struck in the forehead by a stone out of a slingshot" (p. 157). She had been Miss Julia's successor and special protégée, but then we learn of their troubled split over Gloria's marriage to Jack. Most touches of pathos are lightning quick. Lifted to a table top, Granny does a determined little dance routine: "She danced in their faces"—not only visibility, but a little defiance. She starts absentmindedly to walk off the table, is caught by Jack making a cinematic split-second entry, and in her "eyes gathered the helpless tears of the rescued" (p. 308).

In the past there were destructive fires as well as floods; the Beechams' parents were drowned in strange circumstances; the woman whom the Beechams take to be Gloria's mother attempted suicide and, though prevented, died of the aftereffects; Gloria's years at an orphanage and teacher's college were bleak ones; the most admired of the Beecham boys, Sam Dale, died young; much neighborhood damage, as well as losses for the Renfros, was due to a piratical transient named Dearman (possibly Gloria's father). We see Uncle Nathan's artificial hand, then the stump of his arm, and we assume a self-dismemberment as the center of a lifelong penance (wandering endlessly and putting up religious signs). Suddenly he blurts out the reason: "I killed Mr. Dearman with a stone to his head, and let 'em hang a sawmill nigger for it" (p. 344). The death of Miss Julia on reunion day brings forth many reminiscences of her zealous pedagogical career and quotations from her. The key one is "All my life I've fought a hard war with ignorance. Except in those cases that you can count off on your fingers, I lost every battle" (p. 298)—the source of Welty's title. Her dying words were, "What was the trip for?" (p. 241). The implicit despair, quick hints suggest, also has a place in Judge Moody's inner reflections on her career and last months; dying, she had to make heroic efforts to mail letters through a strange barricade by Miss Lexie Renfro, a nurse-companion who had mysteriously become a kind of jailer. The funeral of Miss Julia is the penultimate episode; it is followed only by a short tender scene between Jack and Gloria.

IV

Yet all such actions and effects are contained within the comic framework: the pattern is survival within a world in which one accepts, makes do with, a prevailing disparateness where much is out of whack with logic or desire. The diversity of narrative materials, however, does not imply a diversity of style. Not that a uniformity of manner disregards heterogeneity of matter: "each face as grief-stricken as the other" and "Ella Fay Renfro in front tossing a sweat-fraught pitcher's glove," which are only two lines apart (p. 288), use different vocabularies, and even so few words reveal difference in tone. But both are brief absolute phrases; they suggest, without proving anything, that Welty likes certain basic syntactic arrangements. Ordinarily she does not write very long sentences or use complex structures; she coordinates a good deal; she has almost none of the involutions (such as parentheses within parentheses) of Faulkner, and she does not draw on different traditions of style as much as K. A. Porter does. To say this is to identify a difference, in no way to assert a shortcoming. Welty does not make much use of the logical, analytical, judicial manner (she uses very few abstract nouns) and the comedy of manners style (wit framed in syntactic formalities) ideally represented in Jane Austen and at times equally available to Charlotte Bronte (who thought Austen trivial) and George Eliot—Bronte with her unique emotional intensity of vocabulary and rhythm, and Eliot with her dual at-home-ness in a concrete natural world and a reflective or philosophical one. Porter likewise can combine sensory concreteness with an Austen wit and a sort of combed-out, almost Jamesian thoughtful hovering. Welty has an enormous idiom of homely actuality, domestic and rural; she is still more earthy than George Eliot, handicapped by neither the Victorian reticences (Eliot could not have an Aunt Nanny say to a spelling-bee victor, "You got it spelled but wet your britches" [p. 289]), nor by the chic vulgarities now often mistaken by the naive for proofs of vitality, liberty, honesty, etc. A varied and rampaging actuality of animals, nature (weather, earth, growing things), and even objects is what her bounding style throws us into; though the resulting atmosphere is occasionally sharpened by witty observations, on the whole it is rather suffused by humor, a tireless sense of incongruities, human fallibility, the grotesque, and the jokes of circumstance, even when disaster may be dimly underfoot or just around the corner.

Welty's language falls into two not wholly distinguishable categories— her own words when she acts as scene-shifter, and the speech of her characters. The vast extents of dialogue are never flat; they rush on colloquially like the freshets of spring, splashing with expletives, exclamations, loose connections, pronouns without antecedents, verbs without subjects, and now and then a local vocabulary. Syntax can be enormously compact. Jack: "Here's Papa something to open" (p. 31), and, of the new roof, "I could see it a mile coming" (p. 73). Granny: "I'm in a hurry for him back" (p. 51). Lexie: "I listened hard to be asked for and I wasn't" (p. 337). Uncle Noah Webster of the jail-keeper: "Drunk and two pistols. Makes his wife answer the phone" (p. 50). Verbal or prepositional phrases may hold off stubbornly or hang on loosely. Willy Trimble: "Told him better to stay put with who he's with" (p. 154). Beulah: "Cleo, what in the name of goodness did you think we ever started this in order to tell?" (p. 39) and "Vaughn's got the teacher to tell he's misput the bus" (p. 373). Miss Lexie, of Miss Julia's retirement: "So, where she had left to go, when they put her to pasture, was across the river" (p. 296). The colloquial may substitute for an expected solemnity, as in two comments on Miss Julia's coming funeral. Uncle Homer to Brother Bethune: "And you can have your whack at her. I think you can look for a good crowd" (p. 339), and Brother Bethune, "I'm just good enough to get her into the ground" (p. 351). Scores of such locutions, unhackneyed and unpretentious, make for wonderfully lively speech.

Willy Trimble, who found Miss Julia's body, likes his phrase for her demise and uses it twice: "Down fell she. End of *her*" (pp. 162, 230). This is clipped and unsolemn, but instead of tumbling out, it is patterned. Likewise Beulah can put words into more of a pattern than we expect in colloquial style: "Well, you have to trust people of the giving-stripe to give you the thing you want and not something they'd be just as happy to get rid of" (p. 243). Frequently speakers use phrases that have a slightly more formal (or even bookish or archaic) flavor than the context suggests. Some instances: Miss Lexie, "I at present call Alliance my home" (p. 18); Uncle Noah Webster, "Cleo, I wish it had been your privilege to be with us our day in court" (p. 51); Jack, referring to the late Grandpa Vaughn, "I miss his frowning presence just as I get myself ready to perform something" (p. 102); Jack to his father, "What brought you forth?" (p. 138); uncouth Curly Stovall, "I'll come back and see what story the night has told" (p. 152); Mr. Renfro, a "thing surpassing strange" (p. 294); Uncle Nathan, "I must needs," followed first by "be on my way" and then by "not stop to take comfort" (p. 375); and Jack again, "Mr. Comfort elected to put in his appearance" (p. 418). Some repetitions go beyond the casual: Beulah, "She run-run-run down the hill . . . followed behind 'em trot-a-trot, trot-a-trot, galloping, galloping" (p. 217), and Miss Lexie or Miss Julia, "pencil racing, racing, racing" (p. 283). Beulah can combine singular precision and balance: "I'm ashamed *of* her and *for* her" (p. 296). Often speakers use so organized a locution as the series, from Jack's quick summary for his jailer—"I got my daddy's hay to get in the barn, his syrup to grind, his hog to kill, his cotton to pick and the rest of it" (pp. 44–45)—to Beulah's remarkably shaped "But the truth is you don't know, nor I don't, nor anybody else within the reach of my voice, because that ring—it's our own dead mother's, Granny's one child's wedding ring, that was keeping safe in her Bible—it's gone, the same as if we never had it" (p. 40). Beulah uses such series in describing Gloria (p. 69) and her late brother Sam Dale (p. 221), Jack in picturing the beleaguered Buick ("Singing along, good as gold, fighting along against the laws of gravity, and just daring you to come near her" [p. 150]), Gloria of the normal school, "Not enough of anything to go round, not enough room, not enough teachers, not enough money, not enough beds, not electric light bulbs, not enough books," setting off the catalog with a quick irony, "It wasn't too different from the orphanage" (p. 245). Mostly the series provide compact and speedy summaries, as in Vaughn's list of the bonds holding together the parts of the tow-train at the end, "Trace chains, well rope, Moody towline, fence wire, and Elvie's swing" (p. 399), but a series can produce a pounding intensity à la Bronte, as in Miss Julia's last letter: "Something walls me in, crowds me around, outwits me, dims my eyesight, loses the pencil I had in my hand. I don't trust this, I have my suspicions of it, I don't know what it is I've come to. I don't know any longer" (p. 299).

Welty can have characters speak in antithetical form, as in Judge Moody's "I'm not asking for a Good Samaritan, I'm asking for a man with some know-how" (p. 125); Gloria's double antithesis that has almost an Austen ring, "Jack, I don't know which is worse. . . . What you thought you were going to do, or what you're ending up doing. For the sake of the reunion you were willing to run Judge Moody in the ditch. Now for his sake you are just as willing to break your neck" (p. 126); and Mrs. Moody's exclamation over their fate, "To be saved from falling to the bottom of nowhere by getting blown sky-high with a stick of dynamite!" (p. 140). Others can generalize with the pith of the epigram—Beulah's "You can die from anything if you try good and hard" (p. 279), and Aunt Beck's "Feelings don't get old! . . . We do, but they don't. They go on" (p. 346). And Miss Lexie can annotate an epigram with a series: "But they die. . . . The ones who think highly of you. Or they change, or leave you behind, get married, flit, go crazy—" (p. 272), another quick touch of the occasional pathos. Beulah can manage a paradox: when a night-blooming cereus produces, though "not a drop of precious water" was ever diverted to it, she comments, "I reckon it must have thrived on going famished" (p. 349).

Welty has been praised for her "listening," for her "ear." No need to reaffirm that, or dispute it. Yet the passages that I have just been quoting, with their air of the formal or the formed, have a tone or orderedness that is created by the rhetoric of a self-conscious controlling mind rather than that of lay talkers letting fly with native woodnotes wild. To say that Welty has an ear, then, is not the same thing as to say that she is a human tape recorder whose authenticity in dialogue would be confirmed by a linguistic survey of the region where her characters live. We have rather to say that she composes dialogue which has an impressive air of authenticity. Now it may be that certain locutions and that even certain parallelisms and antitheses do come out of a heard speech, but I suspect that Welty is hearing—what? a probability rather than a going practice of speech. That is, given the feelings they have and a rhetorical impulse (rather than a contentment with an unplanned dribble of words about the things to be expressed), the speakers might speak as she makes them do. The special orderings of words symbolize an element—a mood, an ambition, perhaps even a parodic sense—not lacking or unimaginable in these characters. In making such a surmise I am seeking an approach to the authenticity, as I have called it, of unexpected elements in colloquial style.

A writer with a good ear for regional or dialectal speech has of course other sources of style. Hardy can suddenly shift from a fluid Wessex idiom to a heavy-weather cumbersomeness and even the pedantries of the autodidact. Welty, however, has not a trace of the academic or the inadvertently pretentious. She does not philosophize, as Hardy does; as I have already said, she is rarely analytical or interpretative. Hence she has little need for the kind of logical language used by virtually all nineteenth-century novelists, who were constantly doing formal commentary. In her nondialogue passages she rarely shapes sentences up by balance, symmetry, counterpoise, and so on. She characteristically uses a series not to control the materials but to hurry over them unsentimentally, as Meredith often did. Jack pursues Gloria, she "rounding the bank its whole way around, swiftly past the piecrust edge, streaking by the peephole, clicking across the limestone, bounding over the hummocks, taking the hollow places skip by skip without a miss, threading serpentine through the plum bushes, softly around the baby, and back to the tree, where he reached with both hands and had her" (p. 111).

Choice and ordering of words both serve an anti-sentimental effect. Granny "put kisses on top of their heads like a quick way to count them" (p. 10); Jack "bounced kisses . . . on cheeks and . . . chin" (p. 228); Uncle Noah Webster "kissed [Beulah] with such a bang that she nearly dropped" his present (p. 12). There are unexpected combinations: the boy's "stubborn voice still soft as a girl's" (p. 8); the moon "going down on flushed cheek" (p. 3); the honey's "clover smell as strong as hot pepper" (p. 11); a "stinging veil of long-dead grass . . . hid cowpats dry as gunpowder" (p. 98); Brother Bethune's fingers "rainbow-colored with tobacco stain" (p. 106); and the busload of funeral-bound schoolteachers "rainbow dressed" (p. 157); and Gloria's phrasing of her devotion to Jack: "I love him worse than any boy I'd ever seen" (p. 320). Visual images abound, fresh in themselves or in combination. A single abstract word adds a note of mystery to an early-morning scene: "Mists, voids, patches of wood and naked clay, flickered like live ashes, pink and blue" (p. 4). Several strong-action verbs and an engineering simile picture the hairdos of Renfro females: they "raked their hair straight back, cleaved it down the middle, pulled it skintight into plaits. Miss Beulah ran hers straight as a railroad track around her head" (p. 7). A special eye appears in many visual images. Once there is a "wall of copper-colored dust" (p. 8); later "bales of dust tumbled behind" a truck (p. 153). Welty distinguishes "solid" mud like "the balled roots of a tree out of the ground" from a "thinner, fresher mud like gingerbread batter" (p. 395). She can do the quick snapshot—"She prisses to meet him" (p. 30)—or the more painstaking camera study, as of the child's eyes "open nearly to squares, almost shadowless, the blue so clear that bright points like cloverheads could be seen in them deep down" (p. 47), or make what sounds commonplace very suggestive, as in hills "near but of faint substance against the August sky" (p. 99). Some effective verbs:

"The baby . . . peep-eyed at Judge Moody with the puff of her sleeve" (p. 141); the wagon "tunnelled into the shade" (p. 229); the "cutting smell of coal oil" (p. 347). Auditory images can be very original: "the air shook with birdsong" (pp. 46–7); the mockingbird was "singing the two sides of a fight" (p. 22); a man's "thready voice" (p. 22). The numerousness of "loud" words for speaking—"screamed," "shouted," "shrieked"—gives point to the ironic "again quiet threatened" (p. 340). A subtle and often beguiling use of the auditory appears in synesthetic metaphors, which more than once define the seen by the heard, as in "A long thin cloud crossed [the moon] slowly, drawing itself out like a name being called" (p. 3); dresses "rattling clean" (p. 8); a quilt looking "rubbed over every inch with soft-colored chalks that repeated themselves, more softly than the voices sounding off on the porch" (p. 46); a burning caterpillar web made "an oval cottony glow, like utterly soft sound" (p. 348). Once Welty interprets the olfactory by the tactile—"a smell, more of warmth than wet" (p. 3)— and a sound by a striking use of the visual: a "female voice, superfine, carrying, but thin as a moonbeam" (p. 359). Welty then goes on into a rare lyric description of the night as perceived by twelve-year-old Vaughn Renfro, a passage that might have a place in *A Midsummer Night's Dream*. In this, she has a flux of images for the moonlight: it had "the thickness of china" (p. 362); the world "had been dosed with moonlight, it might have been poured from a bottle" (p. 363); Vaughn "waded through the moonlight"; the flowers "looked like big clods of the moonlight freshly turned up from this night" (p. 366). Then, in contrast with this viscous, palpable light: "Lightning branched and ran over the world with an insect lightness" (p. 367). She can get the same kind of speed in the one long sentence in the novel (about 175 words) by a quick succession of relatively short syntactic units joined by ten *and*'s (pp. 407–8).

Welty has another stylistic device which amplifies the sense of vibrant life: she uses verbs that imply will, intention, and feelings in animals, plants, and even inanimate objects. The dogs "tried to bark [the teetering car] on over as fast as possible" (p. 120), one dog "barked the truck off the road in spite of a dozen hounds" (pp. 381–82), and dogs along the road were "barking everything on past" (p. 403). Stovall's pair of oxen would be a dubious rescue team since they are, Mr. Renfro alleges, "as set on mischief as they can be . . . as you'll know if you can read the glints in their eyes" (p. 140). Plant life can be libertine or cooperative. The cactus "grew down in long reaches as if trying to clamber out of the tub," and Beulah is sure "it's making up its mind to bloom tonight" (p. 18); when it does, Aunt Birdie claims, "We scared it into blooming" (p. 349). The Renfro-dynamited tree exposes a mass of roots, "bringing along their bed of clay, as if a piece of Boone County had decided to get up on its side"; Jack says it's "clinging. . . . Waiting to see what's the next thing to come along," and Welty adds a brilliantly imaginative note, "Nothing but memory seemed ever to have propped the tree" (p. 378); when it finally falls over the edge, Gloria interprets, "Mrs. Moody scared it down" (p. 393). A cyclone animated many objects: "our stove, waltzing around with our lunch pails, and the map flapping its wings and flying away, and our coats was galloping over our heads with Miss Julia's cape trying to catch 'em. And the wind shrieking like a bunch of rivals at us children!" (p. 237). The wind ruined the Methodist church but spared the close-by Baptist church; Mr. Renfro concludes, "I'll tell you something as contrary as people are. Cyclones" (p. 238). When a tire on the stranded Buick blows, Jack has a recipe for saving the others: "let the air out of the others before they start copying" (p. 142). Jack is sure that the car is "Just breaking its heart to go over" (p. 148); Beulah says that someone is "going to have to coax that car *down*" (p. 199), and Gloria's analysis of the situation is, "I scared it up. . . . I only wish it was in my power this morning to scare it down again" (with that elegant moving forward of "this morning" from the final spot where it would normally clomp down: one of these occasional modifications of ordinary run-on speech by a special control over some part, p. 377).

In trying to describe Welty's style—with its speed, bounce, freshness, and frequent unexpectedness, and with its creation of a sense of movement and life in all the elements of the world—I have saved last place for her most frequent rhetorical device: her comparisons. She uses "like," "as," "as if," "as though," and "as-adjective-as" almost 700 times (a casual count induced by my own curiosity and claiming only approximate accuracy); of these, almost 400 are similes with "like." Welty instinctively— perhaps obsessively, provided the word is not used pejoratively—presents people and things by means of resemblances. She may portray one element more sharply, bring quite different things together into one existence, or heighten attention by surprise or shock. She wars against clichés and the hackneyed; she makes familiar life take on newness from striking or even thrilling comparisons. To show the range, here are three different sensory effects on succeeding pages: visual—"her vaccination scar shone at them like a tricky little mirror" (p. 13); olfactory—"white organdy, smelling like hot bread from the near-scorch of her perfect ironing" (p. 14); auditory—"four yards of organdy that with scratching sounds, like frolicking mice, covered all three steps" (p. 15). She can make an old taste new—"fall plums . . . whose sucked skins tasted like pennies" (p. 101)—and give unusual reality to an embrace by means of a surprising tactile effect: "Their hearts shook them, like two people pounding at the same time on both sides of a very thin door" (p. 99). A machine may be pictured through the animal—"The truck sprang up like some whole flock of chickens alarmed to the pitch of lunacy" (p. 392); the animal through the human—hounds "loudly sniffing, like ladies being unjustly accused" (p. 142); and nature through the human—"whirly-winds of dust marched, like scatterbrained people" (p. 21).

Visual surprises are constant: "The distant point of the ridge, like the tongue of a calf, put its red lick on the sky" (pp. 3–4); "trees . . . lit up, like roosters astrut with golden tails" (p. 4); "butterflies . . . whirling around each other as though lifted through the air by an invisible eggbeater" (p. 30); "hair . . . red as a cat's ear against the sun" (p. 47); dust "climbed . . . in clouds like boxcars" (p. 105), "went up like a big revival tent with the flaps popping" (p. 153); "There stood the moon, like somebody at the door" (p. 286); "The moon, like an eye turned up in a trance, filmed over" (p. 367); a part of the truck "motor . . . glistening like a chocolate cake" (p. 402); a "horse ran lightly as a blown thistledown" (p. 434). Auditory images have the same novelty. Watermelons, "spanked" by Mr. Renfro, "resounded like horses ready to go" (p. 63); the tin roof made a "sound like all the family spoons set to jingling in their glass" (p. 71); the "song of the locusts" was "a long sound like a stream of dry seed being poured into an empty bucket" (p. 271). Welty can impute a palpable body to sound—"a sound . . . thin as that of a veil being parted" (p. 118); a mockingbird "threw down two or three hard notes on him like a blacksmith driving in nails" (p. 119); to light—the "substance fine as dust that began to sift down . . . was moonlight" (p. 311); "lights hard as pickaxe blows drove down from every ceiling" (p. 312); as Jack and Gloria came into a shady spot, "The final glare dropped from them like a set of clothes" (p. 99); to smell—"The smell of the cloth flooded over them, like a bottle of school ink spilled" (p. 78); to atmosphere—a "shaft of heat, solid as a hickory stick" (p. 4). Welty can be ironic—insect bites make the baby look "like she's been embroidered in French knots"

(p. 358)—or playful and fantastic: a cake of ice is "Dense with ammonia, like fifty cents' worth of the moon" (p. 184).

The similes that increase the liveliness of an already pulsating and bounding prose by declaring or hinting the likeness of unlikes (numerous metaphors do this too) may also hint at thematic elements which are not much articulated openly. " 'I bet you Banner School had a library as long as your arm,' cried Aunt Birdie as though she saw a snake" (p. 274). The "as though" clause tells us something about the local state of mind that makes the scene a trying one for teachers. The high heels of Gloria "tilted her nearly to tiptoe, like a bird ready to fly" (p. 19); later we learn that Gloria would take Jack and fly away if she could. But we already have got, and continue to get, figurative hints about such aspirations: "flickered the yellow butterflies of August like dreams" (p. 20). The same image and idea soon surface again: "Out there with her [Gloria] flew the yellow butterflies of August—as wild and bright as people's notions and dreams, but filled with a dream of their own; in one bright body, as though against a headwind, they were flying toward the east" (p. 39). Again, "The old man came . . . climbing the path like a rickety ladder of his dreams" (pp. 103–4). If Welty does not openly interpret man's fate, such figures give a furtive imaginative clue to her sense of how things go.

The encyclopedic quotation in this section is risky. I can only protest that I have been highly selective, so much so as constantly to feel that I am not adequately communicating Welty's rich campaigns that win stylistic wars. But quoting and quoting and quoting, be it too much viewed one way or too little viewed another, can alone give a sense of a literary reality. The other alternative is the critic's abstract words of identification and praise, words which cannot absent themselves for a long while but which at their best remain a large distance from the objects they strive to account for.

V

Welty's natural tendency to juxtapose, and often unite, diverse matters— many local stories of past and present, farcical and disastrous events, dramatic dialogue and novelistic description of scene and tone, and above all the sharply contrasting materials brought together in the comparisons that gush forth inexhaustibly—appears more in her themes than in her characters. There is a very large cast of characters, too many to distinguish fully: we tend to be more aware of their common elements as members of a community than of their individualizing traits of personality. They all adhere to the same basic ideas, customs, rites; they have the same general emotional contours. The four married Beecham brothers and their wives can hardly be separated without special effort. Yet no characters are ciphers; virtually all of them have great general vitality; the Dickensian humor that I mentioned earlier appears in the characterization. We see types, key motives, psychological colorations providing the felt life of reunionists and others. Granny is frail, forgetful, and free to mow down anybody at any time. Mr. Renfro is the born loser—his mishaps with the dynamite to which he is addicted symbolize the way things go with him—who still manages a singular equanimity. His wife Beulah, the reunion hostess, is an energetic manager, immensely talkative, sharp on occasions, ironic, an immense admirer of her son Jack, but able to say of him, since he wrote no letters during his eighteen months in the pen, that he "never did unduly care for pencil and paper" (p. 16) and to "hope" that his Grandpa's death will "help him grow up a little" (p. 69). Aunt Beck is regularly identified as "gentle," Aunt Nanny as ballooning and hearty. Aunt Cleo is blunt and disparaging: of the home towns of reunionists, "Never heard of any of it" (p. 18); of Gloria's wedding ring, "What'd you have to do? Steal it?" (p. 48); of Jack's having a truck, "You-all [the Renfros] don't look like you was ever that well-fixed" (p. 67). Vaughn Renfro, aged twelve, is a bit jealous of the heroic stature that all attribute to Jack, and can show considerable competence in the tasks he takes on. Gloria, the teacher who married into the Beechams, passionately longs not to be a Beecham; in marrying Jack, she chose "feeling" over a teaching career and over Miss Julia's opposition; she is aloof but not rude, and can be strong at key moments. Hero Jack is strong, lively, helpful, fond of the hill country, devoted to the family, tender and affectionate to his wife and daughter; he takes charge of the Buick rescue but is not very effective except for one astonishing strong-man feat; normally considerate, he surpasses himself in thinking of his imprisonment as a kind of penance for the murder committed by Uncle Nathan: "maybe it's evened up, and now the poor old man can rest" (p. 431). Judge Moody and his wife have tasted a thin slice of a larger world, and their occasional ironic remarks have a shade more of self-consciousness and knowingness; the judge goes beyond the others in a mildly sad reflectiveness upon the human state as reflected in Miss Julia's career and demise. Mrs. Moody fluctuates between a narrow-gauge ordinariness and occasional sharp insight, as when she says of Miss Julia, "A tyrant, if there ever was one. Oh, for others' own good, of course!" (p. 325).

But even with certain identifying marks that help us keep Jack and Jill, or Tom and Dick, apart, the individual psyche is not quite the business of the novel; individuals may have idiosyncrasies, but basically they participate in the group consciousness—the style, the attitudes, the mores, the traditions of their time and place. The men and women enact parts in the myth that orders their lives. We are not centrally held by the problem of how individual experiences are going to turn out; for the most part we know, or at least are allowed to think we do. There are no demanding plot lines to make us focus on the development of relationships or the resolution of conflicts. But in the medley of passing actions and endless talk that embrace an annual ritual, a social day's trivialities and serious moments, and a few hours' recollections of past crises that helped shape present life—in these there is a kind of plot of meanings that, though we may be incompletely conscious of it, is what holds us. These people's assumptions and values appear, sometimes explicitly but often only implicitly, in thematic strands woven into a quite variegated texture.

Of the themes that operate through gossip, jest, remembered events, and domestic and roadside small movements, the chief one is that of community. To take a fairly obvious phase of this first: Banner is a "Christian community." No one is antichurch, church talk is frequent, a reunion needs a preacher-orator, and nobody works on the Sabbath, especially if work means helpfulness. But what Welty finds underneath this is a kind of secular ecclesiasticism: denominational allusions make us picture the rivalry of clubs or lodges. The Methodist and Baptist churches are across the street from each other, and it is doubtless equally symbolic when they are brought closer together by a cyclone which "picked the Methodist Church all up in one piece and carried it through the air and set it down right next to the Baptist Church!" (p. 238). When Brother Bethune rambles on in his reunion discourse, Aunt Beck demands, "Can't you make that church rivalry sound a little stronger?" (p. 193). Mrs. Moody is sure that Curly Stovall, who has a phone in his store, can be got to open up even on the Sabbath; she argues, "I'm sure he's no more than a Baptist" (p. 128). On the other hand, when Grandpa Vaughn, a "real, real Baptist," went to a Methodist revival and unexpectedly found "infant Baptism" going on, he gave unequaled "heartfelt groans" (p. 182). Rachel Sojourner, Gloria's presumptive mother, may have got into trouble, it is proposed, when she "took to going Sunday-riding with call-him-a-Methodist." Aunt Beck annotates, "Well, you know how Baptists stick together. . . . They like to look far afield to find any sort of transgressor" (p. 265). The style of both Baptists and Methodists leads Mrs. Moody to declare, with the candor that nearly all practice, "I'm neither one, and gladder of it every minute" (p. 406). When a churchful of Methodists, homeward bound after service, indifferently drive by the stranded Buick, Mrs. Moody comments, "I'd just like to see a bunch of Presbyterians try to get by me that fast!" (p. 134). She is a Presbyterian, and she wishes that the graveside service for Miss Julia were in charge of a "down-to-earth Presbyterian"[2] instead of a Catholic priest, once a student of Miss Julia's who, observers declare, "Worshipped himself, didn't he?" (p. 430). Several years before, Uncle Noah Webster had identified Judge Moody as a Presbyterian because "The whole way through that trial, his mouth was one straight line" (p. 61). Aunt Beck approaches closest to tolerance of Presbyterians. Miss Julia, she says, "was a Presbyterian, and no hiding that. But was she deep-dyed? . . . There's a whole lot of different grades of 'em, some of 'em aren't too far off from Baptists" (p. 277). "Deep-dyed" beautifully conveys the sense of an alien other which, however, may not descend as far into gross error as it might.

Though ecclesiastical affiliation is an important bond, the Bible behind the churches enters the story in only a few casual allusions.[3] (There are, I think, no allusions to classical myth.) Of these, three are used to illustrate Brother Bethune's fuzziness: he calls Jack, just home from prison, "The Prodigal Son" (pp. 105, 107); he calls the reunion dinner "Belshazzar's Feast," remembering only belatedly to add, "without no Handwriting on the Wall to mar it" (p. 177); and he alludes to Granny Vaughn and her late husband as "David and Jonathan" (p. 184). One Biblical allusion, rather funny at the moment of utterance, may have some value as a pointer. When Jack resolves to use main strength to bounce the Buick off its nose into a more functional position, his mother Beulah "cried frantically," i.e., with ebullient pride, "Now watch! Reminds me of Samson exactly! . . . Only watch my boy show the judgment Samson's lacking, and move out of the way when it starts coming!" (p. 394). Jack does—double

---

[2] Despite all their setbacks and her husband's ironic attitude, Mrs. Moody has a persisting faith in a Providence attentive to their needs (pp. 142, 145, 149, 151, 165, 207).

[3] To Lucifer (p. 81), the Crack of Doom (p. 129), the book of Romans (p. 183), the Flood (p. 250), Job (p. 404), the parting of the Red Sea (p. 406), Solomon (p. 432). There are a number of references to the family Bible, mainly as the container of the family record of births, marriages, etc.

success. We recall this passage in the final scene when Jack and Gloria look at all the problems that still do not cancel hope. Jack says, "And I've got my strength" (p. 434) and again, "But I still got my strength" (p. 435). Gloria is no Delilah to his Samson; indeed, rather than enslave him to another people, she would save him from what she takes to be bondage to his own.

If churches provide some of the ritual forms of local life, place and family appear to be more fundamental sources of community. All the Vaughns and Beechams are, or once were, Bannerites; Aunt Cleo's rude inquisitiveness seems to be that of an alien; and the condescension of the Moodys from Ludlow is less a valid judgment than outsiders' instinct for shortcomings. Jack's love for this hill country, droughtstricken though it now is, is the aesthetic affirmation of local loyalty. What an unsympathetic outsider might call provincialism also comes through as a unifying sense of place. Yet this is several times managed humorously rather than solemnly. When a "boy cousin" thinks that Jack, not yet arrived, may be in Arkansas, Beulah exclaims, "Arkansas would be the crowning blow! . . . No, my boy may be in Parchman, but he still hasn't been dragged across the state line" (p. 70). The sentiment arises even more emphatically when all learn that Jack and Gloria may be first cousins, who according to a recent Mississippi law may not marry, and when Judge Moody suggests that they could avoid legal trouble by heading out to Alabama, "not over a few dozen miles" away. " 'Alabama!' cried Jack, a chorus of horrified cries behind him. 'Cross the state line? That's what Uncle Nathan's done! . . . leave all we hold dear and all that holds us dear? . . . Why, it would put an end to the reunion' " (p. 321).

The reunion is the preeminent symbol of family feeling. In fact, to lack the symbol is to lack right feeling, the substance that earns respect. Uncle Curtis finishes off the Comfort family: "The Comforts don't know what the word reunion means" (p. 60). The Beechams won family honor because Jack's trial "drew" large crowds from all the villages that Beechams live in. Uncle Curtis provides consolation for the family's temporary loss of Jack to Parchman: of his nine sons, he says, "maybe not a one of 'em had to go to Parchman, but they left home just the same. Married. . . . All nine! And they're never coming home" (pp. 66–67). Beulah sums up the Beechams as a "strict, law-abiding, God-fearing, close-knit family, and everybody in it has always struggled the best he knew how and we've all just tried to last as long as we can by sticking together" (p. 344). The day ends with "the joining-of-hands" as they form a circle, sing "Blest Be the Tie," and hear Brother Bethune's benediction (pp. 348–49). The reunion even provides a metaphor for the feelings of Vaughn Renfro on a moonlight mission: "the world around him was still one huge, soul-defying reunion" (p. 363).

Behind the esprit de corps, which of course does not eliminate sarcasms and clashes, lie certain patterns of thought and feeling which govern family style and actions. Before Jack arrives on stage, all the talk about him builds him up as a heroic figure—a man of charisma and with the talents of the culture hero: he can right wrongs and solve problems such as those of the droughtridden farm. When he crashes in, there are epic signs and portents—dogs barking, people screaming, the new roof "seemed to quiver," "the floor drummed and swayed, a pan dropped from its nail in the kitchen wall" (p. 71): half great hurrah and half parody. With little delay a new large task is imposed on the hero. In thumbing his way back from Parchman, he had got one ride by clinging to the spare tire on the rear of a car. When the car went into a ditch, Jack was there to play Hercules as Good Samaritan: "Put shoulder to wheel and upped him out" (p. 79). Now he learns that the driver was the very Judge Moody who had sentenced him to jail, and everyone censures Jack for rescuing an enemy (pp. 81ff.); the consensus is that he must retaliate. As Aunt Birdie puts it, "Now you can make a monkey out of him. . . . That's all the reunion is asking of you" (p. 86). Family feeling develops the spirit of the feud; it gets to Jack, and all the men (with dogs) happily prepare to set off on an anti-Moody skirmish without any clear plans. Jack insists on his "family duty . . . to get Judge Moody tucked away in a ditch like he was in" (p. 103) and "announce myself to him" (p. 117). But the feudist spirit of getting even is not unanimous; Beulah sees only trouble in the plan, Gloria votes her "common sense" (p. 112) against it (we remember the women in *Coriolanus*), Aunt Beck is "always in danger of getting sorry for the other side" (p. 293), and Jack's father a little later takes "a shine" to the judge (p. 359). What finally aborts the feudist foray, however, is wonderfully ironic, as we have seen: not a change of heart, but a combination of farce and melodrama in which the judge is a victim, not of a Beecham plot, but of his own humanity, running his car not down into a ditch but up on to an impossible perch. Jack promptly turns retaliation into gratitude because the judge "saved my wife and baby" (p. 198), and shifts his role from wrecker to rescuer of the car.

The theme of the feud is thus metamorphosed into two other themes. The first is the most amply developed of the Biblical materials—the story of the Good Samaritan. There are several roadside scenes in which helpfulness is possible, and Welty's pictures of human responses are always partly ironic. Hitching rides home from jail, Jack was helped by several Good Samaritans but wearied of the pious discourses to which they treated him. Then he hopped onto the rear of the Moody Buick, reporting that "Judge Moody was one and didn't know it" (p. 196). The judge's unconsciousness of role is contrasted with Jack's great consciousness of his; referring to his various roadside efforts, he quite likes to call himself a "Good Samaritan" (pp. 125, 149, 163). He in turn is contrasted with other passersby who are indifferent, unhelpful, or profit-seeking, and then his good will with his overall competence, so that the judge can wish for expertise instead of Good Samaritanism (p. 125). Thus Welty provides several perspectives on the myth.

While the ethic of the feud is reversed in the Good Samaritan theme, it is continued in another theme implicitly present—that of chivalry: in both, life focusses on recurrent combat. Welty introduces substantial, if subtle, suggestions of the chivalric, this in a village scene where subsistence problems are onerous: another mark of her originality. The relations between the Beechams and Curly Stovall are basically feudist, clearly. But then when Curly and Jack meet, they fall into each other's arms, pound happily on each other, and trade amiable insults; Jack calls Curly "skunk" (p. 146), "rascal," and "greedy hog" (p. 148)—all this in the tradition of frontier humor. But they have been opponents in a way that keeps reminding us of tournament competition; the initiating action of the novel was a duel of theirs in the past, and near the end there is another. In each of these the take-off point is a little interchange between Jack's sister Ella Fay, sixteen, and Curly; thus Jack is not too distant from the traditional defender of womanhood. Further, in a flashback narrative in mid-novel we learn that a duel broke out when Curly aspired to the favors of Gloria—a battle that came "close to taking the cake," even though Jack "got beat" (p. 205). A truck has the status of a tournament prize, so that uncertainties over its ownership lead the uncles to happy anticipation: "*Now* we've got a war on that's like old times! Jack and Curly buttin' head-on again!" (p. 206). The final duel has interesting ramifications. After Jack knocks Curly down, Ella Fay hints that she may be engaged to Curly, and this leads to some delicate considerations of decorum. At first Jack sees a political marriage that will bring the opponents into "one happy family"; then on second thought he backs off and advances a substitute motion: he will make Curly a "present" of the truck "not to marry into us" (p. 412). Curly is offended by the thought of receiving a present from Jack (as by an antagonist's boast), and Jack by the refusal; Curly swings, Jack is the loser again, and Curly cuts off his shirt-tail (p. 413)—a trophy of his victory in the lists. Though the word is never used, what is at stake is "honor."

There are other intimations of an underlying chivalric code. Jack constantly uses a formal "sir" in addressing men; he tells some yokels to mind their language, since "There's ladies present" (p. 132); he imagines himself disciplining an unwilling helper of the judge by "sitting on his chest where I could pound some willingness in him" (p. 143). Curly doesn't want to play second fiddle while Jack "save[s] one more lady" but insists, "*I'm* going to go ahead and save her while you watch" (p. 151). Shortly after Jack's returning home, he and his brother Vaughn got hold of a "pair of dried cornstalks" and "jousted with them" (p. 72); "every day" in the pen Jack and his friend Aycock Comfort called Judge Moody "Sir Pizen Ivy" (p. 83), a soubriquet repeated several times later (pp. 116, 117, 130). Jack has a chivalric sense of obligation; first he is "beholden to the reunion . . . to meet that Judge . . . [and] sing him my name out loud and clear" (p. 112)—a symbolic throwing down of the gauntlet; and then he is totally committed to saving the Buick of the driver who saved his family (p. 130). He craves the glory of single combat: when Judge Moody wants to call in his garageman to help with the Buick, Jack responds with "a stricken look" (p. 128; cf. p. 134). Perhaps his nicest touch of honor appears in his escape from jail one day before the end of his sentence. "Today was my last chance of making my escape. . . . One more day and I'd had to let 'em discharge me" (p. 360). Discharge on schedule: the commonplace routine of the law rather than the heroic romance of escape.

VI

These low-key hints of the chivalric add charm to the character who is primarily the strong man, the culture hero, and the affectionate family member. Yet there is no case-making for Jack: he is not a magically successful competitor, the legal or political or actual may supersede the chivalric at any time, and both his mother and his wife think Jack not altogether grown up. Telling him about the lost shirt-tail, Gloria positively forbids a resumption of jousting with Curly. Against Jack as agent of Beecham feudist feeling, Gloria sets out to "pit her common sense" (p. 112); she demands that he modify his Good Samaritanism by using "some of my common sense" (p. 126); opposing Mr. Renfro's application of dynamite to the Buick problem, Gloria insists that all the help Jack needs "is a wife's common sense" (p. 140); and if she does not name her common sense, it is implicitly present in her urging him to give up tilting with Curly (p. 153) and to forget about his pet truck—"a play-pretty. . . . A man's something-to-play with" (p. 425). But there is no case-making for Gloria either; of the competing values, none is espoused as an absolute. Jack is ironically ambivalent about Gloria's common sense. When Gloria tells him about her split with Miss Julia over her marriage to him, Jack asks, "wouldn't she pay regard to your common sense?" (p. 171). On the other hand, Jack can allege that his first Buick-rescue scheme failed because "Gloria run in too quick with her common sense" (p. 140), and on another occasion Welty makes a deadpan comment that Jack "gave a nod, as when she mentioned her common sense to him" (p. 172).

If Gloria wants to detach Jack from the youthful heroic games that add zest to community life, she wants even more to detach him from the Beechams. "When will we move to ourselves?" (p. 111) she asks him soon after they are alone for the first time, and her last words are "And some day . . . some day yet, we'll move to ourselves" (p. 435). In part this is the conventional desire for a private "little two-room house" (p. 431). But it is also Gloria's revolt against the old community, the pressuring Beecham way of life. Symbolically, she sits outside the family group at the reunion. She presents herself—an illusion? a part truth?—as trying to "*save Jack* . . . save him! From everybody I see this minute! . . . I'll save him yet! . . . I don't give up easy!" (p. 198). Again, "I was trying to save him! . . . [From] this mighty family!" (p. 320). She never articulates the Beecham shortcoming; she perhaps believes that they take rather than give. She tells Jack, "The most they ever do for you is brag on you." But Jack insists that, despite her book learning, "about what's at home, there's still a little bit left for you to find out" (p. 137). Near the end they have an argument, both of them affectionate and tender, but both holding to their positions; the summary lines are "Honey, won't you change your mind about my family?" and "Not for all the tea in China." She adds, "You're so believing and blind" (p. 360).

Miss Lexie declares at one point, "The world isn't going to let you have a thing both ways" (p. 280). But the author says, in effect, that you can't help living with it both ways: in this central action we see Jack clinging to two loyalties—to old family and new—and feeling them as equally valid. The two communities are mutually jealous. Gloria's worst moment comes when an old postcard message indicates that her father may have been the late Sam Dale Beecham. Being a Beecham is "ten times worse" than anything else. "Welcome into the family!" cries Aunt Nanny, and they force Gloria through an initiation rite which is a mixture of farce and humiliation. It is a baptism by total immersion—in the watermelon hyperbolically provided for the reunion. They rub her face in it and order her to say "Beecham," but she keeps on denying the identity (pp. 268–70). Later Jack says it was just a family welcome, but Gloria bitterly harps on one detail that may be symbolic: "They pulled me down on dusty ground ... to wash my face in their sticky watermelon juice" (p. 313). "Pulled me down": the rite was various things, and leveling was clearly one of them. The outsider, the teacher, the individual who felt apart, must be cut down to community size. Community survival would demand that.

The matter of Gloria's identity—her actual parenthood remains at least partially speculative, as if facts themselves partook of the "ambiguity" which Welty has recently said is the nature of life—is thematically relevant to her would-be secession from the Beechams. Jack wants her to have only a present, not a past, identity: "She's Mrs. J. J. Renfro, that's who she is" (p. 346). Gloria spells this out more fully: "I'm here to be nobody but myself, Mrs. Gloria Renfro, and have nothing to do with the old dead past" (p. 361)—her version of a recurrent human dream. She is not merely bucking Beechamhood; in general she treats the present not as a residue of the past but as the genesis of a future. Her "common sense" is mingled with a visionary tendency: she constantly looks ahead expectantly, just as she did in settling on a teaching career (p. 47). "All that counts in life is up ahead," she says (p. 315). "That's for the future to say," she says on two occasions (pp. 65, 320), on the second of which she falls into romantic prophecy, "We'll live to ourselves one day yet, and do wonders." Another time she humorously modifies her teacher's aspirations: she would no longer "change the world" but "just my husband. I still believe I can do it, if I live long enough" (p. 356). One episode is funny and painful and symbolic. Jack is in his tug-of-war with the Buick, and there is this exchange between Gloria and him:

"I don't see our future, Jack" she gasped.

"Keep looking, sweetheart."

"If we can't do any better than we're doing now, what will Lady May think of us when we're old and gray?"

"Just hang onto my heels, honey," he cried out.

"We're still where we were yesterday. In the balance," Gloria said. (p. 390)

The moment of doubt enriches a picture that is mostly in another color. Once Gloria says that Lady May is "our future" (p. 358); throughout the Buick ordeal she "tried to keep my mind on the future" (p. 421), and at the end she promises, "I'll just keep right on thinking about the future, Jack" (p. 434).

So there is thematic significance in the clashes between the hereditary community—the embracing Banner-Beecham world summed up in the reunion and its rituals—and the small new community that lives only in the imprecise visions of the orphan-teacher-young wife. But the *only* is inaccurate. For Gloria is carrying on, in her own way, the tradition first voiced by Miss Julia Mortimer, the by now mythical figure whose career was an espousal of values different from those that rule the local scene. She dies on reunion day, the very day when her protégée Gloria starts her life with Jack, just home from prison; Julia was "in love with Banner School" (p. 294), Aunt Beck says (we also learn that Julia was attractive enough to have suitors), while Gloria, over Julia's protests, has married a Beecham. Different arena, but same battle, as key words show. While Gloria eyes the future but no longer seeks to "change the world," Miss Julia writes, just a little before her death, "I always thought . . . I could change the future" (p. 298). Or, as Gloria puts it, Julia "didn't want anybody left in the dark, not about anything. She wanted everything brought out in the wide open, to see and be known" (p. 432). Gloria still hopes for some success; Julia reports that she herself has failed. But through Judge Moody we also learn that she has had some spectacular successes: she coached good pupils and pushed some of them into careers of note, and, early mindful of what we now call the "delivery" of professional services, persuaded the young lawyer Moody to stay in his home county—for which he "never fully forgave her" (p. 305)—instead of following her other protégées into a larger world.

Though we learn much about Miss Julia from her deathbed letter to the judge and from his account of her, the heroic antagonist of the local status quo is presented mainly by a technical tour de force: the memories and commentary of ex-pupils who thus portray both themselves and their relentless quixotic challenger. At times they praise her for having taught them all they know, for having made them what they are; more often they portray her as a tormentor, a dragon, a fiend to be escaped. Julia and later Gloria put teaching above everything; it had to go on, come cyclone, flood, fight, angry parents, or local spectacles. But Miss Beulah says that no children of hers can be kept "shut up in school, if they can figure there's something going on somewhere! . . . They're not exactly idiots" (p. 27), and she promises a chastised child, "And for the rest of your punishment, you're to come straight home from school today and tell me something you've learned" (p. 374). Many such remarks give body to Gloria's assessment of Julia: "All she wanted was a teacher's life. . . . But it looked like past a certain point nobody was willing to let her have it" (p. 294). Having heard some of the facts of "that teacher's life," Jack is sure it sounds like "getting put in the Hole [at the pen]! Kept in the dark, on bread and water, and nobody coming to get you out!" (p. 312). Miss Julia, reports Gloria, "saved me from the orphanage—even if it was just to enter me up at Normal" (p. 316)—an inadvertent picture of the education of an educator. Jack nicely sums up the local view of education when he says he's "thankful I come along in time to save my wife from a life like hers" (p. 313).

This world is not an easy one in which to spread light. Miss Julia was independent, solitary, single-minded, respected, feared, a thorn in the flesh of the community, a Quixote with longer career, more bite, less laughableness. Perhaps in retirement she was a little mad; perhaps it served the ends of Miss Lexie, her attendant, to think her so; or more likely Miss Lexie did think her so. Miss Lexie imprisoned her, "tied her. . . . Tied her in bed" (p. 278), and Miss Julia had to be desperately heroic to get letters out to Judge Moody. At the funeral her former student Dr. Carruthers says briefly, "Neglect, neglect! *Of course* you can die of it! Cheeks were a skeleton's! I call it starvation, pure and simple" (p. 430). It is entirely possible that, through a nurse unimaginative enough to treat illness with tyrannous severity, Welty is satirizing a community for callousness amounting to cruelty. And yet the main drift of her art is not in that direction; the fate of Miss Julia, important as it is, is not made a predominant issue but is one of many matters presented in many tones. Welty does not tend to discover goodies and baddies. She is not bitterly condemning viciousness but rather symbolizing a neglectfulness that may, alas, crop up in any human community.

Miss Julia is the spokesman for one value, not an allegory of an ideal. Nor, on the other hand, do the three B's of folk life—Banner, Baptist, Beecham—simply define a culpable crassness. If this life is limited, it still has its own virtues of clan solidarity, humor, hopefulness; it has been molded by a succession of disasters which in the chatter and clatter of a busy day's doings we may almost lose sight of but which surface now and then in flickers of distressed awareness. As Mr. Renfro says on one occasion, "It's all part of the reunion. We got to live it out, son" (p. 211)—the reunion as not only jolly get-together but as shared re-experiencing of many troubles. His wife Beulah puts this still more strongly after they have gone to bed: "I've got it to stand and I've got to stand it. And you've got to stand it. . . . After they've all gone home, Ralph, and the children's in bed, that's what's left. Standing it" (p. 360). We can't help thinking of Faulkner's "They endured."

If Welty is not a satirist, she is even less a regional historian. A regional idiom she does use—the idiom of spoken style and social style. Yet it is a medium, not of local reportage, but finally of a wide and deep picture of American life. The dualism of this life—or better, one of its dualisms— is the larger reality implicit in the confrontation between Miss Julia and Gloria on the one hand, and Banner and Beechams on the other. On the one hand there is the family, the historical community, with its sustaining and unifying legacy of habits, customs, rites, and loyalties; its sense of actuality, its tendency to see the way things were as the way things are, its embodiment of "the system." On the other hand are the teachers—outsiders in Banner (the Ludlow belle and the orphan) and hence natural voices for alteration of the status quo. In them we see the side of the national personality that turns away from the past and toward the future, places a high value on change, has unlimited faith in education, believes in "enlightenment," is full of aspiration, longs for a "better life," can become visionary and utopian and may bring forth, to borrow from Mrs. Moody's description of Miss Julia, "tyrants . . . for others' own good." Still there are no allegorical rigidities; Miss Julia remains the lifelong prod from without, Gloria marries and hopes to bore from within. Her "future" may turn out to be no more than her small private acreage within the system; feeling superior to the Beechams, she must tearfully acknowledge, "One way or the other, I'm kin to everybody in Banner" (p. 313). If the teachers are in one sense quixotic visionaries, still Gloria believes in her own "common sense," and she turns it against that other chivalry that Jack has imbibed from local tradition. "Family" and "future" both want to possess hero Jack; drawn both ways, he may embody an unresolvable division or foreshadow such reconciliations as now and then we come to for a time. He may refertilize the drought-plagued wasteland or simply duplicate the Beechams in a new Renfro family. Talk of the future though she does, Gloria can still sadly ask, at the very end, "Oh, Jack, does this mean it'll all happen over again?" (p. 435).

On all this Welty looks with a vast, but never bitter, irony.

VII

In sketching the ways in which a Mississippi story plays variations on a central American myth—"variations" of course means hitting on innovations, altering patterns, mixing perspectives rather than taking sides—I am trying to communicate the sense of magnitude that this novel creates (as satire, which mostly gratifies prejudices, rarely does). The sense of magnitude is also served by the undercover wispy reminiscences of European myths and specifically of two wholly dissimilar works, a Greek tragedy and an English comic novel—Sophocles' *Oedipus* and Fielding's *Joseph Andrews*. To propose such analogies may seem pretty portentous, a laborious artifice of magnification, but since the resemblances came to me as a spontaneous overflow of powerful impressions on first reading, and since, recollected in tranquillity, they do not die away, I will take the risk.

During the reunion-day conversation, the talk occasionally takes a turn which Beulah tries to head off. In doing this, she somehow reminded me of Jocasta, who catches on to the truth before Oedipus does and urges him not to go further. Neither Jocasta nor Beulah succeeds. Just as Jocasta's son-husband had committed a murder in the past, so, we learn, had Beulah's brother Nathan; both men suffer self-mutilation and exile. Oedipus, coming to Thebes, returns unknowingly to his native city; so does Gloria when she comes to Banner (as Aunt Birdie says, in folk Sophoclean, "you was coming right back to where you started from. . . . Just as dangerous as a little walking stick of dynamite" [p. 319]). Both are "orphans." Oedipus marries a woman who turns out to be his mother; Gloria marries a man who, it turns out, may be her first cousin, which would mean, at that time and place, statutory incest. Oedipus's mother-wife and Gloria's unwed mother are both suicides. Oedipus's horror at discovering his relationship to Jocasta and Laius is paralleled by Gloria's sense of disaster in the discovery that she may be a Beecham. The banishment undergone by Oedipus and Nathan is a possibility for Gloria and Jack.

The identity myth that starts with unknown parenthood and proceeds to a crisis of possible incest is an old romantic device that appears in Roman comedy and then resurfaces in moralistic melodrama in the eighteenth century and in comic form in Fielding's *Joseph Andrews* (which happens also to have a very fine roadside Good Samaritan episode). In the world there depicted, people have a habit of mislaying children, and the last of the vicissitudes that afflict the love of Joseph Andrews and Fanny (the Jack Renfro and Gloria of the story) is that they may be brother and sister. Before bringing in the prestidigitation of parenthood that removes the difficulty, Fielding, who is not given to the ambiguity that Welty elects even here, notes different responses to the possibility. Everybody believed it "except Pamela, who imagined, as she had heard neither of her parents mention such an accident, that it must certainly be false; and except the Lady Booby, who suspected the falsehood of the story from her ardent desire that it should be true; and Joseph, who feared its truth, from his earnest wishes that it might prove false" (IV, xiii). Aunt Beck says simply, of Beulah's response to the story that Gloria may be a Beecham, "if the right story comes along at the right time, she'll be like the rest of us and believe what she wants to believe" (p. 267). The psychological comedy is the same as Fielding's.

Fielding, who revels in allusions, makes another joke about Joseph and Fanny: "They felt perhaps little less anxiety in this interval than Oedipus himself, whilst his fate was revealing" (IX, xv). Welty abstains from such allusions, but her plot does have its sketchy analogies to those of Sophocles and Fielding. Likely she never thought of either. The primary critical point is that in imagining human probabilities she fashioned experience in ways that bring to mind the situations developed by such predecessors. That is, she instinctively moved toward fundamental patterns of action that get at basic springs of human experience. Her materials are central rather than eccentric; or, to risk a rather overused word, they are archetypal. But I want especially to stress the fact that her management of materials clustering about the possible incest is reminiscent of *both* Sophocles and Fielding: that the tragic possibility is often just around the corner, or just under the surface, when the main lines of action in the foreground are comic and often, indeed, farcical. We are plunged into tall tales, folk humor, slapstick episodes of unruly persons and objects, all these mediating a life in which wit, non sequiturs, flashes of pathos and anguish, natural disasters, old patterns of feeling (feudist, chivalric, familial, partisan), and a dominantly good-humored, if not successfully channeled, energizing are kaleidoscopically reflected in indefatigable dialogue. Many tones, often side by side unexpectedly, emerge in this presentation of community: community with a time-created coherence that satisfies but constrains, that is filtered through moment-by-moment diversities of manner and positive inconsistencies of attitude, and that is always troubled by the periodic educational evangels with excelsiors that flicker for a while and then give off a dim persistent light. The characters enact the old modes of existence and the change-bound disturbances of them; the author says little. If she spoke from the shadows in which she remains, she might, we surmise, allude to the *comédie humaine*, pointing out that a wide spectrum of the laughable contains bits of the pitiable and the admirable; that *plus ça change, plus c'est la même chose*, that everyman comes to discover, like Gloria, that he is kin to everybody. But she makes no such observations; she simply sets the scene and makes the actors talk their lives. She does both tasks with immense variety and vitality of style; most characteristically she brings apparent unlikes together. This central habit of style is a symptom of her overall method, which in *Losing Battles* conspicuously wins the artist's war against the chaos of tumbling history and sprawling experience—wins it even while camouflaging the victorious form in the multiplicity and miscellaneousness of the defeated antagonist.

SEYMOUR
GROSS
A Long Day's Living:
The Angelic Ingenuities
of *Losing Battles*

" 'Gloria, we won our day,' said Jack."
                                    Losing Battles (1970)

"... it does lie in my nature to praise
and celebrate things."
                        Welty, an interview (1972)

THERE IS A sense in which the title of Eudora
Welty's major work in the comic mode, *Los-
ing Battles*, is unfortunate. It does seem to sound the note of defeat, as if it
were introducing a novel whose epigraph might be Hemingway's "all
stories end in death, and he is no true storyteller who does not tell you that"
—or some such thing—rather than the affirmative epigraphs I have chosen
for this essay. The title would perhaps merit little remark except that I
suspect that it has subtly encouraged readings of the novel somewhat too
somber, readings which tip the novel toward what is known in Shake-
spearean criticism as "dark comedy." Louise Gossett, for example, calls it
a "comedy of loss," in which "Miss Welty keeps us company—both tender
and robustious—as we edge along avoiding doom."[1] For me, such a reading misses the essence of Welty's comic vision, which is basically celebrative, joyous, and affirmative ("My natural temperament is one of positive
feelings," she remarked in an interview for the *Paris Review*[2]). Her comic
fiction, the culmination of which is *Losing Battles*, displays an enchantment with the energy, diversity, and indomitability of what Emerson in
less self-conscious times would have capitalized as Life; it bears testimony
to a vision which sees life as skirting free of the social, moral, and philosophical formulations which would command it into shape; it exhibits a

[1] Louise Y. Gossett, "Eudora Welty's New Novel: The Comedy of Loss," *Southern
Literary Journal*, 3 (Fall 1970), 137.
[2] Linda Kuehl, "The Art of Fiction XLVII: Eudora Welty," *Paris Review*, No. 55
(Fall 1972), 90.

reverence for freedom, a condition in which people and their feelings are not fixed, defined, and labelled, where life has preserved something of its dazzling mobility and dramatic variousness. Clearly this is no shallow optimism; for Welty, like the Emerson or Whitman whom she in some general ways resembles, knows the conditions out of which praise and celebration must be won.

I said in an earlier essay that Welty is in the American Transcendentalist comic tradition; the statement has no significance beyond what the analogy might reveal. The nineteenth-century Transcendentalist wrote no fiction and liked very little of it, perhaps because fiction, being the most reality-laden of the literary forms, finds it most difficult to convincingly "earn" a celebrative vision. A depiction of the world we know works against such a vision. It would be hard to imagine a serious novel in which the ringing affirmations of an Emerson or a Whitman in the mouth of a character would not sound ridiculous.

A more useful comparison for *Losing Battles* is to the fiction of Jane Austen, or, rather, to Eudora Welty's reading of the older author in a fine little appreciation she wrote while working on her novel.[3] This is not to suggest "influence" as traditionally defined in literary scholarship. Instead, a kindred spirit recognizes in another writer some of the qualities of her own talent and talks about them. And as is the case with most such "shock of recognition" essays, we learn as much about the recognizer as we do about the recognized. For the reader of *Losing Battles*, Welty's "Jane Austen" can offer some very suggestive insights into the way Welty's novel is to be taken. I think it not too much to suggest that the essay is almost a generalized summary of the informing vision and method of the novel.

Jane Austen's "comic masterpieces" are, for Welty, "wholly affirmative." The "noise" and "commotion" in her pages flow from "a tireless relish of life," which is a rejoicing in the "clamorous joys and griefs" of her characters. Her fictional stage is small in size but drawn exactly to scale. Take one household, add a neighbor, and there is "the full presence of the world"—"Life . . . is instantaneously at hand and astir . . . with news, arrivals, tumult and crises." Austen "was born knowing a great deal," and among the things she knew was "that the unit of everything worth knowing in life is in the family," that "the interesting situations of life can, and

---

[3] Eudora Welty, "Jane Austen," *Atlantic Brief Lives: A Biographical Companion to the Arts*, ed. Louis Kronenberger (Boston: Little Brown, 1971), pp. 23–5. See a revised version of this essay in *The Eye of the Story*.

notably do take place at home." Her comedies avoid nothing humanly essential for not being tragedies: they too "are nourished at the primary sources." They never deny "the emotions their power," they encompass "the argument of souls," they explore the range of human motives (which "can still be counted on [one's] fingers"), they pertain "to what goes on perpetually in the mind and heart." But the perspective is always comic; that is, "the effect of the whole is still that of proportions kept, symmetry maintained, and the classical form honored—indeed celebrated." Austen's "comic genius" impels a world in which "she sees and defines both sides," presenting them in their turns "in a continuous attainment of balance: moral, esthetic, and dramatic balance." This "symmetry of design," which Welty characterizes as an "angelic ingenuity," is the projection into art of a "generous dispensation of the understanding."

Losing Battles is a family novel written along just such lines. Its spiritual ebullience is the result of Welty's grand understanding of the joys and griefs of her large cast of characters who, do what they will to tip the world, cannot upset its balance. There is something in the universe which does not like a fall—call it the life force or the natural order or whatever. This impulse is most obviously and hilariously caught in the image of the Moody car, which was kept from crashing with its occupants into the ravine by one of Uncle Nathan's religious signs—"Destruction Is At Hand"! There it remains throughout most of the novel impossibly suspended on Banner Top—its motor running, its tires exploding, its precarious equilibrium depending on an amiable simpleton in the back seat—waiting to be saved. And it is. The salvation is not exactly the kind Nathan had in mind, but it is the kind of salvation that occurs in the world of *Losing Battles*: it's a bit battered but it'll run.

Much the same impulse, though in this instance tonally quite different, occurs in the very brief night scene, which is the literal and symbolic dark time of the novel. Granny, anguished by the end of the reunion, pleads with Vaughn, neither knowing nor caring who he is, to get into bed with her. And Miss Beulah lying in bed says to her husband, "I've got it to stand and I've got to stand it. And you've got to stand it.... After they've all gone home, Ralph, and the children's in bed, that's what's left. Standing it" (p. 360). Although Welty allows her characters their nocturnal loneliness, she does not allow the scene to be taken over by it. After all, another day is coming. Describing Vaughn's ride through the moonlight, Welty, in one of the rare times when she speaks in her own voice, comments, "Even after people gave up each other's company, said goodbye and went home, if there was only one left, Vaughn Renfro, the world around him was still one huge, soul-defying reunion" (p. 363). And the night scene significantly ends with Miss Beulah rushing onto the porch to snatch up her grand-daughter, Lady May, and carry her back to her own bed "as if a life had been saved."

Generally speaking, critics have been reluctant to give full assent to the novel's "wholly affirmative" comic vision. As I have indicated, the tendency has been to darken the novel, this darkening coming in various shades. It has been characterized as "elegiac," as another Welty treatment of "the illusions with which people protect themselves in the losing battles of their experience," as a story of "the separateness of each of us isolated within our shells of individuality."[4] But nowhere is this inclination more apparent than in an interview with Eudora Welty conducted by Charles T. Bunting for the *Southern Review*. When he remarked that "Miss Julia Mortimer has, of course, lost her battle to educate the Renfros, but really it's a losing battle for everybody in the novel, isn't it?" Welty gently but firmly disagreed: "I wanted to show indomitability there. I don't feel it's a novel of despair at all. I feel it's more a novel of admiration for the human being who can cope with any condition, even ignorance, and keep a courage, a joy of life, even, that is unquenchable. But I see human beings as *valuable*. Each life is very valuable in itself, regardless, and in spite of everything."[5] And in the *Jackson Daily News* (5 April 1970), she characterized her novel as being "about all the battles which we *seem* to be losing." The operative word here is the one I have italicized.

One should note in these remarks that Welty's "admiration" is not selective: it apparently applies to *both* sides of the "battle"—Julia Mortimer and the Renfro/Beecham family. Welty loves all of her characters (Cleo perhaps excepted) and, as Jack says, "You can't blame who you love." This love, which comes of the author's "generous dispensation of the understanding," manifests itself primarily as "an angelic ingenuity" in the way of narrative—an almost magical balancing of all the elements in the novel.

---

[4] The quotations are respectively from: M.E. Bradford, "Looking Down from a High Place: The Serenity in Miss Welty's *Losing Battles*," *Récherches Anglaises et Américaines*, 4 (1971), 96; Carol A Moore, "The Insulation of Illusion and *Losing Battles*," *Mississippi Quarterly*, 26 (Fall 1973), 658; John F. Fleischauer, "The Focus of Mystery: Eudora Welty's Prose Style," *Southern Literary Journal*, 5 (Spring 1973), 78.

[5] Charles T. Bunting, " 'The Interior World': An Interview with Eudora Welty," *Southern Review*, 8 (Autumn 1972), 720.

In contrast to such grand impartiality, the critics of the novel have tended to take sides, to give their allegiance (albeit some with agreeable qualifications) to the "anti-family" forces—Miss Mortimer and all those (like Gloria) who fight against what has been variously characterized as the suffocating insularity, pettiness, smug ignorance, and prejudice of the back country family. This negative response is at least partly the result, I believe, of two separate but related things: the ease with which the reader can identify the greatness in Julia and the powerfully concentrated accounts we are given of her suffering in the service of that greatness; and the ease with which we can miss, or at least slight, the sufferings of the family because they come to us either in a ritualized form which deliberately deflects the pain or in an almost offhand and glancing manner.

Julia's losing battles are so overpowering because they are so painfully concentrated in Lexie's account of her last days and in Julia's final letter to the world. Early in the novel when Gloria has torn her knee protecting Lady May from the Buick, Etoyle says to her, "I'm on your side now, Gloria. . . . Know why? Because you're the one that's bleeding" (p. 153). Precisely: we can *see* Julia bleeding. A mind watching itself going back on itself; the desperate attempt to hold onto some vestige of what she has given her life for, if only symbolically, like the speller she sleeps on; the waiting for ex-students who never come; her summation, without self-pity, of her failure to transform the community; her refusal to quit fighting even though she knows she's just about licked—"I'm ready for all they send me"; her lonely death on the road, her last words—"What was the trip for?"—shadowed with the ultimate doubt. It could, indeed, as the judge says, "make a stone cry."

That the family's sufferings might not make a stone cry is hardly the sign of their lack of human cost—that has been enormous. It is rather the index of the family's capacity for absorbing private anguish into its communal life, of which the reunion is the annual rite. They have not come together for lamentation, so what we do learn of their griefs is either undramatically imbedded in their "history" or comes to us in scattered fragments, often impelled against their inclinations by such circumstances as Cleo's vulgar prying or the puzzle of Gloria's parentage. It is harder to be on their side because it is harder to *see* them bleeding.

The family has nothing; they inhabit, as Welty put it in the *Paris Review*, "a bare stage." The Renfro store was easy prey for a sharpshooter like Dearman; the farm, mortgaged acres of clay on which it rains too much or not at all, can no longer raise enough for them to eat; with Jack in jail, they have had to trade the horse for food "to keep us alive" and the beloved truck for pride—to put up a new roof which will say that they have not gone under yet. Life has been, as Beck quietly puts it, "a lot of doing without." If they speak of their material deprivations laconically, it is not because they can't, like the inhabitants of some Tobacco Road, feel them. One passage—the only one like it in the novel—points to feelings that go deeper than the words they choose for them. "Cleo," Noah remembers, "the old place here was plum stocked with squirrel when we was boys. It was overrun with quail. And if you never saw the deer running in here, I saw 'em. It was filled—it was filled!—with every kind of good thing, this old dwelling, when me and the rest of us Beecham boys grew up here . . ." (p. 193).

The downward path to government handouts is in some ways the least of what they suffer. There are more grievous hurts, of which Nathan's cutting off of his offending hand for his double murder is both the most obvious and the most terrible. The seven Beecham children have not only early lost their parents by drowning, but have had to face the awful possibility that their mother and father were running away from *them*. Beneath Noah's raucous, life-loving hilarity there is a rod of iron guilt: he has always blamed himself for his parents' death because he was in the road, having intuited the disaster, when they rode off into the night, but couldn't stop them. Significantly, it is the only family story he has shared with his new wife before she comes to the reunion. Beneath Beulah's powerful and commanding presence is similar anguish: she has lived with the belief that she is responsible for the emasculation of her brother Sam Dale, the darling of the family in her generation as Jack is the darling in his. For those brief moments that the family entertains the possibility that Sam Dale is Gloria's father, the intensity of Beulah's secret hurt breaks out into the open. With the exultation born of exquisite relief, Beulah cries out, "Gloria's here, and she's proof, living proof! I didn't do hurt to my own, after all. I can die happy! Can't I?" (p. 268). Only gradually do we learn what lies beneath Nanny's jolly obesity, why she can't keep loving hands off any child that passes her, why any talk of children evokes a bemusement that approaches the tragic. Her mother gave her away when she was a baby, and all she has ever had of motherhood are what lies beneath those two small stones in the cemetery "bearing the same one word, 'Infant.'" Beck and Curtis have had nine sons but they're all gone. "All nine!" twice in the novel Curtis murmurs with appalled disbelief, "and they're never coming home." Mr. Renfro, a man so gentle and modest that he "bows to the day," has been a lifelong cripple from an accident he suffered shortly before his marriage. He carries his twisted body as if apologizing for the fact that he has not ever been able to do a whole man's work on the farm. And his sister Lexie's hardness of manner only imperfectly hides the disappointment that she was too unattractive ever to be a wife and too dumb to learn Virgil so that she could become a teacher.

The sufferings of the family have been formidable, although to bunch them up as I have done gives them an intensity they are not meant to have in the reading of the novel. But it is necessary to acknowledge them in order to keep the family and therefore the novel in perspective. When Julia says that "there's a measure of enjoyment" in having spent a lifetime in what she considers a losing battle, we assent to the affirmation because we know the conditions out of which that modulated affirmation has been won. The same should be true of the family. In response to Gloria's self-dramatizing remark that she was having a baby "and you can die from that," Beulah, speaking for the family, wryly replies, "You can die from anything if you try good and hard" (p. 279). I have tried to indicate what gives such a remark authority.

If, however, only Julia and her "losing battles" are taken as normative, then inevitably "the other side," those (in her words) "who held the fort" against the learning and rational intelligence she championed, becomes the negative force in the novel. Such a view, as I will try to show, distorts the comic design of the novel, the "continuous attainment of balance."

First of all, as others have noted, Julia is a marvelous woman who is a teacher of fierce dedication, not (thankfully) another saintly schoolmarm. The will, energy, and sacrifice she expended in the service of teaching her pupils are only to be admired, especially since much of what we learn of her as a teacher comes from the mouths of those who consider her zeal to have been their "bane." Her kindness to the sick and rejected Rachael Sojourner, whom she taught to sew when she realized the girl could not do "mental arithmetic," and to Willy Trimble, whom she taught to do carpentry when she realized that he could not learn academic subjects, reveals a woman of both sense and sensibility, not some kind of teaching machine; so too does her hauling a ten-gallon can of milk to school each day and her teaching the kids to swim because at times the Bywy River got high enough to drown in. Her handsomeness—in her youth she was the

best-looking woman around—reminds us that she chose her life by conviction not default. And in her letter to Judge Moody we see a fine mind
groping honestly and painfully toward some kind of understanding and
wisdom. But, it should be stressed, what is grand about Miss Julia Mortimer,
teacher, belongs to her and not to her profession. This is a necessary distinction because the novel does not authorize the wholesale elevation of
Education over what has been learned in the way of the reunion, what in
the *Paris Review* Eudora Welty has called, "a narrative sense of human
destiny": "They learn and teach and think and enjoy that way." The other
teachers we meet, those riding in the church bus to Julia's funeral, are not
a particularly attractive lot. "Isn't it the luckiest thing it's a Sunday she
picked?" one of them says. "Suppose it had been a school day, like tomor-
row. We'd been cooped up" (p. 158). Hardly bearers of what Gloria calls
"the torch" of learning. And by no stretch of the imagination could anything we know of Gloria lead us to believe that had she not become Mrs.
Jack Renfro she would have been another Miss Mortimer. That she once
entertained the idea that she would eventually outshine her mentor is the
index of her naiveté, of her rather aggressive over-evaluation of herself.[6]
Finally, it should be recalled, the most grievous error in judgment belongs
to Judge Moody, who, because he does not understand the amiably antag-
onistic game that Jack and Curly play ("never got it through his head what
it was all about"), sends Jack to jail as "a lesson to the rest" that there must
be respect for the law and for those who have been "raised to office." Considering the real situation, the principle is absurdly misapplied.

Julia Mortimer has been, until nearly the very end of her life, a romantic
empiricist (her letter to Moody, as Gloria disapprovingly recognizes, exhibits "a change");[7] it is what has given shape and meaning to her existence

[6] The admiration for Gloria is puzzling. Welty in the Bunting interview called her
"the most naive soul there; she's not Miss Julia Mortimer at all, by any means. And she
totally lacks imagination" (p. 721). She has an unrealistically inflated opinion of herself, an almost neurotic concern for herself (won't drink Banner water) and for her
daughter (won't give Lady May the food that the child is perfectly capable of eating),
and a penchant for self-dramatization that verges on the ludicrous. Much has been made
of the family's watermelon-cramming, but nothing of the ways she constantly insults
the family and refuses to see anything in them but "a pile," even to hoping Nathan
won't come to the next reunion because he only bathes in the Bywy River. Her concentration on herself, her search for Personal Identity, leads to her failure to go to Parchman
to plead for Jack and so get him out of jail early, as Mississippi wives customarily do
and as Judge Moody assumes she has. What, of course, redeems Gloria is her powerful
love for Jack and the promise of a family which that love will bring in its natural course.
[7] When Jack compliments Julia for being wise as Solomon, "away up over our heads,"
Gloria replies, "Once. But she changed. I'll never change!" (p. 432). What Gloria dis-

and has been the source of many of the fine things she has done with her life. She had a rationalistic program for the improvement of society—"She wanted everything brought out in the wide open, to see and be known"— and had no doubt that if you firmly pointed out to people what was expected of them—progress—they would "measure up." She believes that any question rationally framed (such as who is Gloria's father) can be rationally answered by "a good brain." "She said every mystery had its right answer—we just had to find it. That's what mysteries were given to us for" (p. 252).

The comic side of Julia's character emerges from the odd, even irrational, twists her passionate convictions are made to take—teaching in a cyclone; telling Gloria that all she (Julia) needs to know to decide if a boy is right for Gloria is "his name and age and the year I taught him"; rejecting Jack as a husband for Gloria because he received only two-thirds of a point over 75, "And 75 is passing"; demanding that she be buried under the schoolhouse. As for her belief that every mystery can be solved, the novel demurs. The identity of Gloria's father is never established; what Mamma and Papa Beecham were doing when they rode off in the middle of the night remains forever "something between man and wife . . . and it's what no other soul would have no way of knowing"; exactly why Nathan killed Dearman is never explained; "lost's lost." Julia's last spoken words on earth—"what was the trip for?"—are repeated by the first words of Lady May's life—"What you huntin', man?" Two forms of one question, to which there is no answer given, save, perhaps, one which begs it: the trip is for the trip, life is for the living of it.

The balanced characterization of Julia is important to the novel's comic poise. But more important is the true fate of "what happened to what she was." Julia (mostly) considers her life to have been a failure, "except in those cases that you can count off on your fingers." The text, however, does not support such a sad summation. Julia has won more than she and "the other side" realize. I do not mean here simply the barefoot boys she prodded into becoming professors, physicians, lawyers and clergymen or the fact that "all Alliance, half of Ludlow, and most of Foxtown" attend her funeral. I mean what she "won" in the camp of her presumptive enemies in the battle, the Beecham/Renfro clan. Perhaps Julia herself, at the end,

---

approves of is Julia's recognition, expressed in the letter Gloria heard Moody read, that both sides "fought faithfully and single-mindedly, bravely, maybe even fairly" (p. 298). Gloria can't abide anything good being said about the family.

had an inkling of such a possibility when she wrote that "when the battle's over, something may dawn there—with no help from the teacher, no help from the pupil, no help from the book" (p. 298).

On several occasions Miss Beulah remarks with exasperation that Julia's funeral has become a part of the reunion. It has indeed. (The reverse is also true: the reunion has become a part of the funeral.) Resist as it may, the reunion is nevertheless forced to listen to an account of Julia's last days, to hear her last will and testament read to them, and to have to accept the incredible news that Julia will be buried not under her beloved schoolhouse but in their sacrosanct burial ground. This last fact is not, however, merely an unexpected comic reversal, though it is that too; it is, rather, a symbolically apt finale to what has not been much noted—that Julia is to be buried with those whom she has deeply touched in all the days of their lives. It turns out to be one of Welty's angelic ingenuities that the battle between the family and Julia Mortimer, like Jack and Curly's fistfights or the family's sworn enmity towards Judge Moody, is not the collision of discrete antagonisms but, paradoxically, of "foes well-matched or sweethearts come together." The novel suggests that the relationship between Julia and the family, as with all the other relationships in the novel, is that of interpenetrating polarities, foes *and* sweethearts; only the "foes" has been emphasized, however, to the detriment of Welty's extraordinary balancing act.

First of all, the family is not a univocal chorus. Different voices speak differently and even the same voice does not always sound the same. Certainly the strophe (so to speak) of the family "ode" sounds the note of hostility—carping, perverse, even mean-spirited; and in Lexie's account of her battle with Julia in the last days of the teacher's life, apparently something worse.

"Yes'm," says Dolphus, "she taught the generations. She was our cross to bear." For Nanny and Birdie, too, Julia's obsessive commitment to learning—"She'd follow you, right to your door"—took the joy out of childhood for "the poor little children." "She put an end to good fishing" says it all. Some of them take a curious pleasure in their successful resistance to learning, perversely proud that Julia didn't penetrate their "pore hot skulls." "It was so far fetched," says Birdie, [but] "I've gone a long ways ahead of it now!" Yet Percy, with outrageous unreason, complains that Julia didn't make them "*stay* in school, and learn some profit." Like any self-satisfied ignoramus, some of them dismiss what they do not know as not worth knowing and those who know it as not worth emulating. She expected too much out of people and "never did learn to please"; she was a cracked old maid driven slightly batty by devoting herself to accumulating books rather than children. How else, they ask, can one explain a grown healthy woman reading in the afternoon, throwing herself on the dictionary during the cyclone, spending all she had on a library, and wasting her lovely voice on poems, multiplication tables and other such "rigmarole."

These moral vulgarities (as Julia herself finally realizes) are the result of the family's deep-seated and passionate commitment to surviving in the only way it knows how: "we've all just tried to last as long as we can by just sticking together," Beulah says. Julia's assault on that value—"She wanted us to quit worshipping ourselves so wholehearted"—is both an unbearable insult and a powerful threat aimed at the very nerve center of the family's life. So they fight back in the only way they know how, and it disfigures them. How marring "the desperation of staying alive against all odds" can become is, symbolically speaking, revealed in the family's climactic rejection of what Julia stood for—Lexie's refusal to give the dying Julia a pencil to write with or a book to read.

The "antistrophe," which takes various forms, both actual and symbolic, is, I believe, more decisive, thus justifying, as I've already indicated, the site where Welty has Julia finally laid to rest—with the family. Side by side with the criticisms of Julia, but almost never offered as literal responses to them, are quite different views of Julia as teacher and human being. Curtis, for example, recalls Julia as someone who "was ready to teach herself to death for you. . . . Whether you wanted her to or not didn't make any difference. But my suspicion was she did want you to *deserve* it" (p. 240). Beck, with "awe and compassion" in her voice, says that Julia "put a little more of her own heart" into teaching than she even knew, which is why she went at it "just as hard as a steam engine." Lexie pays homage to Julia's vision in her recollection of the teacher's first words to Banner School— "Nothing in this world can measure up to the joy you'll bring me if you allow me to teach you something" (p. 273). Most surprising of all is Beulah. As the novel's most vociferous defender of the value of "the splendid mothers at home," she is apparently Julia's chief antagonist, and has been accused of viewing Julia "with unreasoning hatred." Yet she confesses, in an unguarded moment, that Julia is "responsible for a good deal I know right here today" (p. 234), and has evidently accepted with equanimity her daughter Elvie's ambition to follow in the teacher's footsteps—"A fine way to get to be a teacher," she tells the child when Elvie expresses a preference for attending the rescue of the Buick rather than school.

Beulah's actual if unperceived congruence with Julia, the coming together of foes as sweethearts, is delicately reinforced and amplified by a symbolic pattern involving spelling. Julia's great public triumph, it will be recalled, was when her Banner pupils spelled down the Mississippi legislature. But for the family, spelling would seem to be just another kind of "far-fetched" memory work, the use of which escapes them. Yet when Willy Trimble produces the speller which lay under Julia's pillow, Beulah instinctively reaches out to take it in her hands; and then suddenly, as if remembering what she is supposed to feel, thrusts it back. But the contact has been made, and it evokes for Beulah the precious memory of her own public triumph—the day she spelled the school down "like a row of tin soldiers," so excited that she wet her britches. The full implications of this convergence at the speller emerge in the figure of Vaughn, Jack's younger brother, about whom until the night scene we know little more than that "He'll never be Jack" and that he is presently the best speller in his class. The scene in which Vaughn, "moonlit," rides the mule through the night to pull the school bus from the ditch is stylistically unlike any other part of the novel; the prose is reminiscent of, for example, "First Love"—mysterious, evocative, resistant to paraphrase, as if it were a projection of and a tribute to a sensibility still mute. The reason this change occurs is revealed when we discover that Vaughn loves school with a passion that is almost pain and watch him with the new geography book he traded out of Curly Stovall: "He dragged it to his cheek, where he could smell its print, sharper, blacker, dearer than the smell of new shoes." The last time we see him tells us where he is going. Clutching his school books to his side, he leaps towards the new teacher he "was so ready to worship" and lands almost in her arms (p. 409). He has, in effect, landed in the arms of Miss Julia. "When the battle's over, something may dawn there—with no help from the teacher, no help from the pupil" (p. 298).

Julia not only moves forward through Beulah to Vaughn but backward to the family's beginnings. Early in the novel the family, out of love and need, "bring" Jack out of Parchman to the reunion. In a sense, it has also "brought" Julia. Banner School, we learn, is a creation of the family. Lexie and Ralph Renfro's grandfather believed it was "something they ought to have" (" 'Never dreamed that!' Aunt Nanny cried") and, after a generation, "Miss Julia Mortimer was the living answer to Old Preacher Renfro's prayer" ("'I never knew that either!' cried Uncle Noah Webster" [p. 273]).

What the family proclaims it has learned from the emergence of Julia into their lives is the meaning of the Islamic proverb—Beware of answered prayers! What it does not know, or resists acknowledging, is how deeply Julia is implicated in their personal history. Granny, for example, brings a puzzled hush to the reunion when she recalls how when Julia lived with the family "she and I could set and catch our breath when the day's over, and confab a little about the state the world was in." "But all that happened a mighty long time ago," Birdie objects in an attempt to push back the implications of the image. To which Beck significantly replies, "Feelings don't get old! . . . We do, but they don't. They go on" (p. 346). It is, however, in the relationship between Julia and Nathan, the family's darkest figure, that we can feel how deeply and decisively the souls of Julia and the family are intertwined. No one in the world knows, except some of the family and Julia, to whom he has confessed, that Nathan killed Dearman and allowed an innocent Negro to hang for his crime. His poor wayfaring stranger's life, that he has any life at all, he owes to Julia. "Nathan," she so beautifully told him when he was lost, "even when there's nothing left to hope for, you can start again from there, and go your way and *be good*" (p. 344). Once a year he returns to the only things that he allows to sweeten his self-imposed asceticism: the reunion of the family and "breakfast-time visits" with Julia. And he wanders the world with the memory of the only things he loves—his family *and* Julia. He breaks his silence in the novel with "Many a little schoolhouse I pass on the mountainside today is a sister to Banner, and I pass it wondering if I was to knock on the door wouldn't she come running out, all unchanged" (p. 294).

Just as the force of Julia-as-teacher moves with increasing momentum from the early Renfros through Beulah to culminate in Vaughn, so too does Julia as a moral presence move from Granny through Nathan to Jack. In his long day's living, Jack has been both pulled by the family reunion and pushed to the funeral of Miss Julia Mortimer. Only the uncomprehending figures at the funeral think he has no business being there. Although he has "never laid eyes" on Julia, Jack, in a translucent moment of imaginative sympathy, comes to "love her" because, as he explains to an astonished Gloria, "I heard her story."

Julia, then, willy-nilly, continues to exert an almost mythic force on the lives of the family. They dismiss as absurd Cleo's suggestion that she knew

"one like her"; for them there has been and could only be one Julia. Whatever stance toward Julia they try to take, the irreducible fact is that she is
there, as much (or almost as much) a part of their "story" as their "feeling
of the solidity of the family," which Eudora Welty characterized in the
Southern Review as "the strongest thing in the book." Miss Beulah, "with
some darkness" in her voice, says, "the littler you wish to see of some people, the plainer you may come to remember 'em. . . . Even against your
will. I can't tell you why, so don't ask me. But I can see that old schoolteacher this minute plainer than I can see you, Lexie Renfro, after your
back is turned" (p. 283).

The suggestion that the true relationship between the family and Julia
is one of unconscious congruities, interacting polarities, unperceived af-
finities as well as moral antipodes meets its severest test in the figure of
Lexie. Her treatment of Julia in the last days of Julia's life has been called
sadistic; and she has been accused of taking a perversely cruel pleasure in
recounting that treatment.

Lexie is the hardest member of the family, the least gracious. Her tough-
old-bird personality is, there is ample reason to believe, her way of having
maintained some dignity in the face of a life in which she lives nowhere
and has suffered the double blow of being wanted as neither wife nor
teacher. It's her way, as she puts it, "of being equal to circumstances." Her
home is where she takes care of those too sick and old to take care of themselves; everything she has in the world she carries in a single bag. She comes
to Julia when the teacher, against her will and to her surprise, has been
"put out to pasture," and when old age has worn down Julia's body and
intensified her characteristic indifference to pleasing into an aggressive
hostility. Julia drove everybody away, Lexie says, and "then she wondered
what had happened to everybody." Having no other object, Julia's bitterness turns on Lexie, whom she strikes, calls fool and old woman (though
Lexie is eleven years younger), and insults: "Suppose you take your presence out of here. How can I read with you in the house with me?" (p. 277).
"You get out of my house, old woman. Go home! If you've got a home"
—a cruelly aimed barb.

Lexie fights back: "I reckon what it amounted to was the two of us
settling down finally to see which would be the first to wear the other one
out" (p. 282). Lexie ties Julia in bed to keep her from running off and
hurting herself; refuses her a pencil when she sees that Julia's letters are
attacks on people ("Listen, Julia. If you've got something this bad to say

about human nature, . . . why don't you go ahead and send it to the President of the United States? What do you want to waste it on us for?" [p. 283]), though she does mail them; and meanly refuses to bring Julia a book because Julia doesn't name a specific title. In coming to the reunion, Lexie, it turns out, has left Julia alone to die.

It is important to remember, however, that of all the family Lexie has most loved Julia. "I worshipped her! Worshipped Miss Julia Mortimer!" she suddenly declares. She cried when Julia, her "inspiration," moved from the Renfros to the Vaughns. When Lexie was a child, Julia "encouraged" her to be a teacher, made the little girl feel important, worthwhile. But "the ones that think highly of you," Lexie remarks, "they change, or leave you behind, get married, flit, go crazy—" When Julia beat at Lexie, Lexie asked her, "Why don't you quit fighting kind hands? . . . I *love* you." To which Julia replied, "Only way to keep myself alive!" (p. 281). The answer might serve Lexie too, but it doesn't. Though it is deeply embedded in the rough bluntness of her telling, Lexie is grieving at what she has done. When Beulah, who has tried to cut short the story at several points, says that she hopes that Lexie is now "satisfied" since she got to tell the whole story, Lexie replies, "You don't get over it all that quick—what some of 'em make you do" (p. 285). So far from being motivated by cruel pleasure, Lexie tells the story out of a troubling guilt. Her story of Julia begins in shame and pain and ends in conversion. Suddenly, over one hundred pages later, Lexie, glaring defiantly at the reunion, announces that she knows now how to treat Mr. Hugg, to whose house she is going: "It's to give him every single thing he wants. Everything Mr. Hugg asks for—give it to him" (p. 377). Once again Julia has touched a member of the clan.

The relationship between Julia and the family is only one, though the most important, relationship in the novel in which oppositions turn out to be "like foes well-matched or sweethearts come together," in which collisions are both hurts and comminglings. Jack and Curly Stovall have fought with each other all their lives. Jack is "the sweetest and hardest-working boy . . . in all Creation," who can't blame anyone alive and loves everything from little birds and dead snakes to people; Curly, the spiritual descendant of Dearman, is a goatish "greedy hog," one of those who would take the joy out of life. But when Jack returns from the jail to which Curly helped send him, they embrace each other in a transport of cordiality. And at the end of the novel we learn that Ella Fay is going to marry Curly and so make him, like it or not, a part of the family. The reunion talks a good game of hating Moody ("the Booger") for sending their beloved Jack to jail—"Just let Moody dare to come up in my yard!"—but when he does, what they do is to feed him, treat him with kindness and consideration, give him and his wife the best sleeping accommodations, and rescue his Buick. Mr. Renfro especially takes "a shine to the fellow. . . . I couldn't tell you why. . . . I just did, that's all. If he'd stay a week, I'd take him turkey hunting" (p. 359). Jack must pay back Moody for sending him to jail. Moody, unknowingly, facilitates Jack's escape when Jack rides the back of his car part of the way home from Parchman. But when Moody's car goes into a ditch, Jack, not knowing who he is, pushes it out. When he learns he has helped his enemy, Jack sets out to get Moody into another ditch. But when Moody swerves to avoid hitting Gloria and Lady May and lands his car on Banner Top, Jack sets out to save the Buick. The almost magical way in which disparates are made to link—like the hilarious "chain" of people, animals, and machines which effects the car's rescue—is perfectly caught in the final moment between the family's darling and its villain: "Judge Moody put out his rope-burned hand, Jack put up his bloody one, and they shook." Ultimately, then, in the comic world of *Losing Battles* there are no "sides," though people take them. Like the election posters nailed to trees, "There were the faces of losers and winners, the forgotten and remembered, still there together and looking like members of the same family."

Comedy must make us feel, if for no longer than the enchanted time of reading, that Death and all those little deaths which are its harbingers have been triumphed over. It can do this, speaking largely, by the use of luck, wit, or as in the case of *The Tempest*, literal magic. Welty uses none of these, though her novel is closer to the feel of *The Tempest*; but her magic is the kind that can be assimilated into the texture of a realistic novel. Julia in the family plot and the reunion at the funeral; Jack and Moody clasping hands; sour Lexie sweetly off to give Mr. Hugg everything he wants; awful Curly a member of the family; Gloria, the devotée of Being Nobody But Herself, to have (lucky for her) family "piled" all over her; Grandpa Vaughn traded for Lady May; the Buick, like the people, beating the laws of probability, mechanics, and gravity. Destruction Is At Hand!? Hardly. "There's room for everything, and time for everybody, if you take your day the way it comes along and try not to be much later than you can help" (p. 362). The glory of *Losing Battles* is that it allows you to feel what it would be like *really* to believe in life.

BARBARA
MCKENZIE The Eye of Time:
The Photographs
of Eudora Welty

The Pencil of Nature (1844–46) by William
Henry Fox Talbot, the first photographic book
and the first important treatise on photography, is a very wise and joyful
book, replete with instruction and delight, procedure and artifact, fact and
prophecy. Susan Sontag's On Photography (1977), the most controversial
of recent treatises on the subject, is a wise and very somber book, one that
serves almost as a final reckoning, a domesday book full of judgment and
censure, insight and history. Most of what Talbot predicted about his photographic discoveries has come to pass: Sontag's book deals with the consequences of Talbot's rich and troubling legacy. Both books have a bearing
on One Time, One Place. Similarly the photographs in Eudora Welty's
"snapshot album" have a bearing on the author's fiction.

The second photographic plate in The Pencil of Nature is a street scene
of a Paris boulevard. Talbot explains that the time is afternoon, the weather
hot and dusty, the road partially under repair, and then adds: "A whole
forest of chimneys borders the horizon: for, the instrument chronicles whatever it sees, and certainly would delineate a chimney-pot or a chimney-
sweeper with the same impartiality as it would the Apollo of Belvedere."[1]
With that sentence Talbot anticipates a significant subject matter of photography and delineates one of the most important aesthetic principles of
the new art.

The subject matter is the street and all the dazzling variety of human
life found there, whether that life be in the London streets (John Thomson's Street Life in London, 1877) or the Paris boulevards (Jacques Henri
Lartigue's Diary of a Century, 1970). Chimney sweep or boulevardier,
chimney pot or parasol: each is made beautiful by the phenomena of light

[1] H. Fox Talbot, The Pencil of Nature (New York: Da Capo Press, 1969), unpaged.
First published by Longman, Brown, Green, and Longmans, London, 1844.

and lens. For the camera, like light itself, is no respecter of persons and, like light, has an easeful way of transforming even the grimmest reality of the streets into something beautiful. Sontag discusses the way photography has democratized the concept of beauty. "Traditionally associated with exemplary models (the representative art of the classical Greeks showed only youth, the body in its perfection), beauty has been revealed by photographs as existing everywhere. Along with people who pretty themselves for the camera, the unattractive and the disaffected have been assigned their beauty."[2] The photographs of Thomson's London, of Jacob Riis's New York City, of Dorothea Lange's rural America, of Eudora Welty's Mississippi attest to the transforming power of the camera.

The camera's ability not only to chronicle whatever it sees but to bestow beauty on whatever it chronicles objectified Eudora Welty's own awareness of the singular beauty and joy of her photographic subjects. In the foreword to *One Time, One Place* she talks about the people she met, most of them poor, most of them without much education, some of them having their picture taken for the first time. "I was able to give them something back, and though it might be that the picture would be to these poverty-marked men and women and children a sad souvenir, I am almost sure that it wasn't all sad to them, wasn't necessarily sad at all" (p. 6). The face of the woman in the frontispiece photograph is "heroic," and Welty knew that this picture must come first in the book. The strong slanting light illuminates the woman's features, coming in from above and to the side, highlighting cheekbone, nose, and mouth, revealing the stitch of the torn sweater, rimming the buttons and the selvage, lighting the hand at her side. The camera looks up at the woman (probably because the Kodak that Welty used—"one step more advanced than the Brownie"—was held at the waist rather than the eye for focusing), a placement that increases the dignity of the subject, suggesting, like the buttoned sweater, a steadfastness, a sureness, an inviolacy. The camera could only have acted as a reinforcing agent at this time in the author's life, serving in various and unexpected ways but always affording concrete proof of what she knew intuitively. "Trouble, even to the point of disaster, has its pale, and these defiant things of the spirit repeatedly go beyond it, joy the same as courage" (p. 6). That she took this knowledge and insight to her fiction is evidenced in stories like "Livvie" and "A Worn Path."

[2] Susan Sontag, *On Photography* (New York: Farrar, Straus and Giroux, 1977), p. 103. Subsequent references appear in the text.

The camera's way of chronicling whatever it sees accounts for its occasionally recording details unnoticed by the photographer during the moment of picture taking. Talbot acknowledges this propensity: "It frequently happens, moreover—and this is one of the charms of photography—that the operator himself discovers on examination, perhaps long afterwards, that he has depicted many things he had no notion of at the time" (Plate XIII). Talbot suggests using a magnifying glass. Welty used the clear light of day: "It was after I got home, had made my prints in the kitchen and dried them overnight and looked at them in the morning by myself, that I began to see objectively what I had there" (p. 7). The camera's vision is inclusive; the photographer's vision, no matter how accommodating he or she wants it to be, is exclusive. The eye responds to what the heart and mind, during the act of perceiving, deem important, but the photograph confronts the viewer with everything in the scene that reflected enough light into the camera to form an image. Clearly, the photographer's vision and *not* the photograph itself is closer to the writer's way of seeing. Welty discusses the writer's habit of choosing, combining, blotting out, shaping up, and otherwise altering the outside world for the good of the story. To accomplish this, she says in "Place in Fiction," the writer always sees double: "two pictures at once in his frame, his and the world's." The documentary photograph, for this reason among others, can never do what her writing does—namely, "to make the reader see only one of the pictures—the author's—under the pleasing illusion that it is the world's" (*ES*, p. 125). The camera is a machine with rules of order which have little to do with matters of the spirit, and the photographs that are its products, particularly those that are records of fact, are forever going to show chiefly the world's view.

Describing overlooked details recorded by the camera, Talbot elaborates: "Sometimes inscriptions and dates are found upon the buildings, or printed placards most irrelevant, are discovered upon their walls: sometimes a distant dial-plate is seen, and upon it—unconsciously recorded —the hour of the day at which the view was taken" (Plate XIII). The wall clock in Welty's photograph of the Holiness church (p. 85) has replaced Talbot's "distant dial-plate," but the inscriptions and printed matter, perhaps irrelevant to the church service, are meaningful to the viewer. A moveable blackboard gives a lesson in history that reveals the church's educational mission. A placard reads, "Be Prompt. On Time for Each Service." A drawing of a horse, its front quarters obliterated, is positioned above the placard. Another drawing bears the inscription, "The Lord on the Cloud." In the foreground, a woman faces us, her left hand upraised in prayer. Most of the congregation is turned toward the altar, their faces hidden. The camera is pointed up and at a slight angle, making the room tilt to the right and throwing the already asymmetrical composition more off balance. The camera angle implies that Welty wanted to include the two mystical drawings as well as the worshippers; but her camera chronicled everything else in the room as well: blackboard, coats hung on the wall, a pictorial calendar, chairs, altar, and more. The effect of this plethora of visual details is to create a sense not only of place but of mystery. What Welty said in an essay about the Pageant of Birds, another highly personal and emotional religious observance, applies here: "Everywhere, the life in a town that goes mostly unseen, because it does not happen to the spectacular inhabitants, never fails to make its own spectacular events out of what it has to work and play with."[3]

Eudora Welty describes herself as having a "visual mind, . . . I *see* everything I write."[4] Elsewhere she says, "I see things in pictures. . . . I love painting. I have no talent for it. The only talent I have—for writing, I was blessed with it—is quite visual."[5] The photographs in *One Time, One Place* attest, as does the fiction, to her sensitivity to pictorial detail. Most likely these photographs—taken "out of simple high spirits and the joy of being alive," scrutinized lovingly the next morning—demonstrated more vividly and more profoundly than any textbook on writing the significance and sheer quantity of objects in the everyday world and their contribution to our apprehension of place. But some photographs, like "Speaking in the Unknown Tongue" and "Home with Bottle-Trees" (p. 41), must have taught another lesson—that the exalted things of the spirit often realize themselves through the most mundane objects of unheightened existence, for in "Place in Fiction" she links place with mystery and with poetry, and in her fiction she seldom uses visual details for their mimetic value alone. Almost always, they have a symbolic function that clarifies and extends the meaning of the story. "Livvie" provides a good example.

The visual center of the story is Solomon's house, located on the farthest

---

[3] "Pageant of Birds," *New Republic*, 109 (25 October 1943), 565.

[4] Linda Kuehl, "The Art of Fiction XLVII: Eudora Welty," *Paris Review*, No. 55 (Fall 1972), 89.

[5] Charles T. Bunting, " 'The Interior World': An Interview with Eudora Welty," *The Southern Review*, 8 (Autumn 1972), 725.

reaches of the Old Natchez Trace, where Solomon, an old man, takes his young bride Livvie. The house and its furnishings suggest order, propriety, and nature confined. The front room, its walls decorated with green palmettos "spaced at careful intervals," contains a "double settee, a tall scrolled rocker and an organ . . . , all around a three-legged table with a pink marble top, on which was set a lamp with three gold feet, besides a jelly glass with pretty hen feathers in it" (*WN*, p. 154). The arrangement is precise, circular, and augmented by threes. The elegant mingles with the ordinary, pink marble with a jelly glass, gold plate with hen feathers. The front porch connotes a similar sense of decorum and containment: "On each side there was one easy chair with high springs, looking out, and a fern basket hanging over it from the ceiling, and a dishpan of zinnia seedlings growing at its foot on the floor" (p. 155).

The front yard contributes further to the general orderliness, for "every vestige of grass" has been "patiently uprooted," the bare earth "scarred in deep whorls from the strike of Livvie's broom." Next, comes a description of the bottle trees: a line of crape myrtles "with every branch of them ending in a colored bottle, green or blue." The bottle trees are another manifestation of Solomon's protectiveness, of his desire to keep trouble away from his house, for it was thought that bottle trees trapped evil spirits and kept them from getting in a house. But the trees have broader implications. Solomon allows no visitors because they too may bring trouble by enticing Livvie away from him. Neither does he allow her to leave the house and yard. The trees symbolize his fear of outside contamination. They signify also his desire to fracture and contain nature. "Solomon had made the bottle trees with his own hands over the nine years" of his marriage (p. 156). The bottles capping each branch have prevented the crape myrtle, a tree with profuse red, pink, or white blossoms, from blooming. Solomon has encased nature within the glass bottles in the same way he has encased Livvie by imprisoning her in his house. No matter how determined Solomon is to keep his house safe and decorous, in the end nature will have its way. Solomon's death allows Livvie's escape. In her new freedom she is joined by Cash McCord, one of Solomon's young field hands.

The bottle trees are natural symbols—that is, they exist as tangible phenomena observed and documented photographically by Eudora Welty. Put in the fiction, they impress us with their singularity and therefore contribute to the story's authenticity of setting and "achieved world of appearance" (*ES*, p. 117). But, as importantly, they also exist as symbols of character and theme, extending and enriching meaning.

The subtitle of Welty's book, "A Snapshot Album," is not intended pejoratively. "A better and less ignorant photographer would certainly have come up with better pictures, but not these pictures," she explains. For the most part, the subjects of the photographs in *One Time, One Place* were either unaware of the camera's presense or only peripherally aware. "These ought to be the best," she adds, "but I'm not sure that they are. The snapshots made with people's awareness are, for the most part, just as unposed: I simply asked people if they would mind going on with what they were doing and letting me take a picture" (p. 5). Informality of pose is a characteristic of the snapshot; so is informality of composition. The photographer documenting an extempore situation produces photographs that often appear to lack composition when judged against traditional formalistic standards. "Fisherman and His Boys Throwing Knives at a Target" (p. 40) provides a good example. The three figures overlap in a casual manner: the small boy in the foreground partially obscures the figures behind him. Similarly the father blocks a portion of the taller boy's body, and together they form an unsteady triangle that shields a truck in the background. Although the subjects are centered, the photograph is unbalanced; the trees, the barrel, and the direction of activity make the picture compositionally heavier on the right than on the left. The informality of composition is enhanced by the glaringly bright directional light that throws the faces of the father and the little boy in deep shadow. The photograph is over-exposed, giving it a bleached look and causing loss of detail in the highlight areas. A painter would not have painted this subject in the same way. In all probability he or she would have separated the figures and not allowed their bodies to overlap so ambiguously. Furthermore, the painter might have subdued or changed the direction of the light to illuminate the faces of the father and the little boy. Some painters would have balanced the barrel and trees by the addition of trees interrupting the horizon on the left. Welty's photograph, however unconsciously, is a good example of what critics call the "photographic way of seeing," a reaction, Sontag argues, to the criteria of photographic purity exemplified by Edward Weston and the Bauhaus school. "For a brief time—say, from Stieglitz through the reign of Weston—it appeared that a solid point of view had been erected with which to evaluate photographs: impeccable lighting, skill of composition, clarity of subject, precision of focus, perfection of print quality" (p. 136). She describes this position as bankrupt. Nor is it now acceptable to judge photographs by the "norms of painting, which assume conscious design and the elimination of non-essentials" (p. 103). A more inclusive position has replaced these traditional criteria, one which considers photographs as examples of photographic seeing rather than finished objects. Sontag writes that "what is meant by photographic seeing would hardly exclude Weston's work but it would also include a large number of anonymous, unposed, crudely lit, asymmetrically composed photographs formerly dismissed for their lack of composition" (p. 136). The new position, she says, puts the snapshot alongside the fine-art photograph by finding "no inherent conflict between the mechanical or naive use of the camera and formal beauty of a very high order, no kind of photograph in which such beauty could not turn out to be present: an unassuming functional snapshot may be as visually interesting, as eloquent, as beautiful as the most acclaimed fine-art photographs" (p. 103).

Sontag is careful to separate the fine-art photograph from the snapshot. So is Eudora Welty, but she valued what she was doing enough to try to sell her pictures—to "fiction editors, thinking or hoping if they liked my pictures (which I thought were fine) they might be inclined to take my stories (which I felt very dubious about, but I *wondered* about them—they being what I cared about)."[6] It seems that Eudora Welty was simply ahead of her time. Even the photographs done for the Farm Security Administration by such established and perceptive photographers as Dorothea Lange, Walker Evans, and Arthur Rothstein have a more formal quality. Their subjects are, like Welty's, the rural poor, but their photographs are composed more carefully, exposed more accurately, printed more expertly. Eudora Welty's photographs are closer to the aesthetic of contemporary photographers like Robert Frank (*The Americans*) and Garry Winogrand (*Women are Beautiful*). Not surprisingly, fiction editors in the 1930s were not "decoyed" by them. Nor is it surprising that in 1971 Random House, wanting to pay tribute to Eudora Welty, published this snapshot album.

The way of seeing represented in these photographs has an analogue in the prose style. That photographs should be beautifully composed, Sontag writes, "seems thin now, too obtuse to the truth of disorder" (p. 101). The opening paragraphs of "The Key" recreate verbally the inclusiveness

[6] Bernard Kalb, "The Author," *Saturday Review*, 38 (9 April 1955), 18.

and disorderly truth of a snapshot. The yellow light, to which bugs cling "like idiot bees to a senseless smell," shines indiscriminately on the passengers who sit silently, "their bodies twisted and quietly uncomfortable, expectantly so, in ones and twos, not quite asleep" (*CG*, p. 55). Among them is a little girl who lies "flung back in her mother's lap," and the abandonment of her pose swings attention to her. And then the focus shifts to Ellie and Albert Morgan and settles there, elaborating on their clothes and suitcase, on the differences between husband and wife. A wall poster, "dirty with time," is described, and then attention moves to a young man standing alone and holding a key which he turns "over and over in his fingers, nervously passing it from one hand to the other, tossing it gently into the air and catching it again" (p. 57). The young man watches the other passengers intently, his identity concealed as though, like them, he were merely an anonymous figure in a discarded photograph. "You guessed that he was a stranger in town; he might have been a criminal or a gambler, but his eyes were widened with gentleness. His look, which traveled without stopping for long anywhere, was a hurried focusing of a very tender and explicit regard" (pp. 57–58). The pulsating light prevents his body from casting a definite shadow and denies us the knowledge and dimensionality that shadows allow. When the key falls to the floor, the clatter becomes an almost visible intrusion. "It was regarded as an insult, a very personal question, in the quiet peaceful room" (p. 58). The key comes to rest at Albert's feet and he picks it up, examining it slowly, "with wonder written all over his face and hands, as if it had fallen from the sky. Had he failed to hear the clatter? There was something wrong with Albert . . ." (p. 59). The ellipsis is Eudora Welty's, and with it the suggestion that Albert is retarded, or deaf, or perhaps both. And his wife? We do not know until she begins to talk to him in sign language.

The story from here turns inward with the drama centering on Albert's responses to the key and the young man's compassionate understanding. His complexity is described in metaphors taken from photography. Closing your eyes, the narrator explains, you find that the young man's intensity, along with the room's, impresses the "imagination with a shadow of itself, a blackness together with the light, the negative beside the positive" (p. 62). In photographic printing, a negative is laid against positive printing paper and both are inserted in a contact printing frame. Welty uses that process to describe the fullness and emptiness of the stranger's life. "You felt as though some exact, skillful contact had been made between the surfaces of your hearts to make you aware, in some pattern, of his joy and his despair" (p. 62).

In this story, the humbleness of setting matches the unpretentiousness of the snapshot: how easy to dismiss these unassuming people, how natural to ignore the action surrounding the key, and yet how charged with meaning this simple encounter becomes. Welty creates her human drama from the most ordinary of materials. So does the snapshot, which as Ted Papageorge notes is limited to the surface of things: "that which can be seen. By a passionate extension of this, its most profound meanings have to do with immanence, the indwelling grace of what Zen calls our ten thousand facts. This is not transport, or celestial transcendence, but that more footed joy and grief found near any clear sighting of the world."[7] A small portion of the world, with all its indwelling grace, is sighted very clearly in "A Key."

The snapshot has an application to this story in still another way. The naive imagery of most snapshots has revolutionized how we see, according to John A. Kouwenhoven, "by reshaping our conceptions of what is real and therefore of what is important."[8] Most people see and value only what the pictorial conventions of their time are calculated to show them. The snapshot's influence is distinctly antiestablishment. "The extraordinary thing about snapshots," says Kouwenhoven, "is that they teach us to see things not even their makers had noticed or been interested in." A double argument applies to Eudora Welty here. Her own early viewing of snapshots prepared her to take the photographs she did, but they in turn taught her what was important. "The Key," like most of the seemingly ordinary snapshots in *One Time, One Place*, provides a lesson in seeing.

In other stories visual details of person and place, no matter how clearly presented, remain essentially mysterious, like the bizarre ornamentation in the photograph of the bottle trees and like the characters and setting in the story, "At the Landing." Voluminous specific visual description fails to offset the dreamlike and mysterious effect. This is a place where boats run "over the houses" and where a man carrying a fishing pole walks through the empty streets "like a dreamer." This story begins and ends in darkness; it emerges with the dying dream of an old man and concludes with the forthright questions of an old woman. Everyday activities like houseclean-

---

[7] "The Snapshot," *Aperture*, 19, No. 1 (1974), 27.
[8] "The Snapshot," *Aperture*, 19, No. 1 (1974), 107.

ing and eating, walking and lovemaking, photographic in the specificity of their rendering, partake of fantasy. Jenny cleans house "as if driven, carrying buckets and mops." She scrubs and pries and forgets "even love" in her cleaning. In this "whole new ecstasy," she stretches the white curtains and sheets, rubs the rust off knives until they shine, and wipes the prisms clean. The housecleaning is excessive, the cause which precipitated it dark and mysterious. If there is such a thing as a vague intensity, that is the special quality of life at The Landing. The movements of the town's inhabitants are watched minutely, but they have a way of disappearing "out to the blue distance" like Billy Floyd. Even the cemetery, on the site of the "old landing place when the ships docked from across the world a hundred years ago," is topsy-turvy: "the hanging moss and the upthrust stones" provide "shade where, by the light they give, the moss seems made of stone, and the stone of moss" (*WN*, p. 184).

In this story seeing is blocked by persistent images that push into Jenny's consciousness: "Floyd's face glared before her eyes all the way, it was like something in her vision that kept her from seeing" (p. 196). Images, like glances of love, slip in and out of the mind, in and out of lovers' meetings. The characters and actions are as illusive as the light refracted by the prisms that hang "everywhere in the shadow of the halls and in the sunlight of the rooms, stirring under the hanging lights, dangling and circling where they were strung in the window curtains" (p. 181). The amber beads provide another substance that reflects and changes light as Jenny looks through the outer surface to the core. "Nobody could ever know about the difference between the radiance that was the surface and the radiance that was inside. There were the two worlds. There was no way at all to put a finger on the center of light" (p. 209). Light, like love, eludes; the dream of love does not coincide with the reality of love; the realities of place dissolve into the phantasmagoric and mythic. The downward thrust of realistic detail, linking the story with earth and river, and the upward thrust of light and vision, pushing the story toward mystery, create a truly remarkable tension, as dream is confronted by reality, innocence by experience, the spirit by the flesh.

Eudora Welty describes fiction as using the oblique to accomplish its ends. Fiction writers, she explains, work indirectly, showing rather than telling, revealing character through action and dialogue rather than exposition. "Anything lighted up from the side, you know, shows things in a relief that you can't get with a direct beam of the sun. And the imagination works all around the subject to light it up and reveal it in all its complications."[9] Images of light occur throughout the stories and novels, but no matter how glaringly the sun shines, or how indirectly it is positioned overhead, the characters and actions it lights up remain mysterious, as in "At the Landing," because the light cannot penetrate the core.

Light is, of course, the photographer's medium. In "Introductory Remarks," Fox Talbot describes his pictures as being "wholly executed by the new art of Photogenic Drawing, without any aid whatever from the artist's pencil." The photograph, he explains in "Invention of the Art," "divested of the ideas which accompany it, and considered only in its ultimate nature, is but a succession or variety of stronger lights thrown upon one part of the paper, and of deeper shadows on another." Talbot recognized that under certain circumstances the action of light is sufficient to cause "changes in material bodies." Eudora Welty, as a photographer and as a writer, understands this transformational property of light. In her fiction as in the photographs, light glares and burns and shines; it is life-giving; it casts shadows; it outlines. In the fiction, however, it does more than leave "its image or impression behind, stronger or weaker on different parts of the paper according to the strength or weakness of the light which had acted there," to quote Fox Talbot again. Most often, it serves as the tangible equivalent of intangible qualities, and, like other phenomena of the natural world, is connected to meaning.

In "At the Landing," for example, Jenny leaves her ancestral home to find Floyd as the sun is setting. "The red eyes of the altheas were closing. . . . The last lily buds hung green and glittering, pendulant in the heat. The crape-myrtle trees were beginning to fill with light for they drank the last of it every day, and gave off their white and flame in the evening that filled with the throb of cicadas. There was an old mimosa closing in the ravine —the ancient fern, as old as life, the tree that shrank from the touch, grotesque in its tenderness. All nearness and darkness affected it, even clouds going by" (p. 211). The dominant images are of closing, of the cessation of activity. Jenny looks back at her house glinting in the sun's last rays, "tinted with the drops of light that seemed to fall slowly through the vaguely stirring leaves." The evening opalescence matches Jenny's newly acquired maturity; the tumult of the flood is behind her, similarly the franticness of the housecleaning. Now there is acquiescence, even languor, a soft ripeness. At the river's edge, she sees the blue nets like veils

[9] Bunting, "Interior World," p. 725.

as they hang out to dry. "All things, river, sky, fire, and air, seemed the same color, the color that is seen behind the closed eyelids, the color of day when vision and despair are the same thing" (p. 212). The uniformity of color symbolizes the oneness with which Jenny accepts the world and her place in it.

Images of light, as this passage reveals, are related intimately with time, for seasons affect the quality of light, as does time of day. Descriptions of light provide Welty with a means of depicting changes in time and, almost as importantly, of lessening time's anonymity, of establishing time's elusive but felt presence. In "Some Notes on Time in Fiction," she describes time as a crucial but difficult element in fiction, for it reveals "nothing about itself except by the signals that it is passing" (*ES*, p. 163). Place engenders affection, even love; time is "something of an enemy." Photography is as intimately connected with time as fiction, a fact Welty recognizes. But the photographer's time is not the fiction writer's time, a discrepancy she also recognizes. *One Time, One Place* reveals a good deal about photographic time and, by implication, fictional time.

On the most basic level, the photographs are a "record of fact" that combines "some of the elements of one time and one place." As such, they are of historic interest for what they reveal about Mississippi in the mid-1930s. They depict the past not only through objectively rendered visual details like cars, clothing, and houses but through a more subjectively felt quality which Welty describes as trust. "The photographs of black persons by a white person may not testify soon again to such intimacy. It is trust that dates the pictures now, more than the vanished years" (p. 6). Because these photographs depict an unreclaimable past, they also convey a sense of nostalgia.

Sontag finds one of photography's strongest appeals related to the sense of time, of which nostalgia is a product. "Photography is an elegiac art, a twilight art. . . . All photographs are *memento mori*. To take a photograph is to participate in another person's (or thing's) mortality, vulnerability, mutability. Precisely by slicing out this moment and freezing it, all photographs testify to time's relentless melt" (p. 15). Extending this argument, she says that photographs show the "innocence, the vulnerability of lives heading toward their own destruction, and this link between photography and death haunts all photographs of people" (p. 70). To Sontag, the presence of time in photographs reminds us of our own mortality, and this may account for one of their deepest meanings. Eudora Welty makes a similar claim for fiction: "We are mortal: this is time's deepest meaning in the novel as it is to us alive." The ephemeral is important to fiction because it triggers our sense of "what endures, or strives to endure." The parallel with the snapshot, ephemeral in both form and content, is evident. Welty explains further: "Fiction's concern is with the ephemeral—that is, the human—effects of time, these alone. In action, scene, and metaphor, these are set how unforgettably before our eyes!" (*ES*, p. 168).

Despite the common denominator of mortality, photographic time and fictional time are quite different. A commonplace of photographic criticism is that the photograph freezes time—the "fascination of a photograph of anything is that it imprisons a moment in time," to quote from Eudora Welty's "Literature and the Lens."[10] Sontag writes, "The force of a photograph is that it keeps open to scrutiny instants which the normal flow of time immediately replaces" (p. 111). Neither the story nor the novel freezes time in this way. Although isolated moments may be held up to view, elaborated on, crystallized, and examined from different aspects— like that moment in the garden when Mrs. Larkin contemplates striking Jamey—time in any narrative art posits a continuum. Welty is emphatic on time as duration: "Time is the bringer-on of action, the instrument of change.... Time has the closest possible connection with the novel's meaning, in being the chief conductor of the plot" (*ES*, p. 165). Time is the element "through which, and by which, all things in their turn are brought forth in their significance—events, emotions, relationships in their changes, in their synchronized move toward resolution" (*ES*, p. 167). Welty suggests a sense of continuum in *One Time, One Place* by having three of the four categories relate to days of the week: Workday, Saturday, and Sunday. But these images remain isolated moments, and for that reason photography for her could never be an end in itself: "I learned quickly enough when to click the shutter, but what I was becoming aware of more slowly was a story-writer's truth" (p. 7). The snapshot, she explains, is a "moment's glimpse (as a story may be a long look, a growing contemplation) into what never stops moving." Exposure to the world is essential, but reflection is more important. "Insight doesn't happen often on the click of the moment, like a lucky snapshot, but comes in its own time and more slowly and from nowhere but within" (p. 8). The story-writer's truth requires duration, the unfolding of meaning. "Ever since I had begun taking painting lessons, I had made small frames with my fingers, to look

10 "Literature and the Lens," *Vogue*, 104 (1 August 1944), 102.

out at everything," the narrator of "A Memory" explains. "To watch everything about me I regarded grimly and possessively as a *need*. . . . I was obsessed with notions about concealment, and from the smallest gesture of a stranger I would wrest what was to me a communication or a presentiment" (*CG*, pp. 143–44). The child's hands form a frame not unlike that of the photograph, but imposing one's vision on reality in this manner is antithetical to revelation. Objectifying the world this way does not lead to subjective truth. The child is too young; insight into human behavior will come for her with maturity. For Eudora Welty the photograph's frame had to yield to the more open boundaries of fiction and the possibilities of contemplation, of indwelling, of journeys to the unfathomable core. Sontag finds photography similarly restrictive as a medium for communicating knowledge: "the truths that can be rendered in a dissociated moment, however significant or decisive, have a very narrow relation to the needs of understanding" (p. 112). Photographs give the illusion of communicating wisdom. The error, she argues, lies in the assumption that we know the world when we accept it as recorded by the camera. "This is the opposite of understanding, which starts from *not* accepting the world as it looks." Understanding, she maintains, depends on knowledge of how something functions. "And functioning takes place in time, and must be explained in time. Only that which narrates can make us understand" (p. 23).

For Eudora Welty the camera's mechanical nature was a further distancing factor. Its lens was unable either to see or give pain, or to "catch effervescence, color, transience, kindness or what was not there" (*OTOP*, p. 7). The photographs in *One Time, One Place* provide early evidence of her wish "not to point the finger in judgment but to part a curtain, that invisible shadow that falls between people, the veil of indifference to each other's presence, each other's wonder, each other's human plight" (*OTOP*, p. 8). But to do that more fully she needed words and the causality and duration of narration. The limitations of photography are embodied in a description of a china night light that occurs in "Place in Fiction." The outside of the lamp was "painted with a scene, which is one thing; then, when the lamp is lighted, through the porcelain sides a new picture comes out through the old, and they are seen as one" (*ES*, pp. 119–20). The lamp remembered from childhood showed a view of London until it was lighted, and then it became the Great Fire of London. Photography is the external scene. Fiction is the lighted lamp in which interior and exterior are combined, "glowing at the imagination as one."

Eudora Welty describes every feeling as waiting "upon its gesture" (*OTOP*, p. 8). For her, it now seems, the gesture was writing, for which photography was a very good apprenticeship. At the very least it got her away from stories about the "great world" and Monsieur Boule "inserting a delicate dagger in Mademoiselle's left side." [11] But it did much more than that. The act of photographing turned her eye to Mississippi and to the richness of visual detail there for the observing. And it gave us, four decades later, photographs which are an intimate and gallant record of the eye of time.

[11] Kuehl, "Art of Fiction," p. 89.

MICHAEL   Words into Criticism:
KREYLING   Eudora Welty's Essays
and Reviews

EUDORA WELTY'S essay "Words into Fiction," first published in 1965 and collected in *The Eye of the Story*, opens with an unassuming sentence: "We start from scratch, and words don't; which is the thing that matters—matters over and over again" (p. 134). This assertion seems so obvious that one flirts with naiveté just to point it out. But, as with all of Welty's writing—fiction as well as nonfiction—a world of significance lies just behind it. It is a critical first principle: approach literature with respect and attention, not with hubris and theories, for the artistic thing, the work, is beauty and the theory is only a description of it—not the thing itself. Criticism and fiction, stories and their interpretations, may not have much in common, according to Welty, but they do have a common goal: beauty. This beauty was, as were the words in which it finds or is given embodiment, here before us in the world. Criticism must respect that seniority.

Welty's critical essays and reviews are alive with this trust in and respect for beauty and the authors who work to give it form. Her works of nonfiction are not only models of perception and an appreciation of individual authors she reads as well as or better than anyone else; they are also guides to the reading of fiction in general. Inevitably and fortunately these essays are also valuable windows on Welty's own fiction. Reading and writing about other writers, the novelist shows us how best to read her own work.

Underpinning all fiction and criticism, of course, are words. Words are what we have to express our relationship with the world: *love, joy, fear, pain, loneliness.* Our relationship with the world is original and unique, or so we think, but our words are common property. How do writers transform the common property of words into a unique literary and artistic expression, and thereby give us back our own words enriched and revitalized? A good question with a difficult answer. In "Words into Fiction" Welty hints at the source of the difficulty: "The mystery lies in the use of language to express human life" (p. 137). The process of words into fiction, then, is mysterious, and the work of words into criticism of fiction, it follows, must not only tolerate mystery but rejoice in it. Welty's own critical writings counsel extreme care in the act of reading lest this "carefully laid connection" (p. 137) between author and reader be ruined.

The way in which Welty's literary criticism preserves the mysterious core of imaginative literature, while finding and illuminating it, can be seen by looking at certain words that occur frequently and significantly in her essays and reviews. The words any critic uses in the pursuit of interpretation and appreciation spring from his or her critical sensitivity and, in a material way, free or restrict the experience of literature. Words such as *psychological, anxiety, text, influence, the morality of, the politics of*, immediately advertise certain approaches to literature. And approaches have a lot to do with destinations.

To explore Welty's distinctive critical language, let me offer an example of a different kind of critical writing to serve as a foil. In an exchange of letters to the editor of *The New York Times Book Review* (20 July 1975, pp. 24–25) Welty disputed Richard Gilman's opinion of Reynolds Price's novel *The Surface of Earth* (*NYTBR*, 29 June 1975, pp. 1–2). Welty's protest is stated in characteristic language for her: "But he's [Gilman] plainly not ready yet to recognize this power for what it is, the passionate working of a gifted and highly individual imagination" (*NYTBR*, 20 July 1975, p. 24). Gilman, in his reply, does not acknowledge language such as this as valid in literary discussion. To him it seems vapid, something like the "jargon . . . of the blurb-writer" (*NYTBR*, 20 July 1975, p. 25). Gilman's own critical language is much different and characteristic of another approach to literature: "Price's notion of love as 'simple peace,' 'kindness,' 'welcome,' etc. is extraordinarily soft and lacking in the kind of dramatic tension, the turbulence and sense of extremity that has almost universally characterized the treatment of the theme in serious fiction" (*NYTBR*, 20 July 1975, p. 25).

Words such as *dramatic tension, turbulence, extremity, serious fiction*, characterize a critical consciousness with firm preconceptions about literature, its current trends, the criteria of excellence "universally" accepted. Gilman provides an even more striking example of his approach in his original review (*NYTBR*, 29 June 1975, pp. 1–2), in which he initially sets up a "perspective" for his discussion of the novel. His perspective is not genuinely a perspective at all, but a narrow corridor of terms and assumptions (having to do with Southern literature and its place in or out of the "general consciousness") that excludes all other ways of reading the novel. In other words, the critic's language reigns over the literary work by attempting to allow only a certain kind of reading.

Behind Welty's letter of objection there is not the regional or "cultural paranoia" (*NYTBR*, 20 July 1975, p. 25) that Gilman anticipated from writers who do not benefit from his judgments, but an artist's deeply felt opposition to criticism that becomes resistance and judgment before it has seen what is there in front of it. Welty's criticism, in contrast, is a series of examples of how to see what is there by allowing the imagination full play—not turbulent struggle—to discover and meet the author. Criticism, like writing itself, for Welty is not a statement or doctrine but a living process.

To see her criticism in its fullness one must pay close attention to recurrent words in the reviews and essays. As these words appear, meaning clusters around them; they become fully resonant. Consider the words *analysis, analytic, study* (noun), and the word *criticism* itself. These words point to pitfalls to be avoided, for analysis performed upon literature is too often a form of vivisection.

In *Short Stories*, first published in 1949 and considerably revised for inclusion in *The Eye of the Story*, Welty voices her suspicions of criticism that "can seem blind itself, when it is ingrown and tedious; on the other hand it can see things in large wholes and in subtle relationships we should be only stupid not to investigate."[1] Such ingrown and tedious criticism, Welty continues, might illuminate the what of a story, but it can never get to the why or the how. It might number the bones, but it will never capture the soul, "the starting point of inspiration,"[2] because that has been dissipated in the very act of analysis.

Several years later her reservations were still strong. In "How I Write," first published in 1955 and revised and retitled "Writing and Analyzing a Story" in *The Eye of the Story*, Welty says: "Story writing and critical analysis are indeed separate gifts, like spelling and playing the flute, and the same writer proficient in both has been doubly endowed. But even he can't rise and do both at the same time" (p. 107). Critical analysis, she goes on to say, is the reverse of the creative, synthesizing act. The critic's choices

[1] Eudora Welty, *Short Stories* (New York: Harcourt, Brace, 1949), p. 8.
[2] Ibid., p. 9.

are not similar in character to the choices of the writer. Imagination rather than analysis is the proper way to read a story, for that is the path the author took toward his vision. And "only the story is to some degree a vision" (pp. 109–10).

In her reviews and criticism Welty offers examples of what, to her, literary criticism ought to be and to do. Most paths that do not begin with a reading of the story leave her with misgivings. Of biographical studies, for example, she is sceptical. Reviewing *Selected Letters of William Faulkner* she hints of her lack of enthusiasm for the project of editing the correspondence of a man who was the "fierce guardian of his own privacy" (*ES*, p. 212). The writing human being, Welty reiterates, is the individual whom we ought to remember. And we ought to remember the writer by reading his work: "If you want to know all you can about that heart and soul, the fiction where he put it is still right there. . . . Read that" (pp. 219–20).

Elizabeth Bowen thought literary analysis would have done only limited good service to her work, according to Welty in her review of Bowen's posthumous book about herself and her work. Bowen looked askance at "studies and analyses" (*ES*, p. 270) which, to her, were often "wildly off the mark" (p. 270). Welty is similarly cool to the method of literary analysis employed by Arthur Mizener in his biography of Ford Madox Ford. Ford was a personal friend of Welty's who strove, in the final months of his life, to find a publisher for her first collection of short stories. But this personal connection with Ford plays a small part in the review. Welty's objections center upon the biographer's method and upon what she sees as his restrictive assumptions about literature and "real life" (p. 247). She regrets the way in which Mizener chooses to read *The Good Soldier*, for she fears he does not make the "essential leap of mind to discover the novel as a complete entity, a world in itself and quite freed of its author" (p. 246). She further objects to the critical assumptions about the relationship of art and life: "In effect he [Mizener] implies that all that's not 'real life' is inferior to it, that fiction is at best secondhand life, that fiction is in fact not honest, for it has been stolen from life and is capable of being returned to its original state by reliable critics" (p. 247). Such assumptions about the supremacy of "real life" and the critic's duty to dismantle the fiction run counter to Welty's own artistic and critical intuitions and practices. The critic who goes at literature as if it were a riddle or a specimen too often saps the very living thing he is supposed to nurture with what Welty calls imagination. This is the unfortunate harm that critical analysis might do. The best one might do, on the other hand, would be first to choose a writer with whom one feels an affinity or sympathy. Mizener, for example, approached Ford with insufficient *tolerance* and *sympathy*. In reviews and essays about Faulkner, Bowen, Chekhov, Cather and others, and in comments about her own work, Welty gives a sustained example of her alternative path.

It is the nature of Welty's criticism that it be less an objection and more a celebration and expression of thanks; for the act of writing, the turning of words into fiction, is of greatest importance to her, and the act of criticizing is the outgrowth of a careful act of the imagination: reading. At the heart of the matter, then, is an interchange in words which should leave both writer and reader enriched. Welty uses several words to describe this central act. Her approach to writing and reading is not just a model for criticism; it is, taken in its principles, also a guide to the reading of her fiction.

Imagination is an important word; for Welty it names one of the essential attributes of writer and reader. That reader who fails or is ill-equipped to make the essential leap of mind, to project his vision into and beyond the work of art, fails to supply the vital ingredient to the creative act. That act begins in the imagination of the writer when the raw material of experience and sensitivity begins its translation into words. Welty's most widely known essay, "Place in Fiction," is a discussion of one of the most frequent originating moments: the sense or experience of place. Elsewhere (in "Writing and Analyzing a Story") Welty says she is often "touched off by place," and the metaphor of a spark igniting combustible material is apt, for the imagination is the flammable material which awaits the spark. "The imagination has to be involved, and more—ignited" (p. 139).

The imagination of the writer is engaged not only at the instant of combustion; the writer's imagination, once sparked, embarks upon a sustained and creative discovery of the "living, uncopyable *identity*" (p. 44) of the material, which is inextricably both what is seen and the way of seeing, the world and the self in the world. To use the example of place once again: "Location, however, is not simply to be used by the writer— it is to be discovered, as each novel itself, in the act of writing, is discovery" (p. 129). A novella like *The Robber Bridegroom*, for example, is not primarily history—that is, the recording of statistics and data of location in the attempt to be realistic in setting. It is first fiction in which these particulars of history—place, time, Indians and whites, towns and customs—are discovered in the act of writing to be subtly and meaningfully extended and beyond history, time, and place in a work that reaches far and deep into realms both personal and communal. The connections, to paraphrase E. M. Forster, are everything: "Fictional patterns may well bite deeper than the events of a life will ever of themselves, or by themselves, testify to. The pattern is one of interpretation. There, the connections are as significant as what they join together, or perhaps more so. The meaning comes through the joined and completed structure, out of the worthiness of its accomplishment" (*ES*, p. 48).

The artist's imagination makes these discoveries of integrity, of joined structure and connection. *Awakening* is another word for discovery: "I think it more accurate to call it [*The Robber Bridegroom*] an awakening to a dear native land and its own story of early life, made and offered by a novelist's imagination in exuberance and joy" (*ES*, p. 314). The imagination operates in all of Welty's stories, discovering in *Delta Wedding*, for instance, the multifaceted point of view that is right for the novel's vision of the multiple mysteries of human life; discovering in *The Golden Apples* the intimate dependence of opposites and the many-layered correspondences between mythology and life in a small Mississippi town; discovering in *The Optimist's Daughter* the images and experiences that reveal a meaningful world in what appears, to the imperfect eye, to be a welter of vulgarity, error, and misunderstanding. Each of Welty's works, in its own way, discovers in and through the working of the imagination the vital integrity, the rock of truth, of which art is made and from which it draws the life that keeps it going, that enables it "to bear the responsibility of its own meaning" (p. 135).

The reader is not excluded from this act, even though some of Welty's works—the stories of *The Bride of the Innisfallen*, for instance—are for some readers too difficult to follow. As the imagination of the artist works outward from self and form to finished and separate thing, the beholder must work inward from the surface of the art (words, character, setting, plot) to the originating vision, which is the destination of Welty's own critical path. Thus the reader shares and participates in the making of the art, if he does not succumb to the powers of critical analysis. *Critical analysis* is a pejorative term when it hampers the act of reading by outlawing or constraining the imagination of the reader. If analysis seeks only the data (location rather than the fully-armed place in fiction, for example) then the "leap" from reader's ledge to the terra firma of the story's rock of truth will be misdirected. When the imagination of the reader is vital and life-giving, however, a meeting occurs—not a simple exchange of information—and life is shared. (The frequency of weddings and brides in Welty's fiction, each an instance of such a meeting either actual or symbolic, is not surprising. Meeting is the important aspect of both theme and technique.) For this successful and living act Welty uses a pair of words: *love* and *communication*.

To image the joint act of making literature with the word *love* is to endow it with special importance—for love is the greatest of virtues. *Love* also suggests an aura of mystery, for it is the antithesis of *theory* and *formula*. So often does Welty use the words *love* and *communication* to evoke both the vital importance and the vital mystery of writing and reading fiction that we, as readers, can sense something of the artistic convictions about "each other's presence, each other's wonder, each other's human plight" (p. 355) that are the lifeblood of her fiction.

This act of love, writing, issues from a human nature isolated and bound within a self. The self, along with words and literary forms, is part of the gorgon against which the writer strives. Style is the means of objectifying the self, of placing it in the physical world. A successful style enables the author to transcend his individual self, to overcome the considerable barriers to communication with other selves, to look at the gorgon without being stricken speechless. Style, then, serves communication (p. 140) and is the means to that end. In expressing what is so uniquely the self, the writer may touch upon what is universally the self, and in so doing he creates a community of readers whose company somehow spans time and mortality: the mundane barriers to communication and love, the latter-day gorgons whose looks have paralyzed Eugene MacLain in "Music from Spain." If one looks and listens closely to Welty speaking of her cherished authors (Cather, Chekhov, Woolf), one may witness this process of creation.

Reading Virginia Woolf, Welty senses the great struggle at the core of literary creation: "But the beauty and the innovation of her writing are both due to the fact, it seems to this reader, that the imprisonment of life in the word was with her a concern of the intellect as much as it was with the senses" (p. 98). And, some years later, that intimacy still held, for Welty writes that "at the very core of Virginia Woolf's life" there was a certainty of the ephemeral quality and the mystery of human existence; there was a sense of the ultimate futility of order counterbalanced only by the work of art that keeps life from going utterly to pieces (p. 197).

Woolf's struggle to objectify herself in her art strikes Welty as most draining. For Willa Cather the same struggle is waged among different details of time and place. At the heart of Welty's admiration for Cather is Cather's love: "The desire to make a work of art, and the making of it—which is love accomplished without help or need of help from another, and not without tragic cost—is what is deepest and realest, so I believe, in what she has written of human beings."[3] The act of complete attention to the world (the desire to make) coupled with the effort to wrestle the essence of that attention into words is the complex act of making art that, when the art is made, communicates. The making is attended, at all points and in its totality, by love. The form love takes is attention; at every step it must be perfect: "Focus then means awareness, discernment, order, clarity, insight—they are like the attributes of love" (*ES*, p. 123). The sense of the physical world, the isolating of the attention upon it, the ordering of the experience into words, the objectivity to render this clearly, the insight into the whole which this process affords, are the stages of artistic creation of which love is the essential principle.

Writing about "A Worn Path" Welty suggests an added dimension when she says that her story may be an allegory of sorts for the life of authorship. Phoenix Jackson is the writer who makes the journey over and over (writing) in the hope of "getting there" (making the communicative connection of art). But, as Welty also points out, the ordinary facts, whether the grandson is really dead or alive, whether Phoenix hallucinates or not, are not of the first importance. They are the explanations of the analytic mind seeking answers in the ordinary world. The truth of the story is different. "The path is the thing that matters" (p. 162); and the "habit of love," of striving again and again to give, is the essence of the act of writing, of putting words on paper and into fiction.

This particular kind of love is not exclusive, for all readers are invited to enter at any time. It is not private, although at times it may be difficult, nor is the reader asked to invest hugely for returns the fiction is not ready and able to make. There are, then, limits to style. It is not perceived as an

---

[3] Eudora Welty, "The Physical World of Willa Cather," *New York Times Book Review*, 27 January 1974, p. 20. I quote from this version because the language is not as concentrated as in the revised version in *The Eye of the Story*.

end in itself, a marvelously working jewelled construct protected from the reader's touch. Style in Welty's fiction is inseparably part of the meaning: the self searched and explored in the hope of transcending the self. So the particular kind of perseverance and love of Ellen Fairchild, of Laurel Mc-Kelva Hand, of Virgie Rainey, and of many other heroes and heroines of Welty's fiction can be seen as the heroism of love, the risking of the self in the mission to go beyond it and into the world. This journey—Phoenix's and the writer's—gives back the lovers to themselves enriched. Such a journey, with its meetings and discoveries and setbacks, distinguishes the plots of many of Welty's fictions. Such is the import of Ellen's looking at George Fairchild, of Laurel's gripping the breadboard, of Virgie's crucial moments in the shining rain simply greeted by the old black woman (veteran of journeys). In such characteristic climaxes Welty's fictions stand "as clear as candor itself. The fine physical thing has become a transparency through which the idea it was made to embody is thus made totally visible. It could not have been this visible before it was embodied. We see human thought and feeling best and clearest by seeing it through something solid that our hands have made" (p. 58).

Self is to style, then, as place is to form, for self contains inchoate each strand of connection, each minute filament of nuance and suggestion out of which the whole is knit. The effort first to patiently entice this integrity into one's vision, and then to behold it as reader (to make the essential leap) requires a quality in both artist and reader that is most frequently named by Welty as passion. It cannot be analyzed, yet it is unmistakably present.

Passion, as a significantly recurring word, signifies the antithesis of the cold and technical disassembling of fiction that might take place in the process of critical analysis. When a reader, writer, or critic clings to the validity of everyday life rather than to the validity of the story (cf. *Short Stories*, p. 48); when he or she prefers the ordinary truth to the "*artistic* truth" (*ES*, p. 160); when the reader ransacks fiction for a slogan or political dimension and, failing to find an attractive one, dismisses the whole fiction—then that reader, writer, or critic lacks the passion necessary for the appreciation of works of art. The most apt analogy for passion that I can think of comes from my college physics. Passion is to works of literature what binding energy is to the atom. Binding energy, I was taught, is that energy in excess of what can be determined to be present in the various parts of the atom: proton, neutron, and electron. It is the attribute of the atom which it possesses as an entity, which distinguishes it from the sum of its parts. Passion in a work of literature, or in its maker, is that quality which distinguishes the work as a whole, which distinguishes the maker as a person rather than the sum of his or her attributes. Passion cannot be accounted for by the simple analysis of parts. Writing about Willa Cather, Welty indicates the wholeness which is the mark of artistic passion: "A work of art is a *work*: something made, which in the making follows an idea that comes out of human life and leads back into human life. A work of art is the house that is *not* the grave. An achievement of order, passionately conceived and passionately carried out, it is not a thing of darkness" (p. 58). In her brief account of the imaginative process, passion has the crucial part, for it must mark the conception and the making of the artistic thing while it is itself the thing embodied, made. This is not an impossible situation when we remember the analogy of binding energy, for in literature, as Welty reads it, the thing made is not identical with the parts and particulars. The whole work possesses a nature that is fundamentally different from that of the collected or assembled (or disassembled) parts. The artist's passion confers this different nature upon the completed work of art and is itself the thing conferred. If this were not so, then Austen's fiction would be Cather's, Cather's Woolf's, Woolf's Faulkner's, and so on. That this passion is elusive and mysterious should not bother anyone either. A work of art is not supposed to be as fully reducible as a theorem of a mathematical formula or a political speech.

Passion reigns over all other motives for writing; it even displaces some of the words used to discuss other aspects of writing. In "Place in Fiction" Welty says that the writer "is always seeing double, two pictures at once in his frame, his and the world's, a fact that he constantly comprehends; and he works best in a state of constant and subtle and unfooled reference between the two. It is his clear intention—his passion, I should say—to make the reader see only one of the pictures—the author's—under the pleasing illusion that it is the world's; this enormity is the accomplishment of a good story" (*ES*, p. 125). Any connotations of conscious premeditation, of mapping out, are dismissed with the substitution of passion for intention. The writer embarked on his story, like Phoenix on her worn path, has nothing more definite than herself for destination, no map more specific than hope or the habit of love. For Phoenix the culmination is seeing the diploma with the gold seal in the doctor's office: not the emblem of a man's proficiency but the emblem of her own integral life of love, sacrifice, hardship—her time held for an instant of stillness. How often has Welty's own image of the still moment been invoked in discussions of her fiction?

What passion supplies to fiction, to the writer and to the reader, is truer than anything conscious intention or "crusading" might have given, for it stills the "perishable life" better than slogans (p. 60). The conviction of the perishableness of life and the self infuses Welty's concern with passion. The world without the artist's passion is a fearful place, what Welty imagines it must have been to Virginia Woolf—the constant "splitting asunder" that makes self-destruction a reality. With passion the artist and the reader together discover self in the world, together see the world's multiplicity not as chaos, a sink of ambiguity, but as a lifegiving mystery. Passion, then, is not a ray from the brain but rather a luminous consciousness of the heart in which the integrity of the physical world is sensed rather than intellectually understood.

Passion is, in the end, indefinable; it is like a fingerprint: identifiable, even analyzable in its individual whorls and contours, but possessed by only one person. Passion is also the attribute of the ideal reader who gives himself to the control initiated by the writer. Within the self the writer conceives and then grapples with his experience, trying through imagination to find the words and patterns to contain and to recreate his experience. From his own private self the reader moves on the path worn with the writer's care and love. Meeting to behold the momentary stay against the perishableness of reality, the "ultimate futility" of man in time and on the earth, is the success and the gift of art.

Imagination, love and *communication, passion* are the important words and hallmarks of Welty's criticism, and inescapably of her fiction too. Although writing criticism and writing fiction may be different and separate gifts, they are possessed by the same author. Welty's criticism is not the labor of the literary taxonomist, nor is it the case study of the theorist: "Not rules, not esthetics, not problems and their solutions: not rules so long as there is imagination; not esthetics until after there is passion; not even problems that will always rise again and again for the honest writer. For at the other end of the writing is the reader. There is sure to be somewhere the reader, who is a user himself of imagination and thought, who knows, perhaps, as much about the need of communication as the writer" (pp. 105–106).

At its vital heart Welty's criticism, as well as her fiction, is a reverence for words because they are older than we are, for the physical world because it is both new to each of us and as old as the hills, and for the individual human soul—writer's and reader's—because using words to reach, to lay the connection, from one to the other is the only hope we have.

Looking with Eudora Welty

The *Eye of the Story* invites us to look over Eudora Welty's shoulder at some of the writers she likes, at the story-making process as she has practiced it, at segments of her own life experience as she has remembered it. It is *her* eye we look through, and for readers of her fiction, that is a very lucky way of viewing. It tempts us to glance often at the one who guides our own looking. As she points out and comments, we have all the pleasures of recognition, knowing how much of what she finds remarkable or valuable in others' work appears in her own. We see in action the "willing imagination" enjoined on readers of her own fiction, and its product, the celebration of life in fiction. We see some of the complexities of her views about life and art (or "living and writing," as Elizabeth Bowen called it), and how the language she uses for these essays, reviews and sketches, these explorations and celebrations in the prose of nonfiction, resembles that of her fiction; for both pursue meaning directly, through a language of essences, ideas and feelings plainly stated, and indirectly, through a language of particulars, which is concrete and metaphorical.

The mix is different, of course; where expression in her fiction is almost purely lyrical, metaphor predominates, and the rhythmical Southern voices that take over so much of the time seem, while they speak, to obliterate abstraction. But it is always unmistakably Eudora Welty's mind at work in *The Eye of the Story*, revealed even in the titles of the opening group of essays. The words *imagination* and *reality* ("Henry Green: Novelist of the Imagination" and "Reality in Chekhov's Stories") belong to the language of essences; *eye* and *house* ("Katherine Anne Porter: The Eye of the Story" and "The House of Willa Cather") to the language of metaphor. And what of *radiance* ("The Radiance of Jane Austen")? Like most light metaphors and epithets, the word seems to combine the abstract with the concrete, as in Nashe's beautiful line "Brightness falls from the air," or Milton's "Bright effluence of bright essence increate."

The title essay is one on Katherine Anne Porter, perhaps chosen for that honor not only because of its central metaphor, but for the personal reason that Porter had introduced Eudora Welty's stories in her first collection, *A Curtain of Green*; this could be an oblique act of gratitude. Most of the essays in the volume were originally lectures given to a college or university audience. For and with these audiences of students, teachers, scholars, lovers of the arts and humanities, Welty wants to turn the occasion of a lecture, traditionally a sober form of rational analysis, into a celebration. That lyric impulse—the source, she states, of most fiction, the impulse "to praise, to love, to call up into view" (p. 108)—pervades these lectures and essays. They are bathed in the light of joy, or should I say the joy of light, since these writers all bespeak revelation? *Radiance*: Jane Austen has it preeminently, but so do many others, and the word hints at celestial light. Katherine Anne Porter is called a "*blessed* achiever" (emphasis added); the epithet conveys the sense of a gift twice bestowed, as the word used in modern biblical translations, *happy*, does not.

The writers Eudora Welty has chosen are blessed for their gifts and praised in illuminating litanies. Here is one: "Whoever turns to incantation, just as whoever turns to reasoning, seizes the word. (And might it not be that all Mr. Green's titles go back in turn to one word, that *Living* is the generic title of all his work?) With its vigor, its true gaiety, its satire quick as a nerve, with its tireless glow of beauty, with its blessed oddity, work which has many a strange and never a ponderous line in it, you are left free to find as you will: it is presented as and for itself only, and this to me fills it to the brim with 'what it means': itself" (p. 16).

Here is another: "What is the real secret of the novels' already long life? The answer seems to be: life itself. The brightness of Jane Austen's eye simply does not grow dim, as have grown the outlines and colors of the scene she saw herself while she wrote—its actualities, like its customs and clothes, have receded from us forever. But she wrote, and her page is dazzlingly alive. Her world seems not only accessible but near, for under her authority and in her charge, all its animation is disclosure" (p. 12).

These are hymns of praise to the blessed human creators, each of a new world (and all that's in it) of imagination, the illusion of reality. In Katherine Anne Porter's stories "we feel their making as a bestowal of grace" (p. 40). Something in Eudora Welty, as critic as well as creator, wants to surrender to the focus which brings love, adoration. It is a religion of art, no more impious than surrender to a Vermeer painting. She finds Isak Dinesen's tales like processions in which are mingled "all the queens and lovers. . . , the magicians and children and beasts and hunters and wives and gypsies and country-gods and artists and angels" of fables and actual life—a glorious company (p. 262). She quotes a storyteller in one of these tales: "The divine art is the story. . . . In the beginning was the story . . . Where the storyteller is loyal, eternally and unswervingly loyal to the story, there, in the end, silence will speak . . . We, the faithful, when we have spoken our last word, will hear the voice of silence" (p. 262). A lady asks a storyteller in one of Isak Dinesen's tales, quoted in Eudora Welty's review: "Are you sure that it is God whom you serve?" A cardinal answers the question: "That, Madame, is a risk which the artists and priests of the world have to run" (p. 263).

If storytelling is indeed a divine art, then writers of fiction deserve nothing less than the acclaim Eudora Welty gives them, though not without some careful reservations. In one of her rare differences with a writer chosen for celebration, she declines to make the artist, as did Willa Cather, "perhaps greater, and more deserving to be made way for, than other human beings" (p. 59). Instinctively Eudora Welty would have realized the implicit dangers in such claims; she was, after all, herself one, and supremely modest, blessed beyond her artistic endowments with traits mentioned in the original beatitudes (chiefly, perhaps, that of being pure in heart). Vanity, she thinks, cannot be what Willa Cather implied; rather, it was the "gift of sympathy" which enables the artist to fill his role, "to give himself away, to fulfill the ultimate role of dedication" (p. 59). This religion of art, then, can never become the cult of the artist; in the end it is seen to be the religion of humanity, of "life itself." Those who create, love, capture life's fleeting moments of beauty and pain and joy, those who disclose it, are *blessed*. One *New York Times* critic not notably ebullient concluded his enthusiastic review of *The Eye of the Story*, "I wish I could go on. Miss Welty certainly does, God bless her."[1]

The sympathy, love, and passion which Welty brings to her reading of these writers, described so effectively by Michael Kreyling elsewhere in this collection, do not prevent her from perceiving the features of each writer's work in their full particularity. Her own experience as a writer seems to give her that power, because she speaks of technique in a familiar

[1] Anatole Broyard, "On Literature's Porch," *New York Times*, 22 April 1978, p. 17.

but nontechnical manner. She uses, in addition to such staples of story-talk as *plot, character, symbol, style*, a great many terms drawn from the visual arts. The words *pattern, shape, design, ordering*, come to her more quickly than does *structure*; and *color*, or *atmosphere*, more quickly than does *tone*. The amateur painter and photographer is evident behind the fiction writer and critic; to a lesser extent, the amateur musician. All three are most fully visible in *The Golden Apples*—a truly golden book.

"Looking at Short Stories," Eudora Welty titles her opening essay in the section "On Writing"; one of the earliest (1949) in the collection, it shows her free use of imagery in critical writing. She begins with the metaphor of viewing stories as though each were "a little world, and spinning closely now into our vision." We become astronomers gazing at planets, and the first thing we are asked to notice about them is that each one is "wrapped in an atmosphere. This is what makes it shine, perhaps, as well as what obscures, at first glance, its plain real shape" (p. 88).

Looking first at Hemingway's stories, she points out that they are bathed in action, and "fling off the brightest clouds of obscuring and dazzling light"; but once that atmosphere of primary colors is penetrated, the object inside is shown to be dark, for "our belligerent planet Mars has an unknown and unrevealed heart." Here the image yields to the language of essences. All the show of action, speed, and color, she says, conceals Hemingway's intention, which is to moralize, to tell us that since the world is dangerous and fearful we had better meet it with bravery and "observe the ritual" (pp. 88–89). With Chekhov, on the other hand, plot is not opaque but pure, the inside and outside of the world of his stories being the same. Lawrence's stories are heavy with sensation, always used symbolically as a means to his prophecy of dissent. His stories she finds awkward but beautiful, like tropical birds; when they fly "our eyes are almost put out by iridescence. The phoenix really was his bird" (p. 99).

Faulkner's "The Bear" puts us in a world different from Lawrence's; his bear is not, like Lawrence's fox, a "denizen of the inner world, purely," but belongs to the outer world, for all the story's being so much "an apocalyptic story of the end of the wilderness" (p. 103). Again Eudora Welty reaches for metaphors in her description of Part Four of "The Bear": she finds, there, that "the flimsy partition that keeps the story time apart from whole time is allowed to fly away entirely. So the entire history of the land and a people crowds into a chapter whose expansion, in sentence and paragraph, is almost outrageous to the eye alone." Her imagery here, though paradoxical, is true to our sense of that book: its compression of history and the vast extensions and scope of Faulkner's perspective in it, his destruction of time's chronological order. "Time and space . . . tear through the story running backward and forward, up and down and around, like a pack of beasts themselves out of the world's wilderness." The story, through its "self-destruction, self-immolation, . . . transcends all it might have been had it stayed intact and properly nailed together" (p. 104). The images never stop pouring out of this writer, whatever she sets her hand to evoke or describe. They add grace, speed, lightness, wit, and a palpable pleasure to her criticism.

Celebration does not preclude discrimination, and Eudora Welty's essays contain as much of one as the other. What has she an eye for in another writer's fiction? For one thing, the eye of the writer under consideration, his or her particular way of seeing, selecting from and ordering the real world so as to make the story or novel into a world entirely that writer's own.

With Jane Austen, the emphasis falls on the limitations and opportunities provided a writer because of the outside world to which she belongs. It is on a small scale, intimate—such was the circumference of Jane Austen's world, though the central metaphor Welty uses for it is a public one, that of a stage, especially suitable to the age of the comedy of manners, of clarity, proportion, common sense. Jane Austen's eye focuses on family relationships, the communication and bustle of activity between and among households, the action of wit and repartee, the criticism of absurd behavior. Jane Austen's plots lead, often, to "the argument of souls" (p. 7). Landscape is kept in its place, which is "the middle background, in size proportionately small," never overpowering the more important figures and their feelings. Jane Austen "moralized; she could also be cynical, even at the rare moment coarse" (where, one wonders?)—those too were characteristics of her age (pp. 8–9).

She transcended those limitations in her explorations of basic human traits, "lustrous with long and uninterrupted use," summed up in her titles. Human motivation, unlike the scene a writer creates out of the restrictions of his milieu, and however different from our own, never changes, and hence remains always available, despite our modern fashion for the alienation which eschews understanding. But each Jane Austen character, though fully realized, remains only and forever within the world of the fiction in which he or she takes on life. Welty insists that we, the readers, must "travel" to them, because they can never come from out of their place in the novels to us (pp. 11–13). To Eudora Welty the past is always inert except where it is rediscovered and kept alive in art, in fiction, in legend, or in private human memory.

With another novelist she celebrates, Henry Green, we find ourselves in the modern world, though he is "a romantic artist who has chosen to write from inside the labyrinth of everyday life" (p. 20). Gone are the intimacy and security of Jane Austen's world, the assumption of rational order, stability, of communication among characters and between writer and readers. His wider scope includes, in addition to the comic, "the outrageous, the bizarre, the awful, the inhuman—all that 'home' is not" (p. 15). Gone too is moralizing; the oddest behavior is acceptable. His characters are fearfully vulnerable, helpless before chance, accident, death—Green is "writing against" it; but these people are all too busily occupied with living, loving, hating, "*making* a world," to be self-aware. His "passion to see" leads him "not to copy what is there to his knowledge, but to show you what is there as alive, basically inviolate, a person or a moment in time" (p. 23). He works from "inside his character's *world*" (p. 25), fearless in experiment and risk-taking, never explaining motives but making us surmise them, discovering and revealing an indelible pattern in each of his novels.

Surely a writer this varied, this open and sympathetic to every nuance of human behavior with all its foibles and vulnerability, with his keen ear and encompassing eye, can be said to have captured the real world? Here Eudora Welty seems uncompromising: it is not so. "A Monet painting is a place you can never go. And neither is a novel by Henry Green the land you thought you knew. His work indeed does not represent life, it presents life. What you discover about it is not the 'key' to it, not the 'secret' of his work, which is his only, anyway, but the experience of giving your regard to beauty, to wonder. There you have come slap up against the reality of fiction" (p. 29).

The "reality" of fiction, it emerges, is illusion, a world created by an artist's patterning through the mysterious power of imagination and re-created by the imagination of the reader—paradoxically, for all its picture of instability, a ballast in a highly insecure modern world, personally assuring in an impersonal age. And there you have come slap up against Eudora Welty's paradoxical view of fictional reality.

Why should it seem paradoxical, and mysterious as well? Partly because the mind strains at the distinction between representation and presentation:

wouldn't she seem to be tossing out Aristotle's time-honored principle of mimesis for the reason of making art seem more immediate and compelling than any imitation of life could possibly make it? Or could it be that she regards the "reality" of life as highly dubious, as the Romantic theorists and American Transcendentalists tended to do? It seems fairly certain that her views of imagination and its powers (never defined but always taken for granted) are indeed Romantic, for the imagination, to her, is as mighty and creative a faculty of the mind as love is of the heart. Furthermore, *all* her writing, fictional and critical, displays the validity of Emerson's observation in the chapter on language in *Nature*: "The moment our discourse rises above the ground line of familiar facts, and is inflamed with passion or exalted by thought, it clothes itself in images. A man conversing in earnest, if he watch his intellectual processes, will find that a material image, more or less luminous, arises in his mind, contemporaneous with every thought, which furnishes the vestment of the thought. Hence, good writing and brilliant discourse are perpetual allegories. This imagery is spontaneous. It is the blending of experience with the present action of the mind. It is proper creation." Eudora Welty's writing, in all its passion, does indeed come clothed in images and analogies. Yet despite her view of the immense power of imagination, she never appears to share the transcendental view that the human mind, as a mystical part and (at its best) clear medium of the universal mind, truth, or God, *itself* confers reality upon Nature. There seems to be no doubt in Eudora Welty's mind that Nature, the outside world, exists, that there is such a thing as "real life," regardless of how human beings react to or modify it in their dreams and fantasies (and they do). Places in particular are *there*; steadily they test our truth, and—barring atomic catastrophe (she toys with the possibility in her essay on Henry Green)—will remain so.

Furthermore, her appeal is certainly, by implication, to the principle of mimesis when she speaks of certain of her stories as having been written primarily "by ear." "Petrified Man," for example, comes out of things overheard in a local beauty parlor; "Why I Live at the P.O." from the kind of stories about family squabbles she heard from women talking in her mother's kitchen. Mimesis is implied too in her statements about how many of her stories came directly out of an experience of a person or place: "Powerhouse" out of her excited response to the performance of Fats Waller; "A Worn Path" from her view of an ancient black woman walking solitarily along a country landscape in winter; "Moon Lake" from sundry childhood experiences in summer camp (where there was once, apparently, an orphan named Easter). Yes, the outside world is not the world of illusion, full as it may be of ambiguity, mystery, change: it is the world of art that is illusion.

Turning to the concluding section of her essays, one may in fact speculate as to why Eudora Welty did not turn Ida M'Toy into a fictional character as she did Fats Waller, both being eminently worthy of a lyric celebration: weathered realists ("born in this hand," Ida boasts of many a Jacksonian), dealers in fantasy—Ida M'Toy literally, through her second-hand clothes, Powerhouse through his music. Could it have been because the challenge to create a story was inherent in Fats Waller's music? She did attempt, and successfully, to approximate in language the sense of jazz improvisation, its beat and pulse, the musicians' abandoning to chaos yet holding through it all to order and control, the glory of theme and variations (on "My wife is dead"). It is difficult to conceive an Ida M'Toy more amazing than she is; and yet, had Eudora Welty turned her into a fictional character, might she not also have been more memorable than her real self (pictured in *One Time, One Place*), as Powerhouse is more amazing and indelible than even the great Fats Waller? For we have the jazz music of Powerhouse forever in our imagination along with those unheard melodies of the piper "forever piping songs forever new" celebrated on Keats's Grecian urn. Powerhouse's relation to Fats Waller is figured in his name—in every way he is larger. Powerhouse can not only make music, but he also has a profound understanding of how reality and fantasy mix in life. He is a tragical-comical philosopher. He can sit at a table in a cafe and tease a delighted and humble black waitress with the question of whether or not there is a telegram with grim news in his pocket and whether all this byplay about Uranus Knockwood and the gory details of Gypsy's suicide are the "real truth." And he can say, "No, babe, it ain't the truth. . . . Truth is something worse, I ain't said what, yet. It's something hasn't come to me, but I ain't saying it won't. And when it does, then want me to tell you?" (*CG*, p. 266). The waitress screams—she's not sure she wants to hear the Real Truth, and neither are we. For it's very likely to be either too much or too little.

How strange, and yet oddly appropriate, that this child of her own time and place, Eudora Welty, neither Platonist nor Aristotelian, should have used an analogy of a cave to talk about life in its relation to artistic truth. In "Words into Fiction" she uses, for her parabolic exploration of fictional meaning, a real cave—the Mammoth Cave in Kentucky—and an actual experience—a tourist's visit to this cave which she made as a child with her parents. She was led, she says, "an unwilling sightseer," into the cave; she had told her parents "it would be a bore." It was. A guide led the touring party into "the blackest hole yet," then struck a light. "We stood in a prism. The chamber was bathed in color, and there was nothing else, we and our guide alike were blotted out by radiance." Nobody spoke. Slowly things became visible: a dark river coming out of a wall; on it a rowboat holding other tourists wearing hats, equally mute; the chief sound that of the guide making his memorized speech about myriads of bats who lived there and their strange habits, though none was visible. Then the light was put out again, "as again we stood damp and cold and not able to see our feet, while we each now had something of our own out of it, presumably." Young Eudora did not, for she adds, "I was too ignorant to know there might be more, or even less, in there than I could see unaided." The cave, in all the coldness and blankness of what it represented as experience "*without its interpretation*," is like the raw experience of life without an informing vision. "Without the act of human understanding— and it is a double act through which we make sense to each other—experience is the worst kind of emptiness; it is obliteration, black or prismatic, as meaningless as was indeed that loveless cave. Before there is meaning, there has to occur some personal act of vision" (pp. 136–137).

Eudora Welty saw the cave, doubtless, long before she had read either Plato's allegory of the cave or E.M. Forster's *Passage to India*. What *can* happen in a cave, given the informing imaginative power which Forster possessed, is perfectly illustrated in his projection of his characters' experiences in the extraordinary Marabar Caves. It could bring, he saw, a vision of ecstatic union with God and man for a Godbole, or a vision of the Void, as it so disastrously was for Mrs. Moore and Adele, with their differing psyches. Eudora Welty as a child came unprepared for encounters with even certain natural kinds of strangeness and monstrosity of place or space or the extremes of either darkness or light—still less any sort of mystical vision: it was possibly a child's instinctive protection against whatever experience of awe or nullity a cave might contain. The predicted boredom was probably assumed unconsciously by a child who was both imaginative and susceptible, curious and fearful and loving. In the cave her imagination balked; it shut out the possible meanings to her or others of the bizarre, uncanny, and potentially awesome in life. But as an adult she has shut out nothing she has experienced or guessed at consciously or intentionally. She has ventured into a great many caves and climbed to many higher and brighter spots and told, in fictional terms, what she encountered there.

But to start with, she seems to believe that raw experience, if not a blank, is certainly an unpredictable, even chaotic affair. Chance plays a large role in what happens: it may be happy, like a pleasant surprise, news from past or present, a funny story; or it may be disastrous. Above all, life has no perceptible pattern, except that it starts with birth and ends with death, equally mysterious, and tends to contain a number of fluctuations and alternations, in themselves without meaning or import. Chaos looms everywhere, until the artist, like God at the beginning, calls for light, and starts his creative task of making order out of chaos. After his work is completed he rests, and calls it good; then, unlike God, the artist lets his creation go free, separate from him and autonomous, off on its mission of communication.

If reality, without the shaping hand of the artist, can seem chaotic, it is also fearfully unstable. Time's passage makes it so. In her essay "Some Notes on Time," Eudora Welty states that if place is felt to be the friend, time may be experienced as the enemy (p. 164). Thus the artist's stakes are high—he is writing in time, against time, to preserve life. And preserve it he does—not frozen in some unnatural state, for its energy and zest—its liveliness—are always springing up and running over; but the pain is no less quick, again and again to be endured.

For Eudora Welty the world (or rather, worlds—each author creates his own, a complete one to a story or novel) of fiction, though illusion, is therefore no less *true* than the real world, and the greatest test an artist faces is that of truth to his own vision. "Artistic growth is, more than it is anything else, a refining of the sense of truthfulness": thus Eudora Welty quotes from Willa Cather's *The Song of the Lark*. Art, being of its time and place, may change, but "truth is the rock": Willa Cather saw it as "unassailable," and Eudora Welty concurs (p. 59). Willa Cather's art, she says, was a house built on rocks—but her work was built out of "her perishable life, which is so much safer a material to build with than convictions. . . . Because the house of Willa Cather contained, embodied, a spirit, it will always seem to us inhabited. There is life in that house, the spirit she made it for, made it out of; it is all one substance: it is her might and her heart and soul, all together, and it abides" (p. 60). (The language and allusions, it might be noted, are again biblical and credal.) The artist's truth, then, subjective and relative as it may be and even erring in its assumptions ("our greatest poem made a mistake about the construction of the universe, but this will never bring the poem down" p. 60), has, simply because it is made out of the artist's own life, the rocklike survival power of absolute truth, a truth often implied though never explicitly acknowledged in Welty's work. And it is more present for her, I would guess, in art than in life.

There is no great contradiction, then, in her finding Chekhov's "reality" to include all the variety of the "realities" of his characters. Again using a variant of the light metaphor, she states of his stories that Chekhov's reality is "no single, pure ray, no beacon against the dark. It might be thought of as a cluster of lesser lights, visible here on earth like the windows of a village at night, close together but not *one*—some are bright, some dim, some waywardly flickering. All imply people; there are people there for every light" (p. 63). Each of these small "realities" turns out to have a good mixture of private fantasy in it, for people live inside their own largely self-fabricated worlds, which rarely overlap. Fantasies may bring Chekhov's characters joy, or pain after their withdrawal, but they do not often bring people together. Yet these characters, though "unpredictable and spontaneous," are resilient and hopeful. Destitute peasants fabricate illusions to relieve themselves of the harsh life which lies behind, about, and ahead of them—but we as readers are not spared that knowledge of life's harshness. "The consistent miracle of Chekhov's realism is that in all its fidelity to its density, its shadings of darkness, . . . it is not obscuring. Chekhov makes it a transparency; we look through it at the blaze of human truth" (p. 68). Furthermore, out of his own poised moral freedom as a writer, Chekhov found it unnecessary to coerce his characters. He never moralized about them; he took the leap into any person, however alien from himself, with candor but without criticism. Chekhov "unsheathed reality itself," showing us the mystery of human life, "searching for the truth that is inside it"—and he found it (p. 81).

Though the illusion of life is present in all good stories, Eudora Welty does not believe that there is any necessary or prescribed way of achieving it. The physical world may be evoked, felt, as it is in the fiction of Willa Cather, with spare but telling use of visual detail. Because her place is the wide open plains of Nebraska with distant horizons, persons and objects, like a plow against the red-gold of a setting sun, loom against the sky portentously. As in Chinese painting, there is nothing in the middle distance; characters cast long shadows and seem larger, more heroic than they would in a social framework. And from the reading of Katherine Anne Porter's fiction, Eudora Welty has learned that fiction can be the nearest thing to invisible, since her stories tend to lack the sensory imagery —particularly visual—Eudora Welty had been accustomed to and herself used. Porter's stories transpire in the mind of a character who is alone, in "those subjective worlds of hallucination, obsession, fever, guilt" (p. 32). Memory is the focus of these stories, relentlessly exposing the hatred which comes from love betrayed or denied, from rejection, desertion, personal failure. Pondering the stories, Eudora Welty concludes that their eye is really "the dispassionate one of time," for time makes the judgments and accusations the stories call for, and provides whatever slender hope there may be for some future understanding. However invisible they may be to the sensory eye, Katherine Anne Porter is "writing stories of the spirit, and the time that fills those moments is eternity" (pp. 38, 40).

Often noted is Eudora Welty's objection to the kind of biographical study which invades a writer's privacy and casts no light on his work, but rather draws attention away from it. Her objection does not mean, however, that she thinks a writer's personal experience, in addition to his place and times, has no relation to or bearing on his fiction. It means, instead, that the broad patterns of his fiction, the way he shapes it, will show the effects of his life experience. The most direct statement she makes of this principle is in the essay on Willa Cather, in language, for her, unusually sparing with metaphor. She discusses Willa Cather's move from Virginia to Nebraska at the vulnerable age of nine, which caused a "wrench to the spirit" that was metamorphosed into her "technique of juxtaposition," her placing of widely disparate characters, times, experiences, side by side in her novels. Concerning this technique, Eudora Welty generalizes:

> Personal history may turn into a fictional pattern without closely reproducing it, without needing to reproduce it at all. Essences are what make patterns. Fictional patterns may well bite deeper than the events of a life will ever of themselves, or by themselves, testify to. The pattern is one of interpretation. There, the connections are as significant as what they join together, or perhaps more so....
> In the novel, relationships, development of acts and their effects, and any number of oblique, *felt* connections, which are as important and as indis-

pensable as the factual ones in composing the plot, form a structure of revelation. The pattern is the plot opened out, disclosing—this was its purpose—
some human truth.

Of course, it is a pattern uniquely marked by its author's character; the
nature of personal feeling has given it its grain. . . . The events of a story
may have much or little to do with the writer's own life; but the story
pattern is the nearest thing to a mirror image of his mind and heart. (pp.
47–48)

Readers of Eudora Welty—especially those who come to her fiction
with the qualities of mind and heart she asks for and shows as a reader—
will be grateful for the concluding section of *The Eye of the Story*, devoted to "Personal and Occasional Pieces." We want to know more about
the life, experience, and character of the writer to whom we are devoted,
about the essences which go into the making of fictional patterns. How
eagerly, then, we read that fresh autobiographical piece, "The Little Store"
(pp. 326–335). It tells of a very ordinary kind of experience, an errand
she performed habitually as a child: when something was unexpectedly
needed in the self-sufficient home so capably run by her mother, Eudora
volunteered to fetch it. "The happiness of errands was in part that of
running for the moment away from home, a free spirit" (p. 332). Right
there is the beginning of a pattern: home—domestic order, emotional security; and the trip away from home—adventure, freedom, encounters on
one's own with the expected and the unexpected. Something unusual went
along with that child, who thought, like all children, that she was so "indelible," only to discover years later that it was others who were "making
themselves indelible" to her. Her imagination was simply far greater than
is usual; she was especially receptive to the imprint others would make
on her, many of those others forever to remain indelible merely to themselves, self-enclosed, without insight or outsight. She was not only im-
pressionable, but fanciful; her imagination put the glow of excitement,
mystery, enchantment, ritual ordeal, around every common object, action,
or person she might encounter. She was, as she later said of Elizabeth
Bowen, "a prime responder to this world" (p. 272). She knew even the
sidewalk block "as well as [her] own skin," having skipped along it,
jumped rope, played hopscotch, roller skated, bicycled; it had a rough patch
she took in the partial flight of "skittering hops," free spirit that she was.

Among the indelible people were three teen-aged sisters, thought to be
"popular," who curled their hair, played the victrola, sang and danced

endlessly; their music followed her down the street. And there was the little boy named Lindsey; it was the patch of sidewalk before his house, irregular brick and covered with chinaberries, that was the hazard—the worst of it would have been falling there, for him to see, in "an act of contrition" she might have been performing because she had made up a funny little poem about Lindsey's dying of the "influinzy." The store itself was dark, mysterious, a wonder of strong odors mixed, including licorice, ammonia from the ice, pickles from the pickle barrel, and sometimes mice. On the high shelves the food and other goods were stored in all their plenitude—a confused array (or so it appeared to her), calling out to be bought, captured, tried, while she focused her mind on the one object of her errand: for "enchantment is cast upon you by all those things you weren't supposed to have need for" (p. 330). After the purchase was made there was a nickel left over, spent for candy, cracker jacks, or cold soda pop consumed on the spot. Mr. Sessions, the storekeeper, was a kind man; he and his family lived over the store and were taken for granted. He was tolerant of children, waiting patiently while they made their anguished decisions, lifting them on the scale and keeping track of their progress, letting them linger.

Her account of the journey home discloses several other patterns. The child Eudora would often take the perilous way, in answer to her brothers' charge of her being a "scarecat." She could choose to go through the sewer, not really dangerous because it was probably only a "storm sewer" into which a sandy little stream yielded its slender flow. But the sewer was dark and scary: it was a feat to crawl along and keep a loaf of bread intact and dry. This was a trial she set for herself out of daring and the love of adventure. But she was armed for underworld trials because she had her own "refuge in storybooks." She could be "Persephone entering into [her] six-month sojourn underground" and her mother could be Mother Cēres, who looked wonderingly for her daughter but would be "mad when she knew" (p. 332). Enter, then, the pattern of adventure and risk-taking, the courageous acceptance of a challenge or dare, both emotional or artistic. Such risks taken by a person naturally shy and fearful are all the more remarkable. This tendency is apparent in Eudora Welty's character and in the experimental forms of her fiction, in her urging young writers to take chances and not opt for a tame and less interesting safety, in her admiration of stories narrowly but brilliantly brought off. And how many of her characters are risk-takers, such as George Fairchild in *Delta Wedding*?

In her fiction, every marriage seems a risk taken—a continuing one. Then, the child's supporting herself with an ancient myth while enduring her self-imposed ordeal in the sewer shows also how early and steadily her imagination was attended and shaped by what she got from books—old stories, legends, myths, fairy tales—all coming from her share in the world's storied past.

Once when she came to the Little Store she was astonished to discover, sitting on the steps, the Monkey Man with his monkey. Enter the extraordinary person, the outsider (she saw the Monkey Man only a few times in her life); the exotic, the elusive mystery man, the comic, the entertainer. She'd never know when he'd "favor Jackson" with his presence, or be even as near as the next street. But there he was, and *sitting* quietly, not performing, resting with his grinding organ on the step, like an old man with "an old friend of his that wore a fez, meeting quietly together, tired, and resting with their eyes fixed on some place far away, and not the same place" (p. 333). Here was a dislocation, an apparent change of role—the exotic entertainer and his monkey had become quite ordinary persons. But Eudora endured this slight shock of reality without disillusion; "their romance for me didn't have it in its power to waver." She couldn't disturb them even to step around them; had she gone in the store she would have given them whatever she bought, "putting it into the monkey's cool little fingers"—she would have given them the whole store if she could.

The Monkey Man is a prototype of the performer, like Powerhouse or the Spanish guitarist in "Music from Spain," who appears in her fiction—a kind of hero. Both are also seen off-stage, without the masque of their roles as entertainers. Powerhouse is seen in the cafe, during the break, tired and relaxing with his fellow musicians; but he is no less romantic a figure for being discovered to be human. The power of the Monkey Man with his accordion and monkey and of Powerhouse with his piano and voice and the players near him is their magical gift of and straight appeal to human fantasy. To that kind of person Eudora Welty has always given her fascinated attention, awe, open admiration. She enjoys theatre, the performing artist, and people who, like Ida M'Toy, make life into a stage; those dealers in illusion who turn whole audiences into fellow celebrants. She has been pleased to see her own stories made into plays or musicals. She knows well that the storyteller too is an entertainer, that stories are designed to give pleasure, and do. As a reader of her own stories, she has become an entertainer and performer, a resoundingly effective one, as the members of her large and delighted "live" and television audiences will testify.

Along the street on her way to the Little Store, the child Eudora passed the houses in which lived all the familiar families of the neighborhood. They changed not because people moved away, but "through the arithmetic of birth, marriage and death" (p. 333). Family histories grew, the lives of their members made their own stories, and of them Eudora Welty states simply, "I grew up in those." Enter: family history and legend, with a dash, or a dose, of the dramatized and dramatizing narrator thrown in. This is the "endowment" Eudora Welty has so often referred to as a result of living in a relatively stable and subtly structured society with an oral tradition. Hence part of the pattern of her fiction making is the recreation of family stories and histories—seen most clearly in her novels and in *The Golden Apples.*

Of a certain family story the child had been unaware—that of the Sessions family who lived over the Little Store. (The fact that "Sessions" is a fictional name shows how carefully Eudora Welty preserves human privacy; one cannot imagine her writing a *roman à clef,* and she deplores the openly confessional novel.) Perhaps because their mode of living was irregular (they didn't have a house); perhaps because she seldom saw them together or heard them speaking to each other—saw them only in the dim interior of the store, the woman at the ledgers and the man waiting on customers—she knew nothing about them. She didn't know whether they were husband and wife or brother and sister; she did not know the identity or relationships of other persons of various ages who came and went through the back door. To her these people were hooded; you could not see their eyes clearly because both the man and the woman wore black eyeshades. Enter the element of human mystery. Over against the pattern of the fully known families, the disclosures made by time's passing and human reflections on the lives being lived in the "regular" homes along the street, is the pattern of irregularity, of an obscurity all but total, of the lack of meaning and identity conferred by the stabilizing facts of place and family.

The Sessions family came to her shocked attention by tragedy, "some act of violence." What it was, her parents did not tell her, considering her too young for such knowledge: whether she learned it later she doesn't say; it isn't important. What is important is her child's awareness of all she didn't and *couldn't* know, the mystery of human motivation and its closed-in nature; the fact that violence could come *out* of people as well as be inflicted upon them by the outside world. The Sessions had been patient and kind to her, but they suffered a tragedy, and unlike all the other people on the street, they simply vanished—"the story broke off." Enter then, as part of the pattern of her fiction, all that is hidden and secret and stubbornly remains so, the "otherness" and solitude of people as well as their familiarity; the arbitrary termination of a life story which ends without meaning or resolution; the vast, blank, terrifying wall of death.

She could not, in 1975, have written such a sketch as "The Little Store" without seeing its symbolic importance to her whole life as a person and a writer, and ordering its details in such a way as to reveal the pattern of her *own* fictional patterns. She suggests as much in her final paragraph: "We weren't being sent to the neighborhood grocery for facts of life, or death. But of course those are what we were on the track of, anyway. With the loaf of bread and the Cracker Jack prize, I was bringing home the intimations of pride and disgrace, and rumors and early news of people coming to hurt one another, while others practiced for joy—storing up a portion for myself of the human mystery" (pp. 334–335).

When she was a child, the Little Store had been for her "a center of the outside world, and hence of happiness," and what she found in the Cracker Jack box was "a genuine prize, which was as simply as I believed in the Golden Fleece" (p. 332). All the people she met on her way to or at the Little Store, including the Monkey Man, seemed to be part of the store, "and in a way they were. As I myself, the free spirit, was part of it too" (p. 333). Eudora Welty was not only part of the Little Store, she *was* one, and later developed into a great story writer. Her memory is the place where so much and such intense life has been stored, both details and essences, which she dispenses so kindly and beautifully that we may receive them with the trust and pleasure with which they are offered, not to be purchased, but as a gift.

There are no startling personal revelations in this autobiographical sketch—this was "life as usual" for her as a child. And as she noted in the passages quoted above, "fictional patterns may well bite deeper than the events of a life will ever of themselves, or by themselves, testify to" (p. 48). For the "deeper bite" taken, Eudora Welty will doubtless use fiction rather than autobiography, though there is nothing to prevent us from looking to the sketches and the bare outlines of her own life to aid our own search into the patterns of her fiction. From both we find that Eudora Welty has always been both rooted and a traveler (the errands to the Little Store were only the beginning), an avid reader with catholic tastes, a sensitive and sympathetic observer, a spirited adventurer, a survivor of many private ordeals and personal losses.

Long ago Robert Penn Warren, in a seminal essay on Eudora Welty's fiction, found in it the basic pattern of love and separateness.[2] The words suggest states more or less static, but they rarely seem so in the stories. Rather, one finds all the movement of feeling and response—usually gentle, almost imperceptible; sometimes abrupt, even violent; the alternation of meeting, coming together in ways tenuous or profound, of pulling (or pushing) away, leave-taking. Alone, together, apart.

"Hello and Goodbye" is the title of an amusing and touching sketch, never reprinted, which Eudora Welty did years ago.[3] The words were for a sweet, naive young country "beauty queen" Welty once met and photographed. How many meetings like that she must have experienced, or observed, in those early years of her serious writing when she was on the road doing her "features" for the WPA: obscure, shy, but outreaching; private and respectful of others' privacy; curious, but with a warmth, a soft wondering; quick to laugh, to share pain or joy or amazement. How but out of "hello and goodbye" could she have known those two most memorable of fiction's traveling salesmen, Bowman and Harris, suspended so achingly between the human needs, as strong in their demands as in their alternations, for love and separateness?

From within the more stable love relationships of children or parents, lovers or mates, families or clan members, the movement is still the same —of pulling toward, sharing, uniting; and pulling or pushing away when the self goes opaque and the soul "selects her own society." But not, as with Emily Dickinson, for permanent seclusion. In these deepest love relationships, the alternations repeat themselves endlessly throughout a lifetime and even, as Eudora Welty shows most effectively in *The Optimist's Daughter*, long after death, in the memory of survivors.

If there is another life pattern or design which Eudora Welty's fiction reflects, I think it would be that ancient one of the journey or search. She herself identifies that as one of several basic plots in all fiction; an idea that "simply pervades life" (p. 88). The path may be new and unique, or

---

[2] "The Love and Separateness in Miss Welty," *Kenyon Review*, 6 (Spring 1944), 246–259.
[3] *Atlantic Monthly*, 180 (July 1947), 37–40.

old and worn. How many of her stories are accounts of journeys, external or internal, with a search or objective more or less clearly implied? For all her rootedness in "one dear perpetual place," Eudora Welty has been, and still is, both literally and spiritually, a free spirit, a traveler. The Natchez Trace, a favored locale in her regional fiction, is a path, a *thoroughfare* for man or beast, on their way, going somewhere. The Trace persists through time; though people change, time runs on, and individual time runs out. A fictional journey is fixed, but it is forever renewable in a story. In the close of "The Wanderers" Virgie Rainey, at last free of all ties but those of memory and insight, is forever poised before her long-postponed flight begins, in the presence of the dead buried in MacLain's cemetery, taking shelter from the rain beside the "old black thief" who has already journeyed through a life long and perilous: these two are kin. Old Phoenix wears down the path still deeper—deeper even than the Trace got to be—every time anybody reads the story and takes with her the trip for the soothing medicine. Phoenix's worn path, as Eudora Welty explains in the essay "Is Phoenix Jackson's Grandson Really Dead?" (pp. 159–162), is taken again and again out of dedicated love, with the faith that the mission is life-sustaining, and the hope to persist in that mission even if it should prove illusory. This act of dedication, Eudora Welty concludes, is what the story writer is up to every time he or she attempts a new story. All unconsciously, I would guess, she has attributed to Phoenix and the story writer the three virtues of faith, hope, and love: all three are part of the pattern of Eudora Welty's fiction, as, indeed, of the writer herself. Include a large measure of the comic spirit as part of hope, and you have the whole.

For the revelation of the patterns which "bite deeper," we shall always want to return to her fiction. I would venture to say that *The Optimist's Daughter* alone reveals more than the sum total of *The Eye of the Story* —both as criticism and autobiography—about Eudora Welty's artistic vision of life and the patterns that have gone into its making. Interestingly, both vision and pattern are central images in the novel—or shall we call these essences?—for they are both.

Something happens to Judge McKelva's seeing, the *inside* of it, the doctor explains in nonmedical terms to Fay Chisom: the judge has experienced both an "interference with [his] *seeing*" and a series of flashes (*OD*, p. 6). The revival of memory and a long gaze inward are required of this optimist before his careless and selfish young wife strikes his now enfeebled life out of him. In his blindness and dying, his time had moved backward. His first wife Becky, also a victim of blindness, had acquired a prophetic insight into what would be coming—her time had moved forward. Having unscrambled sequential time, before her death she had "predicted" Fay Chisom. Judge McKelva had not been able to understand her tragedy and her desperation. His simple generosity, desire to please, weakness for what he saw as vulnerability, led him to marry a pretty woman who turned out to be cheap and loveless. Laurel, their daughter (the "'eye" of this story), has to face, through the "somnambulist" memory, every horror of the final rift between her beloved parents and the desecrations of their home and memory perpetrated by Fay. At the end of a long stormy night of revelations endured in the family home after her father's funeral, she must face the apparition of her dead husband, Philip Hand, with his demand for life; the spectre of what her own marriage might have become had he lived. The next morning she must face the other survivor, who lacks the survivor's virtues, for Fay is a woman without the capacity to feel, with no sense of respect for the past or the dead, a frightening harbinger of the future.

Laurel knows that death brings release from the torment of living, and so from the pain of any fresh indignity, to her dead parents. But Laurel is spared no torment. She understands how people who love each other deeply can hurt each other; through no serious fault of their own, people cannot be "saved" from each other. But if memory torments, it also brings the recollection of old patterns and the making of new ones, out of which restoration and comfort return. Laurel has always been a pattern-maker; as a child, while her mother sat at the sewing machine, she would sit on the floor and "put together the fallen scraps of cloth into stars, flowers, birds, people, or whatever she liked to call them, lining them up, spacing them out, making them into patterns, families, on the sweet-smelling matting, with the shine of firelight, or the summer light, moving over mother and child and what they both were making" (pp. 133–134). It is as hushed and softly bright a memory as the mind can conceive of this child and her mother, their hands and imaginations busy, making patterns, with the double benediction of love and light hovering over and between them.

Another pattern is recalled by Laurel in a dream she has on the night of her long vigil, shattered by the revelations of her insight as is the night by the lightning and thunder of a storm. The dream is of a real experience— of her traveling south by train with Phil before their wedding and seeing, from above and below, a grand pattern of confluence in motion: the Ohio and Mississippi Rivers coming together, lined with "marching" trees, "moving as one," the water "reflecting the low, early sun." And Phil had seen, and she then with him, far overhead, "the long, ragged, pencil-faint line of birds within the crystal of the zenith, flying in a V of their own, following the same course down." Laurel had felt that "they themselves were part of the confluence. Their own joint act of faith had brought them here at the very moment and matched its occurrence, and proceeded as it proceeded. Direction itself was made beautiful, momentous. They were riding as one with it, right up front. It's our turn! she'd thought exultantly. And we're going to live forever" (pp. 159–160).

It *had* been their turn—briefly, but perfectly. The story tells us the truth she sees about life—that it can be *nobody's* turn for a *perfect* confluence of faith, hope, and love, for very long. Set and kept in motion by living and by time's passing, they are destroyed from within and without. And yet—in memory and in art—they are not destroyed. Laurel had felt she and Phil were going to live forever, but Phil had died soon afterward in combat. "Left bodiless and graveless of a death made of water and fire in a year long gone, Phil could still tell her of her life. For her life, any life, she had to believe, was nothing but the continuity of its love" (p. 160).

When Laurel finally leaves to Fay her parents' house and every treasured thing remaining in it, she does so with a knowledge purged of every false sentiment. The past, she knows, is impervious, forever dead to the dead. But memory is alive, "vulnerable to the living moment," and so, painful as it may be, finally merciful; it proves to Laurel that she *is* alive, and herself, free from any material attachment to the past or the need of any sacramental object like the breadboard Phil had made for her mother. "Memory lived not in initial possession but in the freed hands, pardoned and freed, and in the heart that can empty but fill again, in the patterns restored by dreams" (p. 179).

There is the fictional pattern, a structure of revelation, which cuts deeper than any event of Eudora Welty's life might testify to. In the language of essences, this passage speaks of the centrality and continuity of love; of its elusiveness to human grasp but its free flow into an open heart emptied of hate and fear and purged by suffering; of the power of dreams—and does it matter whether they are day or nightdreams, real or fictional?—to restore to life the meaning which only love and pattern can give it.

From whatever large fact of a life—like being a survivor; or small de-

tails treasured—like the memory of delicate, fragrant wild white straw-
berries growing in a hidden place in the mountains of West Virginia;
from whatever strong tides of grief and joy or slender filaments of feeling
this fiction was created by an extended and unifying act of imagination,
we can say of it only what Eudora Welty says of the work of her favorite
writers: it is radiant, beautiful, moving, mysterious, and it presents *life
itself*. Why should we not also—for everything she has been to us as a
writer, a reader, a teacher of writers and readers, and a human being—call
her blessed?

Contributors

John Alexander Allen is professor of English at Hollins College, Virginia.

J. A. Bryant, Jr. is chairman of the department and professor of English at the University of Kentucky, Lexington.

Daniel Curley is professor of English at the University of Illinois, Urbana.

Julia L. Demmin is adjunct professor in the Women's Studies Program at the University of Massachusetts, Amherst.

Albert J. Devlin is associate professor of English at the University of Missouri, Columbia.

Chester E. Eisinger is professor of English and chairman of the Committee on American Studies at Purdue University, West Lafayette, Indiana.

Warren French is director of the Center for American Studies at Indiana University-Purdue University, Indianapolis.

Seymour Gross is Burke O'Neill Professor of American Literature at the University of Detroit.

John Edward Hardy is professor of English at the University of Illinois-Chicago Circle.

Robert B. Heilman is professor emeritus of English at the University of Washington, Seattle.

Michael Kreyling is assistant professor of English at Tulane University, New Orleans.

Barbara McKenzie is an associate professor in the Henry W. Grady School of Journalism and Mass Communication, University of Georgia, Athens.

Daniele Pitavy-Souques is a member of the School of Modern Languages at the University of Dijon, France.

Ruth M. Vande Kieft is professor of English at Queens College, City University of New York, Flushing.

Index to Works by Welty

CPSIA information can be obtained
at www.ICGtesting.com
Printed in the USA
BVHW072248160522
637194BV00001B/16